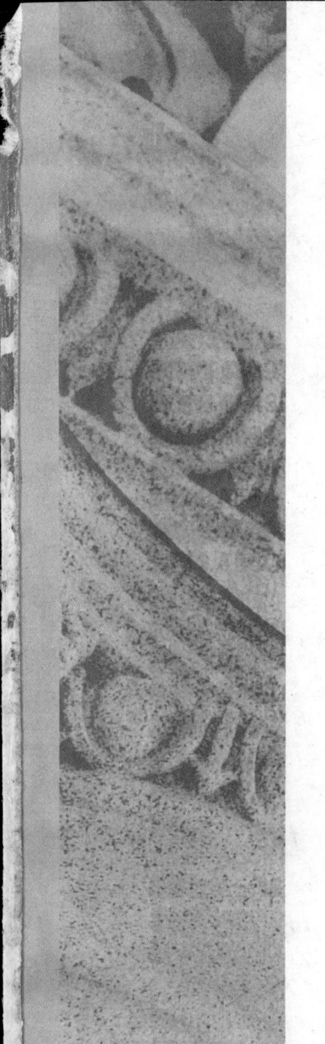

J

Political Science

Library of Congress Classification
2012

LIBRARY OF CONGRESS

Prepared by the Policy and Standards Division
Library Services

LIBRARY OF CONGRESS
Cataloging Distribution Service
Washington, D.C.

This edition cumulates all additions and changes to class J through List 2012/08, dated August 20, 2012. Additions and changes made subsequent to that date are published in lists posted on the World Wide Web at

<http://www.loc.gov/aba/cataloging/classification/weeklylists/>

and are also available in *Classification Web*, the online Web-based edition of the Library of Congress Classification.

Library of Congress Cataloging-in-Publication Data

Library of Congress.
Library of Congress classification. J. Political science / prepared by the Policy and Standards Division, Library Services. — 2012 edition.
pages cm
"This edition cumulates all additions and changes to class J through List 2012/08, dated August 20, 2012. Additions and changes made subsequent to that date are published in lists posted on the World Wide Web at <http://www.loc.gov/aba/cataloging/classification/weeklylists/> and are also available in *Classification Web*, the online Web-based edition of the Library of Congress classification." — Title page verso.
Includes index.
ISBN 978-0-8444-9558-3

1. Classification, Library of Congress. 2. Classification—Books—Political science. I. Library of Congress. Policy and Standards Division. II. Title. III. Title: Political science.
Z696.U5J 2012
025.4'632—dc22

2012038446

For sale by the Library of Congress Cataloging Distribution Service,
101 Independence Avenue, S.E., Washington, DC 20541-4912.
Product catalog available on the Web at **www.loc.gov/cds**.

PREFACE

The first edition of Class J, Political Science, was published in 1910 and the second in 1924. The second edition was reissued with supplementary pages in 1966. A revision of the second edition was published in 1991 integrating all changes that had been made between 1924 and 1991 into the text of the schedule itself. A fully revised new edition was published in 1995, and in 1997 an edition was published that cumulated all changes that were made between 1995 and 1997, and that included for the first time the new subclass JZ, International Relations. Subclass JZ, together with the new subclass KZ, Law of Nations, replaced the former subclass JX. A 2006 edition cumulated additions and changes that were made between 1997 and 2006, followed by an edition in 2008. This 2012 edition cumulates additions and changes that have been made since the publication of the 2008 edition. For reference purposes, the obsolete subclass JX is still included in this edition and will be retained in future editions. All JX numbers are parenthesized. Where possible, see references have been made from the obsolete JX numbers to their counterparts in JZ and KZ.

In the Library of Congress Classification schedules, classification numbers or spans of numbers that appear in parentheses are formerly valid numbers that are now obsolete. Numbers or spans that appear in angle brackets are optional numbers that have never been used at the Library of Congress but are provided for other libraries that wish to use them. In most cases, a parenthesized or angle-bracketed number is accompanied by a "see" reference directing the user to the actual number that the Library of Congress currently uses, or a note explaining Library of Congress practice.

Access to the online version of the full Library of Congress Classification is available on the World Wide Web by subscription to Classification Web. Details about ordering and pricing may be obtained from the Cataloging Distribution Service at:

<http://www.loc.gov/cds/>

New or revised numbers and captions are added to the L.C. Classification schedules as a result of development proposals made by the cataloging staff of the Library of Congress and cooperating institutions. Upon approval of these proposals by the editorial meeting of the Policy and Standards Division, new classification records are created or existing records are revised in the master classification database. Lists of newly approved or revised classification numbers and captions are posted on the World Wide Web at:

<http://www.loc.gov/aba/cataloging/classification/weeklylists/>

Janis L. Young, senior subject cataloging policy specialist in the Policy and Standards Division, is responsible for coordinating the overall intellectual and editorial content of class J. Kent Griffiths and Ethel Tillman, assistant editors of classification schedules, are responsible for creating new classification records, maintaining the master database, and creating index terms for the captions.

Barbara B. Tillett, Chief
Policy and Standards Division

September 2012

OUTLINE

J(1)-981	General legislative and executive papers
J(1)-(9)	Gazettes
	The Library of Congress now classes this material in K
J80-87	United States
J80-82	Presidents' messages and other executive papers
J100-981	Other regions and countries
JA1-92	Political science (General)
JA1-26	Periodicals
JA27-34	Societies
JA35.5	Congresses
JA60-64	Dictionaries and encyclopedias
JA71-80	Theory. Relations to other subjects
JA81-84	History
JA86-88	Study and teaching. Research
JA92	Collective biography of political scientists
JC11-605	Political theory. The state. Theories of the state
JC47	Oriental state
JC49	Islamic state
JC51-93	Ancient state
JC109-121	Medieval state
JC131-273	Modern state
JC177-178	Thomas Paine
JC311-314	Nationalism. Nation state
JC319-323	Political geography
JC327	Sovereignty
JC328.2	Consensus. Consent of the governed
JC328.6-.65	Violence. Political violence
JC329	Patriotism
JC345-347	Symbolism
JC348-497	Forms of the state
JC571-605	Purpose, functions, and relations of the state
JF20-2112	Political institutions and public administration
JF20-1177	General. Comparative government
JF51-56	General works. History
JF225-619	Organs and functions of government
JF251-289	Executive. Heads of state
JF331-341	Parliamentary government
JF491-619	Legislation. Legislative process. Law-making

OUTLINE

	Political institutions and public administration
	General. Comparative government - Continued
JF799-1177	Political rights. Political participation
JF1338-2112	Public administration
JF1501-1521	Civil service
JF2011-2112	Political parties
JJ1000-1019	Political institutions and public administration (North America)
JK1-9993	Political institutions and public administration (United States)
JK1-9593	United States
JK404-1685	Government. Public administration
JK501-868	Executive branch
JK631-868	Civil Service. Departments and agencies
JK1012-1432	Congress. Legislative branch
JK1154-1276	Senate
JK1308-1432	House of Representatives
JK1606-1683	Capital. Public buildings. Government property. Government purchasing
JK1717-2217	Political rights. Practical politics
JK1758-1761	Citizenship
JK1846-1929	Suffrage
JK1965-2217	Electoral system
JK2255-2391	Political parties
JK2403-9593	State government
JK9663-9993	Confederate States of America
JL1-3899	Political institutions and public administration (Canada, Latin America, etc.)
JL1-500	Canada
JL599.5-839	West Indies. Caribbean Area
JL1200-1299	Mexico
JL1400-1679	Central America
JL1850-3899	South America
JN1-9689	Political institutions and public administration (Europe)
JN1-97	General
JN101-1371	Great Britain
JN1187-1371	Scotland
JN1395-1571.5	Ireland
JN1601-2191	Austria-Hungary. Austria. Hungary

	Political institutions and public administration (Europe) - Continued
JN2210-2229	Czech Republic. Czechoslovakia
JN2240	Slovakia
JN2301-3007	France
JN3201-4944	Germany
JN5001-5191	Greece
JN5201-5690	Italy
JN5701-5999	Netherlands
JN6101-6371	Belgium
JN6500-6598	Soviet Union. Russia. Former Soviet Republics
JN6615	Estonia
JN6630-6639	Ukraine
JN6640-6649	Belarus
JN6680-6689	Moldova
JN6690-6699	Russia (Federation)
JN6730-6739	Latvia
JN6745	Lithuania
JN6750-6769	Poland
JN7011-7066	Scandinavia. Northern Europe
JN7101-7367	Denmark
JN7370-7379	Greenland
JN7380-7389	Iceland
JN7390-7399	Finland
JN7401-7695	Norway
JN7721-7995	Sweden
JN8101-8399	Spain
JN8423-8661	Portugal
JN8701-9599	Switzerland
JN9600-9689	Balkan States
JQ21-6651	Political institutions and public administration (Asia, Africa, Australia, Pacific Area, etc.)
JQ21-1852	Asia
JQ200-620	India
JQ1070-1199	Central Asia Including former republics of the Soviet Union
JQ1499-1749	East Asia Including China, Japan, Korea
JQ1758-1852	Middle East Including Turkey, Iran, Israel, Arabian Peninsula

OUTLINE

	Political institutions and public administration (Asia, Africa, Australia, Pacific Area, etc.)
	Asia
	Middle East - Continued
JQ1850	Arab countries
JQ1852	Islamic countries
JQ1870-3981	Africa
JQ3981.5-3986.7	Atlantic Ocean islands
JQ3995-6651	Australia. New Zealand. Pacific Ocean islands
JS39-8500	Local government. Municipal government
JS55-68	History
JS141-163	Executive branch. Mayor
JS171	Legislative branch
JS221-227	Elections. Local elections. Municipal elections
JS241-271	Local government other than municipal
JS300-1583	United States
JS1701-1800	Canada
JS1840-2058.9	West Indies. Caribbean Area
JS2101-2143	Mexico
JS2145-2219	Central America
JS2300-2778	South America
JS3000-6949.89	Europe
JS6950-7520	Asia
JS7510	Arab countries
JS7520	Islamic countries
JS7525-7819.9	Africa
JS7820-7827.9	Atlantic Ocean islands
JS7900-7906.9	Indian Ocean islands
JS8001-8490.9	Australia. New Zealand. Pacific Ocean islands
JV1-9480	Colonies and colonization. Emigration and immigration. International migration
JV1-5397	Colonies and colonization
JV1-9	Periodicals. Serials
JV10-19	Societies
JV61-152	History
JV412-461	Administration
JV500-5397	Colonizing nations
JV6001-9480	Emigration and immigration. International migration
JV6001-6006	Periodicals. Serials
JV6021-6033	History

	Colonies and colonization. Emigration and immigration. International migration
	Emigration and immigration. International migration - Continued
JV6091-6124	Emigration
JV6201-6347	Immigration
JV6403-7127	United States
JV7200-7539	Canada, Latin America, etc.
JV7590-8339.7	Europe
JV8490-8758	Asia
JV8760	Arab countries
JV8762	Islamic countries
JV8790-9024.5	Africa
JV9029-9036	Atlantic Ocean islands
JV9040-9047	Indian Ocean islands
JV9100-9269	Australia. New Zealand
JV9290-9470	Pacific Ocean islands
JX(1)-(6650)	International law, see JZ and KZ
JX(63)-(191)	Collections. Documents. Cases
JX(220)-(1195)	Collections, cases, etc. By country
JX(1261)-(1283)	Codification of international law
JX(1305)-(1598)	Foreign relations
JX(1621)-(1896)	Diplomacy
JX(1901)-(1995)	International arbitration, organization, etc.
JX(2001)-(6650)	International law
JZ5-6530	International relations
JZ5.5-18	Periodicals
JZ24-38	Societies, associations, academies, institutes, etc., for the study of international relations
JZ63-1153	Sources
JZ221-1153	By region or country
JZ1249-1254	Relation to other disciplines and topics
JZ1305-2060	Scope of international relations. Political theory. Diplomacy
JZ1329.5-1395	By period
JZ1400-1454	Diplomatic and consular service
JZ1464-2060	Scope of international relations with regard to countries, territories, regions, etc.
JZ3674-3875	State territory and its parts
JZ3685	Boundaries
JZ3686-3875	International waters

General legislative and executive papers
(1-9) Gazettes
see class K
9.5 General
Americas and West Indies
9.7 General works
United States
(10-75) Congressional documents
see KF12+
Presidents' messages and other executive papers
Class here official messages and documents only
For the collected works of individual presidents, including nonofficial messages and papers, see the appropriate number in class E
For presidential messages on a specific subject, see the subject
For presidential papers see CD3029.8+
For works about presidential messages see JK587
80 Periodicals. Serials
Monographic collections covering more than two administrations
81 Collections issued before 1860
81.2 Collections issued 1860-1899
81.3 Collections issued 1900-1999
81.4 Collections issued 2000-
By president
George Washington
82.A1 Collections (both administrations)
Individual messages. By date (year) of message
82.A11 1789
82.A12 1790
82.A13 1791
82.A14 1792
82.A15 1793
82.A16 1794
82.A17 1795
82.A18 1796
82.A19 1797
John Adams
82.A2 Collections
Individual messages. By date (year) of message
82.A21 1797
82.A22 1798
82.A23 1799
82.A24 1800
82.A25 1801
Thomas Jefferson

Americas and West Indies
United States
Presidents' messages and other executive papers
By president
Thomas Jefferson -- Continued

82.A3	Collections
	Individual messages. By date (year) of message
82.A31	1801
82.A32	1802
82.A33	1803
82.A34	1804
82.A35	1805
82.A36	1806
82.A37	1807
82.A38	1808
	James Madison
82.A4	Collections
	Individual messages. By date (year) of message
82.A41	1809
82.A42	1810
82.A43	1811
82.A44	1812
82.A45	1813
82.A46	1814
82.A47	1815
82.A48	1816
82.A49	1817
	James Monroe
82.A5	Collections
	Individual messages. By date (year) of message
82.A51	1817
82.A52	1818
82.A53	1819
82.A54	1820
82.A55	1821
82.A56	1822
82.A57	1823
82.A58	1824
82.A59	1825
	John Quincy Adams
82.A6	Collections
	Individual messages. By date (year) of message
82.A61	1825
82.A62	1826
82.A63	1827
82.A64	1828
82.A65	1829

Americas and West Indies
United States
Presidents' messages and other executive papers
By president -- Continued
Andrew Jackson
82.A7 Collections
Individual messages. By date (year) of message
82.A71 1829
82.A72 1830
82.A73 1831
82.A74 1832
82.A75 1833
82.A76 1834
82.A77 1835
82.A78 1836
82.A79 1837
Martin Van Buren
82.A8 Collections
Individual messages. By date (year) of message
82.A81 1837
82.A82 1838
82.A83 1839
82.A84 1840
82.A85 1841
William Henry Harrison
82.B1 Collections
Individual messages. By date (year) of message
82.B11 1841
John Tyler
82.B2 Collections
Individual messages. By date (year) of message
82.B21 1841
82.B22 1842
82.B23 1843
82.B24 1844
82.B25 1845
James K. Polk
82.B3 Collections
Individual messages. By date (year) of message
82.B31 1845
82.B32 1846
82.B33 1847
82.B34 1848
82.B35 1849
Zachary Taylor
82.B4 Collections
Individual messages. By date (year) of message

Americas and West Indies
United States
Presidents' messages and other executive papers
By president
Zachary Taylor
Individual messages. By date (year) of message -- Continued

82.B41	1849
82.B42	1850
	Millard Fillmore
82.B5	Collections
	Individual messages. By date (year) of message
82.B51	1850
82.B52	1851
82.B53	1852
82.B54	1853
	Franklin Pierce
82.B6	Collections
	Individual messages. By date (year) of message
82.B61	1853
82.B62	1854
82.B63	1855
82.B64	1856
82.B65	1857
	James Buchanan
82.B7	Collections
	Individual messages. By date (year) of message
82.B71	1857
82.B72	1858
82.B73	1859
82.B74	1860
82.B75	1861
(82.B8-.B85)	Abraham Lincoln see E457.94
	Andrew Johnson
82.B9	Collections
	Individual messages. By date (year) of message
82.B91	1865
82.B92	1866
82.B93	1867
82.B94	1868
82.B95	1869
	Ulysses S. Grant
82.C1	Collections
	Individual messages. By date (year) of message
82.C11	1869
82.C12	1870

Americas and West Indies
United States
Presidents' messages and other executive papers
By president
Ulysses S. Grant
Individual messages. By date (year) of message -- Continued

82.C13 1871
82.C14 1872
82.C15 1873
82.C16 1874
82.C17 1875
82.C18 1876
82.C19 1877

Rutherford B. Hayes
82.C2 Collections
Individual messages. By date (year) of message
82.C21 1877
82.C22 1878
82.C23 1879
82.C24 1880
82.C25 1881

James A. Garfield
82.C3 Collections
Individual messages. By date (year) of message
82.C31 1881

Chester A. Arthur
82.C4 Collections
Individual messages. By date (year) of message
82.C41 1881
82.C42 1882
82.C43 1883
82.C44 1884
82.C45 1885

Grover Cleveland I-II
82.C5 Collections
Individual messages. By date (year) of message
82.C51 1885
82.C52 1886
82.C53 1887
82.C54 1888
82.C55 1889

Benjamin Harrison
82.C6 Collections
Individual messages. By date (year) of message
82.C61 1889
82.C62 1890

Americas and West Indies
United States
Presidents' messages and other executive papers
By president
Benjamin Harrison
Individual messages. By date (year) of message -- Continued

82.C63 1891
82.C64 1892
82.C65 1893

Grover Cleveland II

82.C7 Collections

Individual messages. By date (year) of message

82.C71 1893
82.C72 1894
82.C73 1895
82.C74 1896
82.C75 1897

William McKinley

82.C8 Collections

Individual messages. By date (year) of message

82.C81 1897
82.C82 1898
82.C83 1899
82.C84 1900
82.C85 1901

Theodore Roosevelt

82.C9 Collections

Individual messages. By date (year) of message

82.C91 1901
82.C92 1902
82.C93 1903
82.C94 1904
82.C95 1905
82.C96 1906
82.C97 1907
82.C98 1908
82.C99 1909

William H. Taft

82.D1 Collections

Individual messages. By date (year) of message

82.D11 1909
82.D12 1910
82.D13 1911
82.D14 1912
82.D15 1913

Woodrow Wilson

	Americas and West Indies
	United States
	Presidents' messages and other executive papers
	By president
	Woodrow Wilson -- Continued
82.D2	Collections
	Individual messages. By date (year) of message
82.D21	1913
82.D22	1914
82.D23	1915
82.D24	1916
82.D25	1917
82.D26	1918
82.D27	1919
82.D28	1920
82.D29	1921
	Warren G. Harding
82.D3	Collections
	Individual messages. By date (year) of message
82.D31	1921
82.D32	1922
82.D33	1923
	Calvin Coolidge
82.D4	Collections
	Individual messages. By date (year) of message
82.D41	1923
82.D42	1924
82.D43	1925
82.D44	1926
82.D45	1927
82.D46	1928
82.D47	1929
	Herbert Hoover
82.D5	Collections
	Individual messages. By date (year) of message
82.D51	1929
82.D52	1930
82.D53	1931
82.D54	1932
82.D55	1933
	Franklin D. Roosevelt
82.D6	Collections
	Individual messages. By date (year) of message
82.D61	1933
82.D62	1934
82.D63	1935
82.D64	1936

Americas and West Indies
United States
Presidents' messages and other executive papers
By president
Franklin D. Roosevelt
Individual messages. By date (year) of message -- Continued

82.D65	1937
82.D66	1938
82.D67	1939
82.D68	1940
82.D69	1941
82.D691	1942
82.D692	1943
82.D693	1944
82.D694	1945
	Harry S. Truman
82.D7	Collections
	Individual messages. By date (year) of message
82.D71	1945
82.D72	1946
82.D73	1947
82.D74	1948
82.D75	1949
82.D76	1950
82.D77	1951
82.D78	1952
	Dwight D. Eisenhower
82.D8	Collections
	Individual messages. By date (year) of message
82.D81	1953
82.D82	1954
82.D83	1955
82.D84	1956
82.D85	1957
	John F. Kennedy
82.D9	Collections
	Individual messages. By date (year) of message
82.D91	1961
82.D92	1962
82.D93	1963
	Lyndon B. Johnson
82.E1	Collections
	Individual messages. By date (year) of message
82.E11	1963
82.E12	1964
82.E13	1965

Americas and West Indies
United States
Presidents' messages and other executive papers
By president
Lyndon B. Johnson
Individual messages. By date (year) of message -- Continued

82.E14	1966
82.E15	1967
82.E16	1968
	Richard M. Nixon
82.E2	Collections
	Individual messages. By date (year) of message
82.E21	1969
82.E22	1970
82.E23	1971
82.E24	1972
82.E25	1973
82.E26	1974
	Gerald R. Ford
82.E3	Collections
	Individual messages. By date (year) of message
82.E31	1974
82.E32	1975
82.E33	1976
82.E34	1977
	Jimmy Carter
82.E4	Collections
	Individual messages. By date (year) of message
82.E41	1977
82.E42	1978
82.E43	1979
82.E44	1980
	Ronald Reagan
82.E5	Collections
	Individual messages. By date (year) of message
82.E51	1981
82.E52	1982
82.E53	1983
82.E54	1984
82.E55	1985
82.E56	1986
82.E57	1987
82.E58	1988
	George Bush
82.E6	Collections
	Individual messages. By date (year) of message

Americas and West Indies
United States
Presidents' messages and other executive papers
By president
George Bush
Individual messages. By date (year) of message -- Continued
82.E61 1989
82.E62 1990
82.E63 1991
82.E64 1992
Bill Clinton
82.E7 Collections
Individual messages. By date (year) of message
82.E71 1993
82.E72 1994
82.E73 1995
82.E74 1996
82.E75 1997
82.E76 1998
82.E77 1999
82.E78 2000
George W. Bush
82.E8 Collections
Individual messages. By date (year) of message
82.E81 2001
82.E82 2002
82.E83 2003
82.E84 2004
82.E85 2005
82.E86 2006
Barack Obama
82.E9 Collections
Individual messages. By date (year) of message
82.E91 2009
82.E92 2010
82.E93 2011
82.E94 2012
Administrative papers
83 Collections. Documents of several departments or agencies combined
Department of the Interior
84 Periodicals. Serials
General works see JK868
(85) Other departments or agencies
see the subject

Americas and West Indies
United States
Administrative papers -- Continued
State executive papers
For state legislative documents, see KFA-KFW
For presidential messages of the Confederacy see JK9718+
For legislative and administrative papers of the Confederacy see KFZ8601+

86	District of Columbia (Table J1a)
87.A2	Alabama (Table J1)
87.A4	Alaska (Table J1)
87.A6	Arizona (Table J1)
87.A8	Arkansas (Table J1)
87.C2	California (Table J1)
87.C6	Colorado (Table J1)
87.C8	Connecticut (Table J1)
87.D3	Delaware (Table J1)
	District of Columbia see J86
87.F6	Florida (Table J1)
87.G4	Georgia (Table J1)
87.H3	Hawaii (Table J1)
87.I2	Idaho (Table J1)
87.I3	Illinois (Table J1)
87.I4	Indian Territory (Table J1)
87.I6	Indiana (Table J1)
87.I8	Iowa (Table J1)
87.K2	Kansas (Table J1)
87.K4	Kentucky (Table J1)
87.L8	Louisiana (Table J1)
87.M2	Maine (Table J1)
87.M3	Maryland (Table J1)
87.M4	Massachusetts (Table J1)
87.M5	Michigan (Table J1)
87.M6	Minnesota (Table J1)
87.M7	Mississippi (Table J1)
87.M8	Missouri (Table J1)
87.M9	Montana (Table J1)
87.N2	Nebraska (Table J1)
87.N3	Nevada (Table J1)
87.N4	New Hampshire (Table J1)
87.N5	New Jersey (Table J1)
87.N6	New Mexico (Table J1)
87.N7	New York (Table J1)
87.N8	North Carolina (Table J1)
87.N9	North Dakota (Table J1)
87.N95	Northwest Territory (Table J1)

Americas and West Indies
United States
Administrative papers
State executive papers -- Continued

87.O3 Ohio (Table J1)
87.O5 Oklahoma (Table J1)
87.O7 Oregon (Table J1)
87.P4 Pennsylvania (Table J1)
87.R4 Rhode Island (Table J1)
87.S6 South Carolina (Table J1)
87.S8 South Dakota (Table J1)
87.T2 Tennessee (Table J1)
87.T4 Texas (Table J1)
87.U8 Utah (Table J1)
87.V5 Vermont (Table J1)
Virginia
87.V6 To 1861 (Table J1)
87.V7 1861-1863/1864 (Richmond) (Table J1)
(87.V8) 1861-1863/1864 (Wheeling-Alexandria)
see KFZ8600+
87.V9 1865- (Table J1)
87.W2 Washington (Table J1)
87.W4 West Virginia (Table J1)
87.W6 Wisconsin (Table J1)
87.W8 Wyoming (Table J1)
(95) Puerto Rico
see J164+
(97) Philippines
see J661+
(98) Virgin Islands of the United States
see J166

Canada
100 Lower Canada (Table J2)
101 Upper Canada (Table J2)
102 Province of Canada, 1841-1867 (Table J2)
103 Dominion of Canada, 1867- . Canadian confederation (Table J2)
104 Nova Scotia (Table J2)
105 New Brunswick (Table J2)
106 Prince Edward Island (Table J2)
107 Québec (Table J2)
Including Québec under French regime (New France), 1540-1759; and British regime, 1760-1867
108 Ontario (Table J2)
109 Manitoba (Table J2)
110 British Columbia (Table J2)
110.5 Vancouver Island (Crown Colony, 1849-1866) (Table J2)

	Americas and West Indies
	Canada -- Continued
(111)	Northwest Territories see J118
112	Alberta (Table J2)
118	Northwest Territories (Table J2)
119	Saskatchewan (Table J2)
121	Yukon Territory (Table J2)
125	Newfoundland (Table J2)
126	Greenland (Table J2)
131	Bermuda (Table J2)
132	Saint Pierre and Miquelon (Table J2)
	West Indies. Caribbean Area Including Federation of the West Indies, 1958-1962
133	General (Table J2)
135	Antigua and Barbuda (Table J2)
136	Bahamas (Table J2)
137	Barbados (Table J2)
137.5	Cayman Islands (Table J2)
138	Jamaica (Table J2)
	Leeward Islands Including Leeward Islands Federation, 1871-1956 and including the periods of British and Dutch rule
139	General (Table J2)
139.13	Anguilla (Table J2)
	Antigua and Barbuda see J135
139.5	Montserrat (Table J2)
139.7	Saint Kitts and Nevis (Table J2)
140	Trinidad and Tobago (Table J2)
	Windward Islands Including the periods of British and Dutch rule
141	General (Table J2)
141.2	Dominica (Table J2)
141.4	Grenada (Table J2)
141.5	Saint Lucia (Table J2)
141.6	Saint Vincent and the Grenadines (Table J2)
(144)	Belize see J176
146	Guyana. British Guiana (Table J2)
(148)	Falkland Islands see J227
(150)	Danish West Indies see J166
	Netherlands Antilles. Dutch West Indies
153	General (Table J2)
153.15	Aruba (Table J2)
153.2	Bonaire (Table J2)

	Americas and West Indies
	West Indies. Caribbean Area
	Netherlands Antilles. Dutch West Indies -- Continued
154	Curaçao (Table J2)
154.2	Saba (Table J2)
154.3	Saint Eustatius (Table J2)
154.4	Saint Martin (Table J2)
(154.55)	Suriname. Dutch Guiana see J228
	French West Indies
157	General (Table J2)
(158)	French Guiana see J230
159	Guadeloupe (Table J2)
160	Martinique (Table J2)
(161)	Saint Pierre and Miquelon see J132
	Cuba
162	To 1898 (Table J2)
163	1898- (Table J2)
	Puerto Rico
164	To 1898 (Table J2)
165	1898- (Table J2)
166	Virgin Islands of the United States (Table J2)
167	Haiti (Table J2)
168	Dominican Republic (Table J2)
	Mexico
170	Spanish regime (Table J2)
171	Republic (Table J2)
172.A-Z	States, A-Z Subarrange each by Table J2a
	Central America
175	General (Table J2)
176	Belize (Table J2)
177	Costa Rica (Table J2)
179	Guatemala (Table J2)
181	Honduras (Table J2)
183	Nicaragua (Table J2)
184	Panama (Table J2)
184.5	Panama Canal Zone (Table J2)
185	El Salvador (Table J2)
	South America For regional organizations, see KDZ, KG-KH, or JZ
200	General (Table J2)
	Argentina
201	General (Table J2)
202.A-Z	States and territories, A-Z (Table J2)

Americas and West Indies
South America -- Continued
204 Bolivia (Table J2)
Brazil
207 General (Table J2)
208.A-Z States, A-Z
Subarrange each by Table J2a
211 Chile (Table J2)
Colombia
214 Spanish régime (Table J2)
215 1819-1832 (Table J2)
216 1832-1885 (Table J2)
220 1885- (Table J2)
222.A-Z Departments, A-Z
Subarrange each by Table J2a
225 Ecuador (Table J2)
227 Falkland Islands (Table J2)
Guiana
Guyana. British Guiana see J146
228 Suriname. Dutch Guiana (Table J2)
230 French Guiana (Table J2)
235 Paraguay (Table J2)
241 Peru (Table J2)
251 Uruguay (Table J2)
Venezuela
257 General (Table J2)
259.A-Z States, A-Z
Subarrange each by Table J2a
Europe
For regional organizations, see KJC/KJE or JN
290 General (Table J2)
Great Britain. England
301 General (Table J2)
305 Wales (Table J2)
305.5 Isle of Man (Table J2)
306 Scotland (Table J2)
307.3 Ireland. Irish Republic (Table J2)
307.5 Northern Ireland (Table J2)
307.8.A-Z Channel Islands, A-Z
Subarrange each by Table J2a
307.8.J43 Jersey (Table J2a)
308 Gibraltar (Table J2)
309 Malta (Table J2)
310 Austro-Hungarian Monarchy (Table J2)
Austria
311 General (Table J2)

Europe
Austria -- Continued
States, provinces, etc.
Including extinct jurisdictions
314 Austria, Lower (Table J2)
315 Austria, Upper (Table J2)
316 Bohemia (Table J2)
Cf. J338+ Czechoslovakia
317 Bukovina (Table J2)
317.5 Burgenland (Table J2)
318 Carinthia (Table J2)
320 Dalmatia (Table J2)
321 Galicia (Table J2)
322 Görz and Gradiska (Table J2)
323 Istria (Table J2)
324 Moravia (Table J2)
Cf. J338+ Czechoslovakia
325 Salzburg (Table J2)
326 Silesia (Table J2)
327 Styria (Table J2)
(328) Trieste
see J389
329 Tyrol (Table J2)
329.5 Vienna (State) (Table J2)
330 Voralberg (Table J2)
335 Hungary (Table J2)
(337) Croatia
see J460
(337.5) Slovenia
see J460.3
Czechoslovakia
Cf. J316 Bohemia
338 General (Table J2)
338.2.A-Z States, provinces, etc., A-Z
Subarrange each by Table J2a
338.2.C97 Czech Socialist Republic (Table J2a)
338.2.S577 Slovak Socialist Republic (Table J2a)
338.2.S8 Sudetenland (Table J2a)
338.3 Czech Republic (Table J2)
338.5 Slovakia (Table J2)
(339) Bosnia and Hercegovina
see J460.2
340 Liechtenstein (Table J2)
341 France (Table J2 modified)
341.A Documents before 1789 (Ancien régime)
341.B Documents, 1789-1799 (Revolution)
343 Andorra (Table J2)

Europe -- Continued
345 Monaco (Table J2)
Germany. Germany (Federal Republic, 1949-)
Including German Confederation (1815-1866) and North German Confederation (1866-1870)
351 General (Table J2)
German states, provinces, etc.
Including extinct and mediatized states
352 Germany (Democratic Republic, 1949-1990) (Table J2)
353 Jülich-Berg (Table J2)
353.5 Nassau (Table J2)
354 Alsace-Lorraine (Table J2)
355 Anhalt (Table J2)
355.4 Anhalt-Bemberg (Table J2)
355.6 Anhalt-Dessau-Kothen (Table J2)
356 Baden (Table J2)
Baden-Württemberg see J383.B3
357 Bavaria (Table J2)
357.5 Brandenburg (Table J2)
358 Bremen (Table J2)
359 Brunswick (Table J2)
359.5 Danzig (Table J2)
360 Hamburg (Table J2)
361 Hanover (Table J2)
362 Hesse (Table J2)
363 Lippe (Table J2)
Lower Saxony see J383.S26
364 Lübeck (Table J2)
364.5 Mecklenburg (State, 1990-) (Table J2)
365 Mecklenburg-Schwerin (Table J2)
366 Mecklenburg-Strelitz (Table J2)
North Rhine-Westphalia see J383.N6
367 Oldenburg (Table J2)
367.5 Palatinate (Table J2)
368 Prussia (Table J2)
370 Reuss (Elder Line) (Table J2)
371 Reuss (Younger Line) (Table J2)
Rhineland-Palatinate see J383.R46
372 Saxe-Altenburg (Table J2)
373 Saxe-Coburg-Gotha (Table J2)
374 Saxe-Meiningen (Table J2)
375 Saxe-Weimar (Table J2)
376 Saxony (Table J2)
376.5 Saxony-Anhalt (State, 1990-) (Table J2)
377 Schaumburg-Lippe (Table J2)
378 Schwartzburg-Rudolstadt (Table J2)
379 Schwartzburg-Sondershausen (Table J2)

Europe
Germany. Germany (Federal Republic, 1949-)
German states, provinces, etc. -- Continued
379.5 Thuringia (1920-1952) (Table J2)
379.7 Thuringia (1990-) (Table J2)
380 Waldeck (Table J2)
381 Württemberg (Table J2)
383.A-Z Other, A-Z
Subarrange each by Table J2a
383.B3 Baden-Württemberg (Table J2a)
383.N6 North Rhine-Westphalia (Table J2a)
383.R46 Rhineland-Palatinate (Table J2a)
383.S2 Saarland (Table J2a)
383.S26 Saxony, Lower (Table J2a)
383.W884 Württemberg-Baden (Table J2a)
383.W885 Württemberg-Hohenzollern (Table J2a)
385 Greece (Table J2)
Italy
388 General (Table J2)
389.A-Z Provinces, A-Z
Subarrange each by Table J2a
Malta see J309
389.5 Trieste (Table J2)
Netherlands. Holland
391 General (Table J2)
392.A-Z Provinces, A-Z
Subarrange each by Table J2a
392.B7 Brabant, North (Table J2a)
392.D7 Drenthe (Table J2a)
392.F5 Flanders, West (Table J2a)
392.F7 Friesland (Table J2a)
392.G4 Gelderland (Table J2a)
392.G7 Groningen (Table J2a)
392.H58 Holland (Table J2a)
392.H6 Holland, North (Table J2a)
392.H7 Holland, South (Table J2a)
392.L5 Limburg (Table J2a)
392.O8 Overijssel (Table J2a)
392.U8 Utrecht (Table J2a)
392.Z4 Zealand (Table J2a)
393 Belgium (Table J2)
395 Luxembourg (Table J2)
397 Russia. Soviet Union (to 1991) (Table J2)
Including works on, and proceedings of, the Commonwealth of Independent States, and former Soviet republics (collectively)
397.2 Russia (Federation) (Table J2)

Europe -- Continued
398 Finland (Table J2)
399 Poland (Table J2)
399.2 Ukraine (Table J2)
400 Belarus (Table J2)
400.2 Moldova (Table J2)
400.3 Dniester Moldovan Republic (Table J2)
Baltic States
401 Estonia (Table J2)
401.2 Latvia (Table J2)
401.3 Lithuania (Table J2)
Scandinavia
402 General (Table J2)
403 Denmark (Table J2)
For Greenland see J126
404 Iceland (Table J2)
405 Norway (Table J2)
406 Sweden (Table J2)
Spain and Portugal
409 Spain (Table J2)
Gibraltar see J308
411 Portugal (Table J2)
Switzerland
415 General (Table J2)
Cantons
418 Aargau (Table J2)
419 Appenzell Ausserrhoden (Table J2)
420 Appenzell Innerrhoden (Table J2)
421 Baselland (Table J2)
422 Basel-Stadt (Table J2)
423 Bern (Table J2)
424 Fribourg (Table J2)
425 Geneva (Table J2)
426 Glarus (Table J2)
427 Grisons (Graubünden) (Table J2)
427.5 Jura (Table J2)
428 Lucerne (Table J2)
429 Neuchâtel (Table J2)
430 Saint Gall (Table J2)
431 Schaffhausen (Table J2)
432 Schwyz (Table J2)
433 Solothurn (Table J2)
434 Thurgau (Table J2)
435 Ticino (Table J2)
436 Nidwalden (Table J2)
437 Obwalden (Table J2)
438 Uri (Table J2)

Europe
Switzerland
Cantons -- Continued
439 Valais (Table J2)
440 Vaud (Table J2)
441 Zug (Table J2)
442 Zurich (Table J2)
Southeastern Europe
450 Albania (Table J2)
Bulgaria
451 General (Table J2)
452 Eastern Rumelia (Table J2)
1878-1885, Turkish vilayet with administrative autonomy. In 1885-1886, united with Bulgaria
453 Montenegro (Table J2)
455 Romania (Table J2)
457 Serbia (Table J2)
459 Yugoslavia (to 1992) (Table J2)
460 Croatia (Table J2)
460.2 Bosnia and Hercegovina (Table J2)
460.3 Slovenia (Table J2)
460.4 Macedonia (Republic) (Table J2)
(461) Turkey
see J691
Asia
South Asia. Southeast Asia
India
500 General (Table J2)
States and union territories
Including extinct jurisdictions
Agra see J596+
507 Ajmere-Merwara (Table J2)
511 Andaman and Nicobar Islands (Table J2)
512 Andhra Pradesh (Table J2)
513 Arunāchal Pradesh (Table J2)
Assam see J527+
(519) Baluchistan
see J610
Bangalore see J567
523 Baroda (Table J2)
Bengal and Assam
527 General (Table J2)
528 Assam (Table J2)
529 East Bengal (Table J2)
529.5 West Bengal (Table J2)
530 Bihar and Orissa (Table J2)
Cf. J575 Orissa

Asia
South Asia. Southeast Asia
India
States and union territories -- Continued

530.5 Bihar (Table J2)
531 Bombay Presidency (Table J2)
(535) Burma
see J648
541 Central India (Table J2)
543 Central Provinces and Bera (Table J2)
543.5 Chandigarh (Table J2)
547 Coorg (Table J2)
548 Dadra and Nagar Haveli (Table J2)
549 Delhi (Table J2)
550 Goa, Daman and Diu (Table J2)
551 Gujarat (Table J2)
552 Haryana (Table J2)
553 Himachal Pradesh (Table J2)
554 Kerala (Table J2)
555 Hyderabad (Table J2)
556 Lakshadweep (Table J2)
559 Jammu and Kashmir (Table J2)
563 Madras Presidency (Table J2)
564 Madhya Pradesh (Table J2)
565 Maharashtra (Table J2)
566 Manipur (Table J2)
567 Karnataka. Mysore (Table J2)
Including Bangalore
568 Meghalaya (Table J2)
569 Mizoram (Table J2)
570 Nagaland (Table J2)
571 Frontier Province (Table J2)
North West Provinces see J596+
575 Orissa (Table J2)
Cf. J530 Bihar and Orissa
(577) Pakistan
see J610
(579) Bangladesh
see J603
580 Pondicherry (Table J2)
581 Punjab (Table J2)
581.5 Rajasthan (Table J2)
585 Rajputana (Table J2)
589 Sikkim (Table J2)
593 Sind (Table J2)
594 Tamil Nadu (Table J2)
595 Tripura (Table J2)

Asia
South Asia. Southeast Asia
India
States and union territories -- Continued
United Provinces of Agra and Oudh
596 General (Table J2)
597 Oudh (Table J2)
598 North West Provinces and Oudh (Table J2)
599 Uttar Pradesh (Table J2)
601.A-Z Other Indian states, A-Z
Subarrange each by Table J2a
601.J26 Jaipur (Table J2a)
601.M28 Malpur (Table J2a)
603 Bangladesh (Table J2)
(605) Yemen (Peoples Democratic Republic). Aden
see J703
(608) British North Borneo. Sabah
see J618.S3
(609) Sarawak
see J618.S37
609.5 Brunei (Table J2)
610 Pakistan (Table J2)
611 Sri Lanka. Ceylon (Table J2)
(612) Cyprus
see J691.5
(613) Hong Kong
see J665
Malaysia. Malaya
Including Straits Settlements (to 1942), Federation of Malay States (1896-1942), and Malayan Union (1946-1947)
615 General (Table J2)
618.A-Z By state, A-Z
Subarrange each by Table J2a
Brunei see J609.5
618.J58 Johor (Table J2a)
618.K45 Kedah (Table J2a)
618.K5 Kelantan (Table J2a)
618.P3 Pahang (Table J2a)
618.P4 Perak (Table J2a)
618.P5 Pinang (Table J2a)
618.S3 Sabah. North Borneo (Table J2a)
618.S37 Sarawak (Table J2a)
Singapore see J620
620 Singapore (Table J2)
625 Nepal (Table J2)
626 Bhutan (Table J2)
631 Indonesia (Table J2)

Asia
South Asia. Southeast Asia -- Continued
(638) Pondicherry
see J580
641 French Indochina. Indochina (Federation) (Table J2)
642 Cambodia. Kampuchea (Table J2)
643 Laos (Table J2)
644 Vietnam (Table J2)
Thailand see J681
648 Burma. Myanmar (Table J2)
651 Macau (Table J2)
(651.2) Goa
see J550
(651.3) Timor
see J631
Central Asia
655 Kazakhstan (Table J2)
656 Kyrgyzstan (Table J2)
657 Tajikistan (Table J2)
658 Turkmenistan (Table J2)
659 Uzbekistan (Table J2)
Philippines
661 Spanish rule (Table J2)
662 United States rule, 1898-1946 (Table J2)
663 Republic, 1946- (Table J2)
East Asia. Far East
665 Hong Kong (Table J2)
671 China (Table J2)
For Hong Kong see J665
672 China (Republic, 1949-). Taiwan (Table J2)
674 Japan (Table J2)
677 Korea (Table J2)
Including South Korea
677.5 North Korea (Table J2)
681 Thailand (Table J2)
682 Mongolia (Table J2)
Southwest Asia. Middle East
685 Afghanistan (Table J2)
688 Iran (Table J2)
Caucasus
690 Armenia (Table J2)
690.2 Azerbaijan (Table J2)
690.3 Georgia (Table J2)
691 Turkey (Table J2)
691.5 Cyprus (Table J2)
692 Arabia. Arabian Peninsula (General) Persian (Arabian) Gulf States (Table J2)

Asia
Southwest Asia. Middle East -- Continued
694 Bahrain (Table J2)
695 Iraq (Table J2)
Israel see J698
696 Jordan. Trans-Jordan (Table J2)
697 Lebanon (Table J2)
698 Palestine. Israel (Table J2)
699 Qatar (Table J2)
700 Saudi Arabia (Table J2)
701 Syria (Table J2)
Trans-Jordan see J696
702 United Arab Emirates (Table J2)
703 Yemen (Table J2)
Africa
704 General (Table J2)
English-speaking Africa
South Africa, Republic of
705 General (Table J2)
Provinces and self-governing territories
Including former homelands
706 Bophuthatswana (Table J2)
707 Cape of Good Hope. Kaapland (Table J2)
708 Ciskei (Table J2)
709 Lebowa (Table J2)
710 Mpumalanga (Table J2)
711 Natal (Table J2)
715 Orange Free State. Oranje Wystaat (Table J2)
717 Transkei (Table J2)
719 Transvaal (Table J2)
719.5 Venda (Table J2)
Southern Africa. Central Africa
720 Swaziland (Table J2)
722 Lesotho. Basutoland, 1822-1964 (Table J2)
723 Botswana. Bechuanaland Protectorate, British, 1885-1964 (Table J2)
725 Rhodesia. Federation of Rhodesia and Nyasaland. British Central African Protectorate (Table J2)
725.3 Zambia. Northern Rhodesia (Table J2)
725.5 Zimbabwe. Southern Rhodesia (Table J2)
728 Malawi. Nyasaland (Table J2)
Southwest Africa see J812
East Africa
Including East Africa Protectorate (British)
730 General (Table J2)
731 Kenya (Table J2)
Tanganyika see J801

	Africa
	English-speaking Africa
	East Africa
732	Uganda (Table J2)
733	Zanzibar (to 1964) (Table J2)
735	Somaliland, British (Table J2)
	For Somalia see J825
	West Africa
741	General (Table J2)
742	Gambia (Table J2)
743	Ghana. Gold Coast (Table J2)
	Nigeria
745	General (Table J2)
745.2	Northern (Table J2)
745.4	Southern (Table J2)
745.6	Western Region (Table J2)
745.7	Eastern Region (Table J2)
746.A-Z	Other states, A-Z
	Subarrange each by Table J2a
746.A48	Akwa Ibom State (Table J2a)
746.A53	Anambra State (Table J2a)
746.B38	Bauchi State (Table J2a)
746.B39	Bayelsa State (Table J2a)
746.B464	Benue State (Table J2a)
746.B67	Borno State (Table J2a)
746.D44	Delta State (Table J2a)
746.E34	Edo State (Table J2a)
746.E35	Ekiti State (Table J2a)
746.I474	Imo State (Table J2a)
746.K34	Kaduna State (Table J2a)
746.K364	Kano State (Table J2a)
746.K384	Katsina State (Table J2a)
746.K93	Kwara State (Table J2a)
746.L344	Lagos State (Table J2a)
746.O63	Ondo State (Table J2a)
746.O77	Osun State (Table J2a)
746.O956	Oyo State (Table J2a)
746.P55	Plateau State (Table J2a)
747	Sierra Leone (Table J2)
	Anglo-Egyptian Sudan see J868
753	Ascension (Table J2)
754	Saint Helena (Table J2)
755	Tristan da Cunha (Table J2)
758	Mauritius (Table J2)
759	Seychelles (Table J2)
	Francophone Africa
	Barbary States. The Maghrib

Africa
Francophone Africa
Barbary States. The Maghrib -- Continued
762 General (Table J2)
763 Algeria (Table J2)
Morocco see J881
765 Tunisia (Table J2)
French West Africa
768 Benin. Dahomey (Table J2)
771 Guinea. French Guinea (Table J2)
773 Côte d'Ivoire. Ivory Coast (Table J2)
774 Mali. French Sudan (Table J2)
775 Mauritania (Table J2)
777 Niger (Table J2)
779 Senegal (Table J2)
780 Burkina Faso. Upper Volta (Table J2)
French Equatorial Africa
783 General (Table J2)
784 Central African Republic. Central African Empire (Ubangi-Shari) (Table J2)
785 Chad (Table J2)
786 Congo (Brazzaville). Middle Congo (Table J2)
787 Gabon (Table J2)
788 Djibouti. French Somaliland (Table J2)
791 Madagascar. Malagasy Republic (Table J2)
792 Comoros (Table J2)
792.5 Mayotte (Table J2)
793 Réunion (Table J2)
Other countries
800 German East Africa
801 Tanzania. Tanganyika (Table J2)
For Zanzibar see J733
805 Cameroon (Table J2)
809 Togo. Togoland (Table J2)
812 Namibia. Southwest Africa (to 1967). German Southwest Africa (to 1967) (Table J2)
814 Ruanda-Urundi (Table J2)
815 Burundi (Table J2)
816 Rwanda (Table J2)
821 Italian East Africa (Table J2)
823 Eritrea (Table J2)
825 Somalia. Italian Somaliland (Table J2)
826 Libya (Table J2)
(827) Tripolitania. Cyrenaica
see J762
831 Congo (Democratic Republic) (Table J2)
841 Angola. Portuguese West Africa (Table J2)

Africa
Other countries -- Continued
844 Cape Verde (Table J2)
849 Mozambique. Portuguese East Africa (Table J2)
850 Guinea-Bissau. Portuguese Guinea (Table J2)
851 Sao Tome and Principe (Table J2)
855 Spanish West Africa (to 1958) (Table J2)
861 Ethiopia. Abyssinia (Table J2)
866 Egypt (Table J2)
868 Sudan. Egyptian Sudan (Table J2)
875 Liberia (Table J2)
881 Morocco (Table J2)
Pacific area
903 Australasia
Australia
905 General (Table J2)
907 Central Australia (Table J2)
911 New South Wales (Table J2)
912 Norfolk Island (Table J2)
913 Northern Territory. North Australia (Table J2)
Papua (British New Guinea) see J964
916 Queensland (Table J2)
921 South Australia (Table J2)
926 Tasmania (Table J2)
931 Victoria (Table J2)
936 Western Australia (Table J2)
941 New Zealand (Table J2)
951 Guam (Table J2)
(953-956) Hawaii
see J87.H3
Philippines see J661+
958 American Samoa (U.S. Territory) (Table J2)
960 Micronesia (Federated States). Trust Territory of the Pacific Islands (Table J2)
For Guam see J951
For Gilbert and Ellice Islands. Kiribati see J968.G5
961 Fiji (Table J2)
964 New Guinea (Table J2)
967 Tonga (Table J2)
968.A-Z Jurisdictions, A-Z
968.C6 Cook Islands (Table J2a)
968.G5 Gilbert and Ellice Islands. Kiribati (Table J2a)
Kiribati see J968.G5
968.M37 Mariana Islands (Table J2a)
Including Northern Mariana Islands
968.N57 New Hebrides. Vanuatu (Table J2a)

Pacific area
Jurisdictions, A-Z -- Continued

968.S6 Solomon Islands (Table J2a)
Formerly British Solomon Islands

968.T64 Tokelau (Table J2a)

981.A-Z Other jurisdictions, A-Z

Caroline Islands see J960

Marshall Islands see J960

981.N3 Nauru (Table J2a)

981.N4 New Guinea, British (Table J2a)

981.N42 New Guinea, German (Table J2a)

981.P185 Palau (Table J2a)

Samoa see J981.W3

981.S6 Solomon Islands (Table J2a)
For British Solomon Islands see J968.S6

981.W3 Western Samoa. Samoa (Table J2a)

Political science (General)
Periodicals. Serials
Class here general periodicals by place of imprint
1 United States
4 Canadian
5 Latin American
8 British
11 French
14 German
18 Italian
26 Other countries of imprint
Societies
27 International
28 American
29 British
30 French
31 German
32 Italian
34 Societies in other countries
35.5 Congresses
Collections see JA66+
Yearbooks see JA1+
Dictionaries. Encyclopedias
60 Polyglot
61 English
62 French
63 German
64.A-Z Other languages, A-Z
65 Terminology. Abbreviations. Notation
General works
66 English
67 French
68 German
68.5 Russian and other Slavic
69.A-Z Other languages, A-Z
70 Juvenile works
Theory. Method. Scope. Relations to other subjects
71 General works
Mathematical methods. Quantitative analysis
71.5 General works
71.7 Statistical methods
72 Mathematical models
72.5 Game theory
74.5 Relation to psychology. Political psychology
Relation to astrology see BF1729.P6
75 Relation to law

Theory. Method. Scope. Relations to other subjects -- Continued

(75.5) Relation to international law
see KZ

75.7 Relation to culture. Political culture

Relation to anthropology. Political anthropology see GN492+

75.8 Relation to ecology. Political ecology
Including Green movement
Cf. GE195+ Environmental sciences
Cf. HC79.E5 Sustainable development

76 Relation to sociology. Political sociology

77 Relation to economics

78 Relation to history

79 Relation to ethics. Political ethics

Relation to religion see BL65.P7

80 Relation to science

(80.2) Relation to literature
see PN51

Relation to poetry see PN1081

Relation to drama see PN1643

Relation to dance see GV1588.45

Relation to clothing and fashion see GT523.9

History of political science
For biography of political scientists see JA92

81 General works

(82) Ancient and medieval (to 1500/1600)
see JC51+

83 Modern

84.A-Z By region or country, A-Z

Communication in politics. Political communication
Cf. P95.8+ Political aspects of communication

85 General works

85.2.A-Z By region or country, A-Z

Study and teaching. Research

86 General works

88.A-Z By region or country, A-Z

School cities. School republics see LB3093+

92 Collective biography of political scientists
For biography of statesmen and politicians, see classes D - F
For biographies of individual political scientists and political theorists, see JC under the appropriate time period

Political theory. The state. Theories of the state
11 General works
Political anthropology
General works see GN492+
Tribal government see GN492.5
Village government see JS271
47 Oriental state
(48) Buddhist state
see BQ4570.S7
49 Islamic state
By region or country see JA84.A+
Ancient state. Political theory in antiquity
51 General works
55.A-Z Special topics, A-Z
55.D36 Democracy
55.L43 Legitimacy
55.P7 Plebiscite
61 Assyro-Babylonian Empire
For Code of Hammurabi see KL2212.1
66 Egypt
67 Hebrews
Greece
Including works on the political theory and institutions of Athens
Cf. KL4115.A+ States and city states
71 Contemporary works. Biography
73 General works. History
75.A-Z Special topics, A-Z
75.A48 Altruism
75.A5 Amnesty
(75.A7) Archons
see DF83
Boulē see JC75.V6
75.C44 Central-local government relations
75.C5 Citizenship
75.D36 Democracy
75.D4 Despotism
75.E6 Ephors
75.E9 Exiles
75.F3 Federal government. Federalism
75.F74 Freedom of speech
75.J8 Justice
Kingship see JC75.M65
75.L63 Local government
75.M65 Monarchy. Kingship
75.R4 Resistance to government
75.S4 Secretaries (Grammateus)

Ancient state. Political theory in antiquity
Greece
Special topics, A-Z -- Continued
75.S8 Suffrage
75.V6 Voulē. Boulē
(79) Local
see DF221+
Rome
81 Contemporary works. Biography
83 General works. History
85 Special topics, A-Z
85.C5 Citizenship
85.C55 Civil rights. Human rights
Comitia
85.C7 General works
85.C73 Comitia Centuriata. Centuriate Assembly
85.C76 Corruption. Political corruption
85.D3 Democracy
85.E4 Elections
Espionage see JC85.I58
85.E95 Exiles
85.I58 Intelligence service. Espionage
(85.J9) Judiciary
see KJA3040+
85.L53 Liberty
(85.M2) Magistracy
see KJA2980+
85.P64 Political parties
Political corruption see JC85.C76
85.P9 Provincial administration
85.R4 Referendum
85.S4 Senate
85.S7 Sovereignty
85.T7 Tribunes
By period
88 The Republic
89 The Empire
(90) Local
see DG55+
Byzantine Empire
91 Contemporary works. Biography
93 General works. History
Medieval state. Feudal institutions
For works on the political history of the Middle Ages see D131+
109 Dictionaries. Encyclopedias

Medieval state. Feudal institutions -- Continued
111 General works. History
116.A-Z Special topics, A-Z
116.F8 Frank pledge
116.H7 Homage. Fealty. Allegiance
116.I3 Immunity
Land use see HD141+
116.M4 Ministeriales
116.S4 Scutage
116.S5 Seigneur, Right of. Jus primae noctis
116.S7 Souffrance (Sufferentia)
116.V3 Vassals
(117) City State
see JC352
121 Contemporary works. Biography
By region or country
see JN-JQ
Modern state
131 General works
By period
16th century
134 General works. History
Contemporary works. Biography
137 English
139 French
141 German
143 Italian
Machiavelli, Niccoló, 1469-1527
143.M14 Collected works. By date
143.M142-.M1429 Translations. By language
143.M145 Selected works. By date
143.M146-.M1469 Translations. By language
143.M15-.M399 Separate works. By title
143.M4A-Z Criticism
145 Other
17th century
151 General works. History
Contemporary works. Biography
153 English
155 French
156 German
158 Italian
160 Spanish
163 Other
18th century
171 General works. History

Class number	Subject
	Modern state
	By period
	18th century -- Continued
	Contemporary works. Biography
	English
176	General
	Thomas Paine
	Collected works
177.A3	English. Editions by date
177.A32	French. Editions by date
177.A33	German. Editions by date
177.A34	Other. Editions by date
177.A4	General treatises on Paine's political theories
177.A5	Selections. By date
	Rights of man
	Collected editions (Pts. I-II)
	By date of imprint
177.B3	English
177.B5	French
177.B8	Other
177.B9	Minor collections. "Maxima", etc.
	Rights of man, Part I
177.C11-.C15	English editions of 1791
177.C16-.C19	American editions of 1791
177.C21-.C25	English editions of 1792
177.C26-.C29	American editions of 1792
177.C31-.C35	English editions of 1793
177.C36-.C39	American editions of 1793
177.C41-.C45	English editions of 1794
177.C46-.C49	American editions of 1794
177.C51-.C55	English editions of 1795
177.C56-.C59	American editions of 1795
177.C61-.C65	English editions of 1796
177.C66-.C69	American editions of 1796
177.C71-.C75	English editions of 1797
177.C76-.C79	American editions of 1797
177.C81-.C85	English editions of 1798
177.C86-.C89	American editions of 1798
177.C91-.C95	English editions of 1799
177.C96-.C99	American editions of 1799
177.D2	Later editions. By date
	Rights of man, Part II
177.E21-.E25	English editions of 1792
177.E26-.E29	American editions of 1792
177.E31-.E35	English editions of 1793
177.E36-.E39	American editions of 1793

Modern state
By period
18th century
Contemporary works. Biography
English
Thomas Paine
Rights of man
Rights of man, Part II -- Continued

177.E41-.E45 English editions of 1794
177.E46-.E49 American editions of 1794
177.E51-.E55 English editions of 1795
177.E56-.E59 American editions of 1795
177.E61-.E65 English editions of 1796
177.E66-.E69 American editions of 1796
177.E71-.E75 English editions of 1797
177.E76-.E79 American editions of 1797
177.E81-.E85 English editions of 1798
177.E86-.E89 American editions of 1798
177.E91-.E95 English editions of 1799
177.E96-.E99 American editions of 1799
177.F2 Later editions

French editions

177.G11-.G15 Editions of 1791
177.G21-.G25 Editions of 1792
177.G31-.G35 Editions of 1793
177.G41-.G45 Editions of 1794
177.G51-.G55 Editions of 1795
177.G61-.G65 Editions of 1796
177.G71-.G75 Editions of 1797
177.G81-.G85 Editions of 1798
177.G91-.G95 Editions of 1799
177.H1 Later editions. By date
177.H3A-.H3Z Other languages, A-Z

Works about Rights of man, etc.

177.H5 English. By date
177.H7 French. By date
177.H9 Other
(178.A1-.V4) Other works
see the topic
178.V5 Biography
(178.X2-.X6) Trials
see KD
(178.Z2) Miscellaneous and controversial literature
see the topic
179 French
181 German

Modern state
By period
18th century
Contemporary works. Biography -- Continued
183 Italian
186 Spanish
189 Other
19th century
201 General works. History
Contemporary works. Biography
United States
211 Early works to 1815
212 1818-1860
213 1860-
217 Canada
219 Latin America
223 Great Britain
226 Netherlands
229 France
233 Germany
236 Italy
241 Scandinavia
244 Spain and Portugal
248 Other
20th century
General works. History. Biography
251 United States
253 Canada
255 Latin America
257 Great Britain
259 Netherlands
261 France
263 Germany
265 Italy
267 Russia. Soviet Union
269 Scandinavia
271 Spain and Portugal
273 Other
2lst century
General works see JA66+
History see JA83
Biography
Collective see JA92
274.5.A-Z Individual, A-Z
Nationalism. National state. Nation-state
Cf. JZ1308+ Internationalism

Nationalism. National state. Nation state -- Continued
311 General works
312 Minorities
313 Particularism
314 Political messianism
Political geography. Geopolitics
319 General works
321 Feminist political geography
323 Boundaries. Frontiers
(325) Nature, entity, concept of the state
see JC11
327 Sovereignty
Cf. JZ4034 Sovereign states in international relations
Cf. KZ4041+ Law of nations
328 Allegiance. Loyalty
328.2 Consensus. Consent of the governed
328.3 Opposition. Resistance to government. Civil disobedience
Cf. JF518 Legislative bodies
328.5 Insurgency
Violence. Political violence
328.6 General works
(328.65.A-Z) By region or country
see HN90.A-Z ; HN101+
328.7 Failed states
Cf. KZ4029 Law of nations
Patriotism
329 General works
By region or country
see JK-JQ
329.5 Political obligation
330 Power
Cf. HN49.P6 Sociology
330.15 Public interest. Common good
330.2 Stability
330.3 Political leadership
Social and evolutionary theories of the state
336 General works
337 Civil society
(341) The state as a moral organism
see JA79
Symbolism. National emblems. State emblems
Cf. CD5001+ Seals
Cf. CR191+ Official heraldry
345 General works
By region or country
346 United States

Symbolism. National emblems. State emblems
By region or country -- Continued
347.A-Z Other regions or countries, A-Z
Forms of the state
348 General works
352 City-state
355 Federal state. Federal government. Federalism
357 Confederation of states
359 Empire. Imperialism
(362) World state. Internationalism. Cosmopolitanism
see JZ1308+
Size of states
364 General works
365 Small states
366 Large states
(367) Ideal states. Utopias
see HX806+
(370) Political anthropology
see GN492+
(371) Village. Commune
see JS271
372 Theocracy
Cf. BV629+ Church and state
Ancient state see JC51+
Feudal state see JC109+
Monarchy
375 General works. History
381 Absolute monarchy. Despotism
389 Divine right of kings. Royal prerogatives
391 Consecration. Coronation
392 Abdication. Deposition
393 Education of princes. Duties of kings and rulers. Mirrors for princes
405 Constitutional monarchy. Limited monarchy
(411-417) Aristocracy. Nobility
see HT647+
419 Oligarchy
Democracy
421 History
423 General works
Peoples' democracies see JC474
(471) Democratic centralism
see HX77
Social democracy see HX71+
Federations see JC355
474 Communist state. Peoples' democracies

Forms of the state -- Continued
478 Corporate state
Cf. HD6479 Guild socialism
479 Welfare state
Authoritarianism. Totalitarianism
Cf. JC495 Dictatorships
480 General works. History
481 Fascism. National socialism
Cf. D726.5 History
Cf. DD253+ Germany
Cf. DG571+ Italy
Communism see HX39.5.A2+; JC474
Change of form of the state. Political change
489 General works
491 Revolutions
Cf. HM876 Social change
Cf. HX550.R48 Revolutions and socialism
492 Counterrevolutions
494 Coups d'état
495 Dictatorships
496 Interim governments
497 Legitimacy of governments. Legitimation
Purpose, functions, and relations of the state
(501) General works
see JC11
(510) Church and state
see BV629+ Religion; JC372 Theocracy
State and the individual. Human rights. Civil rights
Including human rights violations
571 General works. History
By region or country see JC599.A+
Conservatism
573 General works
573.2.A-Z By region or country, A-Z
Liberalism
574 General works
574.2.A-Z By region or country, A-Z
575 Equality
578 Justice. Equality before the law
580 Truth commissions
For historical works on truth commissions in specific regions or countries, see the region or country in D-F
Rights of the individual
Liberty. Freedom. Libertarianism
Cf. HM1266 Social psychology
585 General works

Purpose, functions, and relations of the state
State and the individual. Human rights. Civil rights
Rights of the individual
Liberty. Freedom. Libertarianism -- Continued
(589) Freedom of religion. Liberty of conscience
see BV741
(590) Academic freedom
see LC72+
591 Freedom of speech
(593) Freedom of the press
see Z657+
Right of privacy
596 General works
596.2.A-Z By region or country, A-Z
598 Freedom of information. Right to know
Cf. K3255 Law
Cf. Z711.4 Libraries
599.A-Z By region or country, A-Z
Under each country:
.x *General works*
.x2A-.x2Z *Local, A-Z*
Nationality. Citizenship see JF801
Political rights see JF799+
605 Property
Cf. HB711+ Economics
Cf. K721.5 Law
Social rights see HM671
(607) Freedom of association
see K3256

Political institutions and public administration (General)

General. Comparative government

Periodicals. Serials see JA1+

Societies see JA27+

Collections see JF51+

Congresses see JA35.5

Dictionaries. Encyclopedias see JA60+

20 Directories

37 Handbooks, manuals, etc.

General works. History

51 English

52 French

53 German

54 Italian

55 Spanish and Portuguese

55.5 Russian and other Slavic

56.A-Z Other languages, A-Z

59 New states

60 Developing countries

127 Juvenile literature

128 Theory. Method. Scope. Relations to other subjects

130 Study and teaching. Research

195 Civil-military relations

Language policy see P119.3+

197 Regionalism

Organs and functions of government

(201) General works
see JF51+

(221) Sovereignty
see JC327

(223) Referendum
see JF491+

225 Delegation of powers

229 Separation of powers. Checks and balances

Executive. Heads of state
Cf. JC375+ Monarchy

251 General works

Constitutional monarchy see JC405

255 President

256 War and emergency powers
Cf. K3344+ Law

(260) Legislative power
see K3350

(261) Veto power
see K3351

General. Comparative government
Organs and functions of government
Executive. Heads of state -- Continued
(269) Treaty-making powers
see K3342
274 Appointments and removals
285 Election. Succession
289 Installation. Inauguration
Parliamentary government. Cabinet system
331 General works
341 Ministerial responsibility
Parliamentary interpellation see K3313
Civil service see JF1601+
Legislation. Legislative process. Law-making
General works see K3316+
(441) Legislative powers
see K3311
Referendum. Direct legislation
491 General works
By region or country
United States
494 General works
495.A-.W By state, A-W
496.A-Z By city, A-Z
497.A-Z Other regions or countries, A-Z
Legislative bodies. Parliaments
501 History
General works
508 Early through 1800
511 1801-
Bicameralism. Unicameralism see JF541+
513 Election. Dissolution. Term of office
514 Organization. Officers. Officials and employees
515 Parliamentary practice. Procedure
For individual legislative bodies, see class K
518 Opposition
Cf. JC328.3 Political theory
519 Obstruction. Filibusters
(525) Technique. Bill drafting
see class K
527 Legislative reference bureaus. Information services
529 Lobbying. Pressure groups
533 Parliamentary inquiries. Commissions. Committees
536 Salaries of members
538 Limitation of speeches
539 Reporting. Broadcasting of proceedings

General. Comparative government
Organs and functions of government
Legislation. Legislative process. Law-making
Legislative bodies. Parliaments -- Continued
540.5 Publishing of proceedings
Upper House
Including discussions of unicameral and bicameral systems
541 General works
549 Election. Dissolution. Term of office
Lower House
601 General works
619 Election. Dissolution. Term of office
Judiciary see K3367
(751) Federal and state relations. States' rights
see JC355
Human rights see JC571+
Political rights. Political participation
799 General works
801 Citizenship
For law of citizenship, see class K
Cf. JZ1320.4 World citizenship
(811) Naturalization
see K3224+
Suffrage. Right to vote
831 General works
841 Voting age
Women's suffrage. Women's right to vote
847 Periodicals. Societies. Serials
851 General works. History
By region or country
see JK - JQ
Elections. Electoral systems. Voting
1001 General works
1005 Statistics. Election returns. Voting behavior
Including exit polling
(1015) Universal suffrage
see JF831
1023 Plural voting
1031 Compulsory voting
1032 Electronic voting
Including Internet voting
1033 Absentee voting
1047 Abstention
1048 Election forecasting
Campaign management see JF2112.C3

General. Comparative government
Political rights. Political participation
Elections. Electoral systems. Voting -- Continued
Campaign funds see JF2112.C28
Representation. Representative government
1051 General works
Representation of economic and social groups
1057 General works
(1059) By region or country
see JK - JQ
Representation of minorities
1061 General works
(1063) By region or country
see JK - JQ
Proportional representation
1071 General works
1075.A-Z By region or country, A-Z
Political corruption
1081 General works
1083 Election fraud. Corrupt practices
(1085) Election contributions and expenditures
see JF2112.C3
Ballot
1091 General works
1104 Short ballot
Cf. JK2217 United States
1107 Secret ballot. Australian ballot
(1111) Australian ballot
see JF1107
Compulsory voting see JF1031
1113 Voter registration
1128 Voting machines
1161 Vote count. Ballot counting
1177 Electoral college. Indirect election
By region or country
see JK-JQ
Public administration
Periodicals. Serials see JA1+
Societies see JA27+
Congresses see JA35.5
Dictionaries. Encyclopedias see JA60+
Mathematical methods see JA71.5+
Statistical methods see JA71.7
Study and teaching. Research
1338.A2 General works
1338.A3A-.A3Z By region or country, A-Z

Public administration -- Continued
General works. History
1351 English
1352 French
1353 German
1354 Italian
1355 Spanish and Portuguese
1358.A-Z Other languages, A-Z
Civil service
For municipal and local civil service see JS148+
(1411) General works
see JF1601+
1501 Bureaucracy
1521 Records management
1525.A-Z Special topics, A-Z
1525.A26 Accountability
1525.A8 Automatic data processing. Electronic data processing
Including use of the Internet for the delivery of government services
Benchmarking see JF1525.T67
1525.C58 Commissions
1525.C59 Communications
Confidential information see JF1525.S4
1525.C6 Consultants
1525.C65 Correspondence
1525.C66 Corruption
1525.C74 Crisis management
1525.D4 Decision making
Electronic data processing see JF1525.A8
1525.E8 Ethics
1525.I6 Intelligence service. Espionage
Internet, Use of, for the delivery of government services see JF1525.A8
1525.L4 Leadership
1525.M37 Marketing
1525.O35 Office practice
1525.O45 Ombudsman
1525.O6 Operations research
1525.O73 Organizational change
1525.O74 Organizational evaluation. Strategic reviews
1525.P6 Political planning. Public policy
1525.P67 Productivity. Government productivity
1525.P7 Property. Government property. Public buildings
Including government auctions
Public policy see JF1525.P6
1525.P8 Public relations. Propaganda. Government publicity

Public administration
Special topics, A-Z -- Continued
1525.P85 Purchasing. Government purchasing
Records management see JF1521
1525.R46 Report writing. Government report writing
1525.S4 Secret and confidential information
Strategic reviews see JF1525.O74
1525.T67 Total quality management. Benchmarking
1525.W45 Whistle blowing
Administrative law see K3400+
Civil service
1601 General works
1651 Selection and appointment. Dismissal
1655 Job stress
(1658) Minorities
see JF1659.M56
1659.A-Z Special groups of employees, A-Z
1659.E94 Executives
1659.M56 Minorities
Including diversity in the workplace and multiculturalism
1661 Salaries. Fringe benefits
Cf. HD4938+ State labor
Cf. JF536 Legislative bodies
1671 Pensions. Retirement
1673 Political activity
1674 Public relations
(1678) Trade-unions. Civil service societies
see HD8005+
(1800) Martial law
see K4754
1820 Military government
Cf. JF195 Civil-military relations
1900 Federal districts. Capitals
Colonial administration see JV412+
Political parties
2011 History
(2049) Political participation
see JF799
2051 General works
2071 Party affiliation
Organization. Party machinery. Campaign methods
2085 Nominations for office. Primaries. Caucus
2091 Political conventions. Party platforms
2111 Political patronage. Party bosses
2112.A-Z Other topics, A-Z
2112.A4 Advertising. Political advertising

Public administration
Political parties
Organization. Party machinery. Campaign methods
Other topics, A-Z -- Continued
2112.C28 Campaign funds. Election finances. Election costs
2112.C3 Campaign management. Electioneering
2112.D43 Debating. Campaign debates
2112.E44 Electoral coalitions
2112.P8 Public relations
Television in politics see HE8700.75+

Political institutions and public administration (North America)

1000-1019 North America (Table J9)

Political institutions and public administration (United States)
United States
1 Periodicals. Serials
3 Societies
4 Museums. Exhibitions
Directories. Registers
5 Official Register
6 Other directories
7.5.A-Z By region or state, A-Z
Class here directories of federal agencies and employees
For directories of state agencies and officials see JK2701+
(8) Annuals
see JK1
9 Dictionaries. Encyclopedias
(11-19) Constitutional history. Constitutional law. Constitutions
see KF4501+
21 Addresses, essays, lectures
(27) Collected biography
see E176
31 General works
40 Juvenile works
By period
Colonial period. The colonies
54 General works
66 Governor
Legislature
81 General works
83.A-Z Local, A-Z
(91) Judiciary
see KF361+
Suffrage. Right to vote
96.A3 General works
96.A4-Z Local, A-Z
Elections
97.A3 General works
97.A4-Z Local, A-Z
99.A-Z Local, A-Z
Political parties
101 General works
103.A-Z Particular colonies, A-Z
1776-1820
116 General works
(128) Declaration of Independence
see KF4506

United States
By period
1776-1820 -- Continued
(130-136) Articles of Confederation, 1778
see KF4508
(141-148) Constitution of the United States, 1787-1788
see KF4520+
155 Federalist
Class here works on the political theory of the Federalist
For the text of, and legal commentaries on, the Federalist see KF4515
(161) State conventions
see KF4512
(168-170) Amendments
see KF4555+
1788-1789/1800
171 General works
(176) Virginia and Kentucky resolutions, 1798
see KF4621
181 1798/1800-1820
216 1821-1865
246 1866-1898
20th century
271 General works
274 Textbooks
21st century
275 General works
276 Textbooks
(291-295) American and other constitutions compared
see KF4554
Separation of powers
Cf. KF4565 Constitutional law
305 General works
(307) Treaty making power
see KF5055
Federal government. Federal-state relations. Federalism. States' rights
311 General works
By period
316 To 1836
318 1836/40-1860
320 1861-1865
321 1866-1876/78
323 1876/78-1898
325 1899-
330 Civil-military relations

United States -- Continued

339 War and emergency powers
Cf. KF5060 Law

(361) Church and state. Religion and the government
see BR516 Religion; KF4865 Law

Government. Public administration

(401) Directories. Registers
see JK5+

404 Periodicals. Serials

411 History

(416) Administrative law
see KF5401+

421 General works

(448) Recall
see KF4884

467 Business and politics

468.A-Z Other special, A-Z

468.A3 Advertising

468.A8 Automatic data processing. Electronic data processing
Including use of the Internet for the delivery of government services

Benchmarking see JK468.T67

Central Intelligence Agency see JK468.I6

CIA see JK468.I6

468.C7 Consultants. Executive advisory bodies

468.C75 Correspondence

468.C82 Crisis management

Espionage see JK468.I6

468.E7 Ethics

Executive advisory bodies see JK468.C7

468.F5 Field service

468.I6 Intelligence service. CIA. Central Intelligence Agency. Espionage

468.L5 Lie detectors. Polygraphs

468.O4 Office practice

468.O6 Ombudsman
Cf. KF5423 Abuse of administrative power

468.P34 Paperwork

468.P64 Political planning. Public policy

Polygraphs see JK468.L5

468.P75 Productivity

Public policy see JK468.P64

468.P76 Public records management

Publicity see JK849

468.R3 Radio broadcasting

468.S4 Secret and confidential information

United States
Government. Public administration
Other special, A-Z -- Continued
468.T4 Telecommunication systems
468.T67 Total quality management. Benchmarking
468.T7 Transportation
468.W54 Whistle blowing
(469) Other works
see JK421
Executive branch
For executive papers see J80+
501 General works
President
511 History
516 General works
517 Juvenile works
Nomination
521 General works
522 Presidential primaries
Election
History
524 General
For works discussing presidential and congressional elections see JK1967
526 By date of election
Subarrange by main entry
For works discussing individual elections of both president and Congress see JK1968
528 General works
529 Electoral college
536 Inauguration
550 Term of office
Salary. Compensation see JK779
552 Staff. Executive Office of the President
554 Press conferences. Media relations
558 War and emergency powers
Cf. KF5060 Law
(570-573) Treaty-making powers
see KF5055
Relations with Congress. Relations between Congress and Executive departments
585 General works
586 Veto power
587 Messages. State of the Union messages
Cf. CD3029.8+ Presidential papers
Cf. J80+ Texts of messages

United States
Government. Public administration
Executive branch
President -- Continued

606 Ex-Presidents
609 Succession. Disability
Cf. KF5082 Legal status
609.5 Vice President
Cf. JK1224 President of the Senate
Cabinet
610 Directories. Registers
611 General works
616 Relation to Congress
Civil service
Cf. KF5338 Civil service law
Office of Personnel Management. Civil Service Commission. Merit Systems Protection Board
631 Periodicals. Serials
639 General works
641 Presidents' messages
(643) Commissions or committees on departmental methods, economy, efficiency
see JK681+
(645) Relation of the Civil service to Congress
see JK585
(646-656) Congressional documents
see KF16+
661 Directories. Registers
666 Statistics
671 Periodicals. Serials
674 Societies
For trade-unions see HD8005+
677 Congresses
681 General works
Including Civil Service reform
By period
686 Before 1883
691 1883-1977
692 1978-
692.5.A-Z By region or state, A-Z
Class here works on the federal civil service
For state civil service see JK2465+
Biography
692.8 Collective
693.A-Z Individual, A-Z
698 Republican Party and civil service reform

United States
Government. Public administration
Executive branch
Civil service -- Continued
699 Democratic Party and civil service reform
(711) Treatises
see JK681+
Civil service examinations. Civil service schools. Vocational guidance
716 General works
717.A-Z Special subjects, A-Z
717.C54 Clerks. Clerical ability
(717.S7) Stenography
see Z53
717.S8 Supervisors
718 In-service training. Interns
Special classes of employees
Cf. JK766.4 Affirmative action programs
720 Veterans
721 Women
723.A-Z Other special, A-Z
723.A34 African Americans. Blacks
723.A4 Aliens
Blacks see JK723.A34
723.B58 Blue collar workers
723.C6 Communists
723.D4 Deaf
723.E9 Executives
Gay men see JK723.H6
Handicapped. People with disabilities
723.H3 General works
723.H35 People with mental disabilities
723.H55 Hispanic Americans
723.H6 Homosexual men and women
Lesbians see JK723.H6
723.M54 Minorities
723.O4 Older employees. Age and employment
People with disabilities see JK723.H3+
723.S8 Students, College
723.V64 Volunteer workers
723.W5 Without-compensation personnel
Appointments and removals. Patronage. Spoils
731 General works
734 Loyalty and security investigations. Loyalty-security program
744 Dismissal. Reductions-in-force. Layoff systems

United States
Government. Public administration
Executive branch
Civil service
Appointments and removals. Patronage. Spoils -- Continued
761 Political activity
Personnel management
765 General works
766.4 Affirmative action programs
766.5 Personnel records
766.6 Performance appraisal. Rating of employees
767 Promotions
768.3 Incentive awards. Meritorious service awards. Merit increases. Performance awards. Suggestion systems
768.4 Labor productivity
768.7 Discipline
768.8 Grievance procedures
769.5 Hours of labor
770 Annual leave. Sick leave
Salaries. Pensions. Fringe benefits
Class here works dealing with service under the state in all branches (not limited to civil service proper)
Cf. HD4938+ Wages of state labor
Cf. JK768.3 Salary increases as service awards
771 Salary lists
774 Periodicals. Serials
(775) Documents
see JK774 Periodicals; JK776 General works
776 General works
779 Salary of the President
781 Salaries of members of Congress
Including pensions
Salaries of the judiciary see KF8777
791 Retirement. Pensions
794.A-Z Other, A-Z
794.H4 Health insurance
794.L5 Life insurance
795 Travel
849 Publicity. Media relations
850.A-Z Other topics, A-Z
850.A3 Accidents
850.A4 Alcoholism
850.B7 Bribery
850.C53 Charitable contributions

United States
Government. Public administration
Executive branch
Civil service
Other topics, A-Z -- Continued
Crimes against employees see JK850.E49
850.D4 Details and transfers
850.D77 Drug abuse. Drug testing
Drug testing see JK850.D77
850.E48 Employee assistance programs. Problem employees
850.E49 Employee crimes. Crimes against employees
Including employee theft and violence in the workplace
850.E5 Employers' liability. Workers' compensation
850.J62 Job satisfaction
Problem employees see JK850.E48
850.R44 Relocation of employees
850.S45 Sexual activity. Sexual harassment
850.S9 Supplementary employment of civil service employees
850.T44 Telecommuting. Teleworking
850.T85 Turnover of employees
850.U5 Uniforms
Violence in the workplace see JK850.E49
Individual departments and agencies
(851-853) Department of State
For legal works on the Department of State see KF5110+
(854) Agency for International Development
see HC60
Department of the Interior
(864) Periodicals. Serials
see J84
868 General works
(873) Department of Justice
see KF5106+
Executive advisory bodies see JK468.C7
Other departments or agencies
see the subject
(901) Independent regulatory commissions
see KF5406+
Congress. Legislative branch
(1001) Legislative process
see KF4945+
(1003) Legislative reference bureau
see JK1108
1012 Directories. Registers

United States
Government. Public administration
Congress. Legislative branch -- Continued
1021 General works
1025 Juvenile works
Congressional committees
For rules of procedure see KF4946
1029 General works
1029.2 Seniority system
1029.5.A-.W Delegations. By state, A-W
1030 Collective biography
For biographies of individual legislators, see class E
History
By period
Colonial period see JK81+
Continental Congress, 1774-1788
Journals
(1031) General
see KF4505
(1032) Secret journals, 1820-1821, 4 v.
see KF4505
1033 General works
Federal Congress, 1789-
(1036) Debates. Proceedings
see KF16+
1041 General works
1051 Voting by members of congress
For particular numbered meetings of Congress see JK1059
1059 By number of congress
Subarrange by main entry
e. g.
1059 67th 67th Congress
(1061-1081) Constitution. Powers. Prerogatives
see KF4935+
Congressional employees. Staff members
1083 General works
1084 Capitol pages
Salaries of members see JK781
(1091-1106) Procedure
see KF4937
1108 Legislative reference bureaus. Information services
1111 Conference committees
1118 Lobbying. Pressure groups
1121 Ethics

United States
Government. Public administration
Congress. Legislative branch -- Continued
(1123) Investigations
see KF4942
1128 Reporting
1129 Broadcasting of proceedings
1130 Term of office. Term limits
1131 Constituent communication
Senate
1154 Directories. Registers
1161 General works. History
Juvenile works see JK1276
(1166-1197) Constitution. Powers. Prerogatives
see KF4988+
Organization. Administration
1220 General works
Officers
1224 President
1226 President pro tem
1227 Majority leader
Committees
For rules of procedure see KF4986+
1236 Directories. Registers
1239 General works
(1240) Individual committees
see KF4987
1251 Executive session
Employees. Staff members
(1255) General works
see JK1083+
1257 Secretary of the Senate
1259 Sergeant at arms
(1266-1274) Procedure
see KF4982+
1276 Juvenile works
House of Representatives
1308 Directories. Registers
1319 General works
1321.A-Z Representation of specific groups, A-Z
1321.A37 African Americans
(1326-1333) Constitution. Powers. Prerogatives
see KF5053+
Congressional districts. Election districts.
Gerrymandering
1341 General works

United States
Government. Public administration
Congress. Legislative branch
House of Representatives
Congressional districts. Election districts. Gerrymandering -- Continued
1343.A-.W By state, A-W
For election districts of state legislatures see JK2493
1379 Ethics
Organization. Administration
1410 General works
1411 Officers. Speaker
1415 Congressional Black Caucus
1417 Congressional Caucus for Women's Issues
Committees
For rules of procedure see KF4996+
1426 Directories. Registers
1429 General works
(1430) Special committees
see KF4997
(1431) Employees. Staff members
see JK1083+
1432 Clerk of the House
(1435-1443) Procedure
see KF4992
(1507-1603) Judiciary
see KF8700+
1606 Capital. Site of the capital
Cf. F191+ History of the District of Columbia
Cf. KF5750+ Law
Public buildings
Cf. NA4195+ Architecture
1613 General works
Including works on federal buildings
For state buildings see JK1651.A1+
Washington
1616 Capitol
Cf. F204.C2 History
1617 Senate offices
1618 House offices
1621 White House
Cf. F204.W5 History
Departments
1625 General works
1626 State Department

United States
Government. Public administration
Public buildings
Washington -- Continued
1637.A-Z Other buildings, A-Z
1637.C6 Commerce Department building
1637.I6 Interior Department building
1641.A-Z Other cities, A-Z
State buildings
1651.A1 General works. States collectively
1651.A2-.W By state, A-W
Government property
For public buildings see JK1613+
For property of the individual states see JK2701+
1661 General works
1663 Government auctions
Supplies. Government purchasing
(1671) Federal
see JK1673
1672 General Services Administration
1673 General works
1677.A-Z Special kinds of supplies, apparatus, etc., A-Z
1677.A8 Automotive spare parts
1677.C6 Coal
1677.C65 Computers
1677.C67 Copying machines
1677.D3 Data tapes
1677.D4 Desks
1677.D7 Drugs
1677.E4 Electron tubes
1677.L37 Lasers
1677.M7 Motor vehicles
1677.O4 Office equipment and supplies
1677.P3 Paper
1677.P35 Parking facilities
1677.P4 Petroleum
1677.R3 Radio equipment
1677.T4 Teletype
1679 Specifications, standards, product descriptions
Cf. TS155+ Production management
1683 States collectively
For individual states see JK2701+
(1685) Public printing
see Z286.G69

United States -- Continued
Political rights. Practical politics
For civil rights and human rights see JC571+
For political participation see JK1764
1717 History
1726 General works
(1731) Right of petition
see KF4780
(1736) Trial by jury
see KF8975
Citizenship
(1756) Legal treatises
see KF4700+
1758 Manuals for foreign-born citizens. Citizenship test. "Americanization"
1759 General works
(1760) Study and teaching
see JA86+
1761 National holidays. Patriotic holidays
For individual holidays, see the subject or event being commemorated
1764 Political participation
Cf. JK2255+ Political parties
(1800-1836) Naturalization
see KF4706+
Suffrage. Right to vote
For Colonial period see JK96.A3+
1846 General works
(1861-1863) Election laws
see KF4891+
(1872) Voting by psychiatric hospital and mental retardation facilities patients
see KF4896
Absentee voting
1873 General works
1874.A-.W By state, A-W
(1876-1878) Voting by soldiers
see KF4894
Women's suffrage. Women's right to vote
1880 Periodicals. Serials
Societies
1881 National
1883 State
1885 Congresses
(1889) Election laws
see KF4895

United States
Political rights. Practical politics
Suffrage. Right to vote
Women's suffrage. Women's right to vote -- Continued
1896 General works
1898 Juvenile works
Biography
1898.5 Collective
1899.A-Z Individual, A-Z
1911.A-Z By state, A-W
African American suffrage. African American voters
1924 General works
1929.A2 Southern states. South
1929.A3-.W Other states, A-W
(1936) By state
see JK2701+
Electoral system. Elections. Voting
For Colonial period see JK97.A3+
For election of the president see JK524+
Cf. JK1846+ Suffrage
(1961-1963) Election laws
see KF4885+
History
1965 General
(1966) By state
see JK2701+
Statistics. Election returns. Voting behavior
For works discussing presidential elections alone see JK524
1967 General works
1968 By date of election
Subarrange by main entry
For works discussing individual presidential elections alone see JK526
By state see JK2701+
1976 General works
1978 Juvenile works
(1982) Election districts. Voting districts
see JK1341+
(1984) Short ballot
see JK2217
1985 Internet voting
1987 Abstention
Campaign funds. Election finance. Political action committees. Campaign contributions
1991 General works

United States
Political rights. Practical politics
Electoral system. Elections. Voting
Campaign funds. Election finances. Political action committees. Campaign contributions -- Continued
1991.5.A-.W By state, A-W
1994 Election fraud. Corrupt practices
(1997) Publicity of expenditures
see JK1991+
2007 Election forecasting
Election guides. Handbooks for election officials
(2021) General works
see JK1976
Law see KF4885+
(2023) By state
see JK2701+
(2025) By city
see JS
Nominations for office
2063 General works
Primaries. Caucus
2071 General works
2075.A-.W By state, A-W
Voter registration
2160 General works
(2161) By state
see JK2701+
(2164) Laws
see KF4898
Ballot
2214 General works
2215 Secret ballot. Australian ballot
2217 Other systems
Including short ballot, coupon ballot, preferential ballot
(2241-2248) Electoral fraud
see JK1994
2249 Political corruption
Political parties
Including political movements
2255 Party platforms. Political conventions
History
For Colonial period see JK101+
For comprehensive histories see JK2261
2260 1776-1860
2261 1860-
Including comprehensive histories

United States
Political parties -- Continued
2265 General works
2271 Parties and the individual. Party affiliation
2281 Campaign management. Electioneering
2295.A-Z Local. By region or state, A-Z
For individual national parties functioning at the state level see JK2301+
Particular parties and movements
2301-2309 Federal Party (Table J3)
2311-2319 Democratic Party. Republican-Democratic Party (Table J3)
2320 National Republican Party (Table J5)
2326-2334 Whig Party (Table J3)
2336 Free Soil Party (Table J5)
2341 Know Nothing Party. American Party (Table J5)
2351-2359 Republican Party (Table J3)
Greenback Party see HG604
2361-2365 Labor Party. United States Labor Party (Table J4)
2371-2375 Populists. People's Party of the United States (Table J4)
2381-2385 Prohibition Party (Table J4)
2386-2390 Progressive Party (Table J4)
2391.A-Z Other parties and movements, A-Z
Subarrange each by Table J6
2391.T43 Tea Party movement (Table J6)
State government
Class here general works only
For individual states see JK2701+
2403 Periodicals. Serials
2408 General works
(2410-2411) Admission of territories to statehood
see KF4545.S7
(2413-2428) State constitutions
see KF4529+
(2430-2491) Legislation
see KF4933
Public administration
2443 General works
2445.A-Z Special topics, A-Z
2445.A4 Advertising
2445.A8 Automatic data processing. Electronic data processing
Including use of the Internet for the delivery of government services
Benchmarking see JK2445.T67
2445.C58 Communication systems
2445.C7 Consultants

United States
State government
Public administration
Special topics, A-Z -- Continued
2445.E8 Ethics
2445.I57 Interstate relations, agencies, etc.
2445.P76 Productivity
2445.P82 Public records management
(2445.R4) Referendum
see JF494
2445.T67 Total quality management. Benchmarking
(2446) "Short ballot" movement
see JK2217
Executive branch
2446.5 General works
Governor
2447 General works
2454 Veto power
2459 Lieutenant governor
Civil service
2465 General works
2471 Appointments and removals
2474 Salaries. Pensions. Fringe benefits
Class here works dealing with service under the state in all branches (not limited to civil service proper)
Individual departments and agencies
2477 State Department
Other departments or agencies limited to a particular subject
see the subject
2480.A-Z Special topics, A-Z
2480.E4 Employment tests. Civil service examinations
2480.H4 Health insurance
2480.I6 In-service training
2480.L24 Labor productivity
2480.M5 Minorities
2482.A-Z Special classes of officials and employees, A-Z
2482.E94 Executives
2482.W6 Women
Legislative branch
2484 History
2488 General works
2493 Representative districts. Election districts
For individual states see JK2701+
2495 Organization. Administration
2498 Lobbying. Pressure groups

United States
State government
Public administration
Legislative branch -- Continued
2506 Upper House
2508 Lower House
(2521-2525) Judiciary
see KF8700+
2556 Territorial government
Cf. JV500+ Colonial administration
Indians of North America. Indian nations. Tribal government see E98.T77
Confederate states see JK9803
Directories. Registers
For directories of federal agencies and employees at the state level see JK7.5.A+
For directories of agencies and employees of individual state governments see JK2701+
2679 General
2681 New England
2683 Southern states
2685 Central states
2687 West. Pacific states
Individual states and territories
2701-2793 District of Columbia (Table J7)
2801-2893 Maine (Table J7)
2901-2993 New Hampshire (Table J7)
3001-3093 Vermont (Table J7)
3101-3193 Massachusetts (Table J7)
3201-3293 Rhode Island (Table J7)
3301-3393 Connecticut (Table J7)
3401-3493 New York (Table J7)
3501-3593 New Jersey (Table J7)
3601-3693 Pennsylvania (Table J7)
3701-3793 Delaware (Table J7)
3801-3893 Maryland (Table J7)
3901-3993 Virginia (Table J7)
4001-4093 West Virginia (Table J7)
4101-4193 North Carolina (Table J7)
4201-4293 South Carolina (Table J7)
4301-4393 Georgia (Table J7)
4401-4493 Florida (Table J7)
4501-4593 Alabama (Table J7)
4601-4693 Mississippi (Table J7)
4701-4793 Louisiana (Table J7)
4801-4893 Texas (Table J7)

United States
State government
Individual states and territories -- Continued
5101-5193 Arkansas (Table J7)
5201-5293 Tennessee (Table J7)
5301-5393 Kentucky (Table J7)
5401-5493 Missouri (Table J7)
5501-5593 Ohio (Table J7)
5601-5693 Indiana (Table J7)
5701-5793 Illinois (Table J7)
5801-5893 Michigan (Table J7)
6001-6093 Wisconsin (Table J7)
6101-6193 Minnesota (Table J7)
6301-6393 Iowa (Table J7)
6401-6493 North Dakota (Table J7)
6501-6593 South Dakota (Table J7)
6601-6693 Nebraska (Table J7)
6801-6893 Kansas (Table J7)
7001-7093 Indian Territory (Table J7)
7101-7193 Oklahoma (Table J7)
7301-7393 Montana (Table J7)
7501-7593 Idaho (Table J7)
7601-7693 Wyoming (Table J7)
7801-7893 Colorado (Table J7)
8001-8093 New Mexico (Table J7)
8201-8293 Arizona (Table J7)
8401-8493 Utah (Table J7)
8501-8593 Nevada (Table J7)
8701-8793 California (Table J7)
9001-9093 Oregon (Table J7)
9201-9293 Washington (Table J7)
9301-9393 Hawaii (Table J7)
9501-9593 Alaska (Table J7)
Confederate States of America
Cf. E482+ History of the Confederate States of America
9663 Directories. Registers
(9671-9679) Constitution. Constitutional law
see KFZ9000+
(9695-9716) Legislative documents
see KFZ8606+
Executive documents
9717 General works
Messages of the President
9718 Collected
9719 Individual

Confederate States of America -- Continued

(9778-9799) State documents
see KFZ8600+

9803 General works. History

9887 State relations. Equality and sovereignty

Executive branch

9909 General works. History

9919 Cabinet

9925 Civil service

Legislative branch

9933 General works. History

9939 Constitution, powers and prerogatives

9954 Senate

9961 House of Representatives

(9973-9975) Judiciary
see KFZ9108+

Political rights. Citizenship

9981 General works

9989 Suffrage. Right to vote

9993 Electoral system. Elections. Voting

Political institutions and public administration (Canada, Latin America, etc.)
Canada
1 Periodicals. Serials
3 Societies
(5) Yearbooks
see JL1
9 Dictionaries. Encyclopedias
15 General works. History
19 Separation of powers
27 Federal-provincial relations
By period
Early, 1608-1792
41 General works
45 French rule, 1608-1763. New France
48 English rule, 1763-1792
53 Upper and Lower Canada, 1792-1840
55 Province of Canada, 1841-1867
65 Dominion of Canada, 1867- . Canadian Confederation
67.A-Z Special topics, A-Z
67.C58 Civil-military relations
Government. Public administration
71 Directories. Registers
75 General works
86.A-Z Special topics, A-Z
86.A8 Automatic data processing. Electronic data processing. Information technology
Including use of the Internet for the delivery of government services
Benchmarking see JL86.T67
Confidential information see JL86.S43
86.C67 Corruption
86.C87 Customer services. Customer relations
86.D42 Decision making
Electronic data processing see JL86.A8
Informatioin technology see JL86.A8
86.I58 Intelligence service. Espionage
86.O43 Ombudsman
86.P64 Political planning. Public policy
Public policy see JL86.P64
86.P76 Public records
Public relations see JL86.P8
86.P8 Public relations. Propaganda. Government publicity
86.S43 Secret and confidential information
86.T67 Total quality management. Benchmarking
Executive

Canada
Government. Public administration
Executive -- Continued
87 General works
88 Governor general
93 Privy Council
(94) Commissions of inquiry
see KE4765
Departments. Ministries
For departments limited to a particular subject, see the subject
95 General works
Cabinet
97 General works
99 Premier. Prime ministers
103 Department of the Secretary of State
Civil service
(105) Directories. Registers. Civil service lists
see JL71
106 Periodicals. Societies. Serials
108 General works
111.A-Z Special topics, A-Z
111.A4 Alcoholism
111.D4 Details. Relocation
Employee suggestions see JL111.I5
111.E84 Ethics
111.E93 Executives
111.I5 Incentive programs. Meritorious service increases. Employee suggestions
111.L54 Life insurance
Meritorious service increases see JL111.I5
111.M54 Minorities
Pensions see JL111.S3
111.R38 Rating of employees
Relocation see JL111.D4
111.S3 Salaries. Pensions. Fringe benefits
Including legislators' salaries and pensions
Transfers see JL111.D4
111.W6 Women employees
Parliament. Legislative branch
131 Directories. Registers
136 General works
Procedure see KE4535
148.5 Lobbying. Pressure groups
155 Upper House. Senate
161 Lower House. House of Commons

Canada
Government. Public administration
Parliament. Legislative branch -- Continued
Representation
167 General works
168.A-Z By province, A-Z
179 Provincial legislative bodies
(181) Judiciary
see KE4775
186 Government property. Public buildings
186.5 Political rights. Political participation
187 Citizenship
(189) Naturalization
see KE4351
Suffrage. Right to vote
191 General works
192 Women's right to vote
193 Elections. Electoral system. Voting
Political parties
195 General works
197.A-Z Special parties, A-Z
198 Provincial government
200-209 Newfoundland (Table J10)
210-219 Prince Edward Island (Table J10)
220-229 Nova Scotia (Table J10)
230-239 New Brunswick (Table J10)
240-259 Québec (Table J9)
260-279 Ontario (Table J9)
280-299 Manitoba (Table J9)
300-319 Saskatchewan (Table J9)
320-339 Alberta (Table J9)
420-439 British Columbia (Table J9)
460-479 Northwest Territories (Table J9)
480-489 Nunavut (Table J10)
495 Yukon Territory (Table J11)
498 Maritime Provinces (collectively)
500 Prairie Provinces (collectively)
590-599 Bermuda (Table J10)
599.2 Greenland (Table J11)
599.4 Saint Pierre and Miquelon (Table J11)
599.5 West Indies. Caribbean Area (Table J11a)
600-609 British West Indies. English-speaking Caribbean (Table J10)
609.2 Anguilla (Table J11)
610-619 Bahamas (Table J10)
620-629 Barbados (Table J10)
629.5 Cayman Islands (Table J11)

629.6	Grenada (Table J11)
630-639	Jamaica (Table J10)
	Leeward Islands
640-649	General (Table J10)
	Anguilla see JL609.2
649.2	Antigua and Barbuda (Table J11)
649.5	Monserrat (Table J11)
649.7	Saint Kitts and Nevis (Table J11)
650-659	Trinidad and Tobago (Table J10)
	Windward Islands
660-669	General (Table J10)
669.2	Dominica (Table J11)
	Grenada see JL629.6
669.4	Saint Lucia (Table J11)
669.5	Saint Vincent and the Grenadines (Table J11)
670-679	Belize (Table J10)
680-689	Guyana. British Guiana (Table J10)
690-699	Falkland Islands (Table J10)
(740-749)	Danish West Indies see JL1160+
	Netherlands Antilles. Dutch West Indies
760-769	General (Table J10)
769.3	Aruba (Table J11)
769.5	Bonaire (Table J11)
770-779	Curaçao (Table J10)
779.2	Saba (Table J11)
779.5	Saint Eustatius (Table J11)
779.7	Sint Maarten (Table J11)
780-789	Suriname. Dutch Guiana (Table J10)
	French West Indies
790-799	General (Table J10)
810-819	French Guiana (Table J10)
820-829	Guadeloupe (Table J10)
830-839	Martinique (Table J10)
950-969	Latin America (Table J9)
1000-1019	Cuba (Table J9)
1040-1059	Puerto Rico (Table J9)
1080-1099	Haiti (Table J9)
1120-1139	Dominican Republic (Table J9)
1160-1169	Virgin Islands of the United States (Table J10)
1200-1299	Mexico (Table J8)
	Central America
1400-1419	General (Table J9)
	Belize see JL670+
1440-1459	Costa Rica (Table J9)
1480-1499	Guatemala (Table J9)

	Central America -- Continued
1520-1539	Honduras (Table J9)
1560-1579	El Salvador (Table J9)
1600-1619	Nicaragua (Table J9)
1640-1659	Panama (Table J9)
1670-1679	Panama Canal Zone (Table J10)
	South America
1850-1869	General (Table J9)
2000-2099	Argentina (Table J8)
2200-2299	Bolivia (Table J8)
2400-2499	Brazil (Table J8)
2600-2699	Chile (Table J8)
2800-2899	Colombia (Table J8)
3000-3099	Ecuador (Table J8)
	Guianas
	Guyana. British Guyana see JL680+
	Suriname. Dutch Guiana see JL780+
	French Guiana see JL810+
3200-3299	Paraguay (Table J8)
3400-3499	Peru (Table J8)
3600-3699	Uruguay (Table J8)
3800-3899	Venezuela (Table J8)

Political institutions and public administration (Europe)
1 Periodicals. Serials
2 Societies
(3) Collections
see JN5
General works. History
5 General
By period
7 Medieval
Modern
8 General works
9 16th-18th centuries
10 19th century
12 20th century
13 21st century
15 European federation and integration
16 Union of European Federalists
European Council see JN33
16.5 European Movement
18 Council of Europe
For legal works and proceedings see KJE101+
European Union. European Community. European communities
26 Periodicals. Societies. Serials
For official record and documentation, see KJE
27 Directories. Registers
30 General works
32 Executive branch
Including works on public administration
33 European Council
33.5 Commission of the European Communities. European Commission
34 Council of the European Communities. Council of the European Union. Council of Ministers (European Union)
34.3 European Economic and Social Committee
34.5 Regionalism
34.7 Minorities
35 Civil service
36 Legislative branch. European Parliament
40 Political rights. Political participation
45 Elections
50 Political parties
European Union in relation to individual regions or countries see HC240.25.A+
Regions
Northern Europe. Scandinavia see JN7009.2+

Regions -- Continued
94 Western Europe (Table J11a)
96 Central Europe. Eastern Europe (Table J11a)
97 Balkan Peninsula (Table J11a)
98 Black Sea Region
Great Britain
101 Periodicals. Serials
102 Societies
106 Directories. Registers
(111) Constitutional law
see KD3931+
114 Dictionaries. Encyclopedias
General works. By date of imprint
117 Early to 1832
118 1832-
By period
131 To 1066
Medieval, 1066-1485
137 General works
141 Norman Conquest, 1066-1215
147 Magna Carta, 1215
Cf. KD3944+ Law
151 Magna Carta to end of 13th century
158 14th century. Plantagenet to 1399
Modern, 1485-
175 General works
181 16th century, Tudor, 1485-1603
17th century, Stuart. Revolution, 1603-1702
191 General works
193 Early Stuart
196 Commonwealth and Protectorate, 1649-1660
203 Restoration, 1660-1689
207 William and Mary, 1689-1702
18th century, 1702-1832
210 General works
214 Contemporary works
216 19th century, 1832-
231 20th century
238 21st century
248 Commonwealth of Nations. Imperial federation
(266) Church and state
see BX5157
(276) Imperialism. Imperial federation
see JN248
290 Separation of powers
297.A-Z Special topics, A-Z

Great Britain
Special topics, A-Z -- Continued
297.C58 Civil-military relations
297.F43 Federalism
297.I53 Insurgency
297.R44 Regionalism
Government. Public administration
Directories. Registers see JN106
309 History
318 General works
329.A-Z Special topics, A-Z
329.C7 Consultants
329.C74 Correspondence
329.C87 Customer services. Customer relations
329.D43 Decentralization
329.E4 Electronic data processing
329.I6 Intelligence service. Espionage
Lobbying see JN329.P7
329.O43 Ombudsman
329.O73 Organizational change
329.P7 Pressure groups. Lobbying
329.P75 Public records management
329.P8 Publicity
329.S4 Secret and confidential information
Executive branch
Crown
331 General works. History
By period
335 To 1066
336 Norman, 1066-1154
337 Plantagenet, 1154-1485
338 Tudor, 1485-1603
339 Stuart, 1603-1689
340 William and Mary, 1689-1714
341 Hanover, 1714-
(351) Royal prerogative. Divine right, succession, etc. see KD4435+
359 Lord High Steward
365 Privy purse. Royal expenditures
371 Privy Chamber. Royal household
378 The Privy Council
389 Signet Office
Cabinet. Prime ministers
401 History
405 General works
407 Royal commissions

Great Britain
Government. Public administration
Executive branch
Cabinet. Prime ministers -- Continued
409 Executive advisory bodies. Other executive bodies
Civil service
425 General works
428 Civil service reform
431 Civil service examinations
441 Veterans and the civil service
442 Women in the civil service
443 Salaries. Fringe benefits
445 Pensions
447 Retirement. Superannuation
450.A-Z Other topics, A-Z
450.C6 Conflict of interest
450.I5 In-service training. Interns
450.M36 Manpower planning
450.P6 Political activity
450.R38 Rating of employees
450.S88 Suggestion systems. Incentive awards
450.T7 Travel
Departments. Ministries
For departments limited to a particular subject, see the subject
451 General
452 Cabinet Office
453 Home Office
Parliament. Legislative branch
500 Directories. Registers
General works. By date of imprint
505 Early to 1800
508 1800-
History. By period
513 To 1066
515 Medieval, 1066-1485
Modern, 1485-
521 General works
525 16th century
534 17th century
539 18th century, to 1832
543 19th century, "Reform," 1832-1900
550 20th century
Prerogatives of Parliament see KD4246
555 Parliamentary employees. Staff
558 Parliamentary representation

Great Britain
Government. Public administration
Parliament. Legislative branch -- Continued
Privileges see KD4246
581 Salaries of members
Parliamentary procedure
(591-608) General
see KD4210+
611 Reporting. Broadcasting of proceedings
House of Lords
617 Directories. Registers
621 General works
(627-653) Procedure. Prerogatives
see KD4260+
House of Commons
Directories. Registers
671 Debrett
672 Other directories
673 History
677 General works
678 The Speaker
(679) Committees
see KD4358+
(679.8) Individual committees
see KD4361
(681-695) Procedure. Prerogatives
see KD4354+
(750-841) Judiciary
see KD4645
Government property. Public buildings
851 General works
865 Government purchasing
Political rights. Political participation. Practical politics
900 General works
906 Citizenship
(930-943) Naturalization
see KD4056
Elections. Voting. Suffrage. Right to vote
History
945 General
948 Early to 1640
951 1640 to The Reform Bill
955 1832-1945
956 1945-
961 General works
Women's suffrage. Women's right to vote

Great Britain
Political rights. Political participation. Practical politics
Elections. Voting. Suffrage. Right to vote
Women's suffrage. Women's right to vote -- Continued
976 Periodicals. Societies. Serials
979 General works
(1001-1033) Election law
see KD4321+
1037 Election statistics. Election returns
1039 Campaign funds. Election finance
(1041-1071) Contested elections
see KD4380+
1088 Election fraud. Corrupt practices
Political parties
1111 Periodicals. Societies. Serials
1117 General works. History
By period
1118 Early to 18th century
1119 18th century
1120 19th century
1121 20th century
1125.A-Z Local, A-Z
1129.A-Z Special parties, A-Z
e. g.
1129.C62 Communist Party of Great Britain
1129.C7 Conservative Party
1129.L32 Labor Party
1129.L45 Liberal Party
1150-1159 Wales (Table J10)
1170-1179 Isle of Man (Table J10)
Scotland
1187 Periodicals. Serials
(1201-1203) Constitutional law
see KDC750+
1213 General works. History
Government. Public administration
1228 General works. History
1231 Secretary for Scotland. Scottish Office
Executive branch. Crown
History
1233 General works
(1239) Right to the crown. Succession
see KDC779
1243 Civil service
Legislative branch. Parliament
1263 General works. History

Great Britain
Scotland
Government. Public administration
Legislative branch. Parliament -- Continued
1277 Representation
(1281) Procedure
see KDC766
(1282) Private bill legislation
see KDC768
(1283-1285) Judiciary
see KDC840+
Political rights. Political participation. Practical politics
1290 General works
1291 Citizenship
1341 Elections. Voting. Suffrage. Right to vote
1361 Political corruption
Political parties
1370 General works
1371.A-Z Special parties, A-Z
Northern Ireland see JN1572
Channel Islands see JN1573
Ireland
1395 Directories. Registers
(1400-1403) Constitutional law
see KDK1200+
1405 General works. History
By period
1408 To 1500
1409 1501-1781
1411 1782-1921
1415 Irish Free State. Eire, 1922-
Government. Public administration
Directories. Registers see JN1395
1425 General works. History
Executive branch
1435 General works. History
1441 Lord Lieutenant
1442 Governor-General
1443 Privy Council
1444 Cabinet
Civil service
1448 History
1457 General works
1463 Salaries. Pensions
Legislative branch. Parliament
1468 General works

Ireland
Government. Public administration
Legislative branch. Parliament -- Continued
1477 Representation
(1481) Procedure
see KDK1308
(1483-1485) Judiciary
see KDK1580+
Political rights. Political participation. Practical politics
1490 General works
1491 Citizenship
(1505-1511) Naturalization
see KDK1250
1541 Elections. Voting. Suffrage. Right to vote
1561 Corrupt practices. Political corruption
Political parties
1571 General works
1571.5.A-Z Special parties, A-Z
1572 Northern Ireland (Table J11)
1573 Channel Islands (Table J11)
1576 Gibraltar (Table J11)
1580-1589 Malta (Table J10)
Austrian Empire. Austria-Hungary
1601 Periodicals. Serials
1604 Directories. Registers
(1605) Constitutional law
see KJJ2064+
1607 Dictionaries. Encyclopedias
1611 General works
By period
History
1621 To 1273
1274-1804
1623 General works
1625 Pragmatic Sanction
1628 1805-1866
1629 Ausgleich, 1867. Austro-Hungarian compromise
1635 Dual Empire, 1867-1918
Austrian Republic, 1918- see JN2011+
1651 Separation of powers
(1653) Language question
see P119.32
Executive branch. Crown
1713 General works
Civil service
1715 General works

Austrian Empire. Austria-Hungary
Executive branch. Crown
Civil service -- Continued
1721 Salaries. Pensions
Legislative branch
1751 Directories. Registers
1771 General works
1792 Austro-Hungarian Parliament
Austrian Parliament. Reichsrat
1815 General works
1845 Upper House. Herrenhaus
1865 Lower House. Abgeordnetenhaus
Hungarian Parliament see JN2115+
(1901-1929) Judiciary
see KJJ1572+
1941 Government property. Public buildings. Government purchasing
Political rights. Citizenship. Political participation
1951 General works
(1965-1975) Naturalization
see KJJ2440
Elections. Voting. Suffrage. Right to vote
1993 General works
(1998) Law
see KJJ2506
Political parties
1998.8 General works
1999.A-Z Special parties, A-Z
Austrian Republic, 1918-
2011.A2 Periodicals. Serials
2011.A3 Directories. Registers
History
2012 General works
1918-1939 see JN2012
2012.2 1939-1945, Period of annexation by Germany
2012.3 1945-
(2014) Constitutional law
see KJJ2064.5+
2015 Federal-state relations. Regionalism. Federalism
Government. Public administration
(2017) Registers
see JN2011.A3
2018 General works. History
Executive branch
2021 General works
2021.2 President

Austrian Republic, 1918-
Government. Public administration
Executive branch -- Continued
2021.3 Chancellor
2021.4 Departments. Ministries
For departments dealing with a particular subject, see the subject
2021.5 Civil service
Legislative branch. National Assembly
2021.7 General works
2022 Federal Council. Bundesrat
2023 National Council. Nationalrat
(2025) Judiciary
see KJJ1572+
2025.5 Government property. Government purchasing
Political rights. Citizenship. Political participation
2026 General works
(2027) Naturalization
see KJJ2440
Elections. Voting. Suffrage. Right to vote
2029 General works
2029.5 Statistics. Election returns
Political parties
2030 General works
2031.A-Z Special parties, A-Z
2040 Provincial government (General and comparative)
2041.A-Z Provinces, A-Z
Subarrange each by Table J12
Class here provinces of the Austrian Republic only
Hungary
2050 Periodicals. Societies. Serials
2052 Directories. Registers
(2053) Constitutional law
see KKF2064.5+
2055 General works
History
By period
2057 To 1515
2061 1516-1847
2063 1847-1918
Including 19th century general
For Austro-Hungarian compromise, 1867 see JN1629
2066 1918-1989
Including 20th century general
2067 1989-

Hungary -- Continued
(2069) Treatises
see JN2055
2081 Civil-military regions
History
see JN2057+
Government. Public administration
(2083) Directories. Registers
see JN2052
2084.A-Z Special topics, A-Z
Espionage see JN2084.I58
2084.I58 Intelligence service. Espionage
General works
see JN2055
Executive branch
2085 General works
2107 Civil service
Legislative branch. Parliament. Országgyülés
2115 Directories. Registers
2121 General works. History
2135 Representation
(2143) Procedure
see KKF2516
2151 Upper House. Főrendiház
2156 Lower House. Képviselőház
(2161) Judiciary
see KKF1572+
2163 Government property. Public buildings. Government purchasing
Political rights. Citizenship. Political participation
2165 General works
(2171) Naturalization
see KKF2440
2183 Elections. Voting. Suffrage. Right to vote
2187 Political corruption
Political parties
2191.A1 General works
2191.A2-Z Special parties, A-Z
Local. By county see JS4682.A+
Local. By city see JS4685+
(2199.C4-.C46) Croatia
see JN2202
(2199.R8-.R86) Ruthenia
see JN6639
(2199.S44-.S49) Slovakia
see JN2240

2201 Slovenia (Table J11)
2202 Croatia (Table J11)
2203 Bosnia and Hercegovina (Table J11)
2210-2229 Czech Republic. Czechoslovakia. Bohemia (Table J9)
2240 Slovakia (Table J11)
(2250-2269) Bosnia and Hercegovina
see JN2203
2270-2289 Liechtenstein (Table J9)
France
2301 Periodicals. Serials
2303 Directories. Registers
2306 Societies
General works see JN2597
Ancien Régime (To 1789)
(2320) Directories. Registers
see JN2303
2325 General works
History
By period
2328 Early to 511
2331 Merovingian, 511-687
2334 Carolingian, 687-843
2337 Medieval, 843-1493
House of Orléans, 1493-1789
2341 General works
2344 Contemporary works
Executive. Crown
2358 General works
History
By period
2361 Early to 511
2363 Merovingian, 511-687
2365 Carolingian, 687-843
2367 Medieval, 843-1493
2369 House of Orléans, 1493-1789
2375 Succession to the Crown
2377 Crown properties and revenues
(2395) Intendants
see JS4843
2409 Tiers Etat
Parliamentary Assemblies. Etats Généraux
For Assemblies of 1787-1789 see JN2471
For Parlements see KJV3754
2413 General works
2417.A-Z By place, A-Z

France
Ancien Régime (To 1789) -- Continued
(2423) Judiciary. Parlements
see KJV3745+
(2433) Local. Provinces
see JS4845
Revolutionary and modern periods
2451 General works. History
By period
1789-1870
2461 General works
Revolution and First Republic, 1789-1804
2468 General works. History
2471 Assemblies of 1787-1789
2473.A-Z Local assemblies. By place, A-Z
(2475) Assemblée Constituante, 1790-1791
see KJV4074.5
2491 Napoleonic era, 1804-1815
2509 Restoration, 1815-1830
2521 Second Revolution, 1830
2529 Louis Philippe, 1830-1848
2552 Second Empire, 1852-1871
(2554) Gouvernement de la défense nationale, 1870-1871
see DC310
(2557) Commune, March 18-May 22, 1871
see DC310
Third Republic, 1871-1947
2562 General works
2592 Pétain regime
2592.5 Interim regime, 1943-1947
2593 Contemporary works
2594 Fourth Republic, 1947-1958
2594.2 Fifth Republic, 1958-
2597 General works
2606 Separation of powers. Delegation of powers
2610.A-Z Special topics, A-Z
2610.C58 Civil-military relations
2610.D43 Decentralization
2610.E45 Ethics
2610.R4 Regionalism
Government. Public administration
(2615) Directories. Registers
see JN2303
General works see JN2597
Executive
Cf. JN2358+ Ancien Régime

France
Government. Public administration
Executive -- Continued
2625 General works
2665 President
Executive power see KJV4360+
Council of Ministers. Ministries
For ministries dealing with a particular subject, see the subject
2681 General works
2685 Ministry of the Interior
2701 Council of State. Conseil d'Etat
Civil service. Fonction publique
Directories. Registers see JN2303
2719 Dictionaries
2725 History
2728 General works
2738.A-Z Special topics, A-Z
2738.A66 Appointments and removals. Patronage
Confidential information see JN2738.S43
2738.C58 Consultants
2738.C6 Corruption
2738.C74 Crisis management
2738.D43 Decentralization
2738.E4 Electronic data processing
2738.E95 Executives
2738.H35 Handicapped. People with disabilities
2738.I58 Intelligence service. Espionage
2738.O47 Ombudsman
2738.P36 Paperwork
Patronage see JN2738.A66
People with disabilities see JN2738.H35
2738.P8 Public relations. Propaganda. Government publicity
2738.S43 Secret and confidential information
2738.W67 Women employees
2741 Study and teaching. Examinations
(2746) Organization
see JN2728
2748 Salaries. Pensions
(2749) Trade-unions. Civil service societies
see HD8005
Government property. Public buildings
2751 General works
2759 Records management
Legislative branch
2761 Directories. Registers

France
Government. Public administration
Legislative branch -- Continued
2771 History
For Ancien Régime see JN2413+
2791 General works
2794 Lobbying. Pressure groups
(2809) Legislative powers
see KJV4321
(2815) Procedure
see KJV4326
Senate
2819 Directories. Registers
2826 General works. History
National Assembly. Chamber of Deputies
2858 Directories. Registers
2863 General works. History
(2887) Judiciary
see KJV3721
(2913) Government property
see JN2751+
Political rights. Political participation
2916 General works
2919 Citizenship
(2931) Naturalization
see KJV377
Suffrage. Right to vote
2941 General works
2954 Women's suffrage. Women's right to vote
Elections. Electoral systems. Voting
2959 General works
2960.A-Z Local, A-Z
Class here works on local results of national elections
Political corruption
2988 General works
2988.5 Election fraud
Political parties
2997 General works
3007.A-Z Special parties, A-Z
Departmental government see JS4903+
Regional government see JS4902
3100-3119 Andorra (Table J9)
3130-3149 Monaco (Table J9)
Germany
3201 Periodicals. Serials
3202 Societies

Germany -- Continued
3203 Directories. Registers
3211 Dictionaries. Encyclopedias
Constitutional history. Constitutional law. Constitution see KK4443.92+
3221 General works
History
By period
3241 Early to ca. 900
The Holy Roman Empire, ca. 919-1806
3249 General works
(3250) Constitutional history. Constitutional law
see KK290+
(3251-3260) Early Feudal period
see JN3249
(3261-3270) Later Feudal period, 1273-1519
see JN3249
3271 Charles V to the Peace of Westphalia, 1519-1648
3281 Peace of Westphalia to the dissolution of the Empire, 1648-1804
Period of confederation, 1806-1871
3295 General works
Confederation of the Rhine: Rhinebund, 1806-1815
3301 General works
(3303-3307) Constitution
see KK4444
Confederation of 1815. German confederation. Deutscher Bund, 1815-1866
3321 General works
(3323) Constitution. Bundesakte, 1815. Wiener Schlussakte, 1820
see KK4444.2+
(3329) Movements and events of 1848
see DD207
3331 National Assembly. Frankfurt Parliament. Deutsche Nationalversammlung, 1848-1849
North German Confederation and the New Empire, 1867-1918
3357 General works
North German Confederation, 1867-1871
3368 General works
(3371-3379) Constitutional history
see KK4525+
Empire of 1871. Kaiserreich, 1871-1918
3388 General works

Germany
History
By period
North German Confederation and the New Empire, 1867-1918
Empire of 1871. Kaiserreich, 1871-1918 -- Continued
(3391-3444) Constitutional history
see KK4552+
Weimar Republic. Third Reich see JN3951+
1945- see JN3971.A1+
1990- see JN3971.A1+
Government. Public administration
(3445) Directories. Registers
see JN3203
General works see JN3221
Executive branch. Kaiser
Cf. KK4654+ Constitutional law
3463 General works
(3475-3489) Imperial Chancellor. Reichskanzler
see KK4667+
3501 Departments. Ministries
For departments limited to a particular subject, see the subject
Civil Service
(3525) Directories. Registers
see JN3203
3548 General works
3565 Salaries. Pensions
Legislative branch
3571 Directories. Registers
3581 General works
(3593-3615) Parliamentary procedures. Legislative powers
see KK4629
Upper House. Bundesrat
3623 Directories. Registers
3633 General works
(3638-3643) Constitution, powers, and prerogatives
see KK4630+
Lower House. Reichstag
3669 Directories. Registers
(3671) Collections
see JN3674
3674 General works
(3678-3698) Constitution, powers, and prerogatives
(3721-3753) Judiciary
see KK4696

Germany -- Continued
3759 Government property. Public buildings
Political rights. Political participation
3770 General works
Citizenship
(3771) Legal treatises
see KK4590
3774 General works
(3785-3794) Naturalization
see KK4598
Suffrage. Right to vote
3809 General works
3825 Women's suffrage. Women's right to vote
3838 Elections. Voting
(3848-3887) Election law
see KK5272+
3901 Election fraud
Political parties
3925 General works
By period
3931 Early to 1871
3933 1871-1918
(3934) 1918-1945
see JN3970
1945- see JN3971.A979+
3946.A-Z Special parties, A-Z
Weimar Republic. Third Reich, 1918-1945
3951.A2 Periodicals. Serials
3951.A3 Directories. Registers
(3951.5) Constitutional history
see KK4710+
3952 General works. History
3955 Federal-state relations. Federalism
Government. Public administration
(3957) Directories. Registers
see JN3951.A3
(3958-3959) General works
see JN3952
Executive branch
3961 General works
3961.2 President
3961.3 Chancellor
3961.4 Departments. Ministries
For departments dealing with a particular subject, see the subject
3961.5 Civil service

Germany
Weimar Republic. Third Reich, 1918-1945
Government. Public administration -- Continued
National Council. Reichsrat
3962 General works
(3962.A3) Procedure
see KK4821
Reichstag
3963 General works
(3963.A3) Procedure
see KK4813
(3965) Judiciary
see KK4879
Political rights. Citizenship. Political participation
3966 General works
(3967) Naturalization
see KK4736
Elections. Voting. Suffrage. Right to vote
3969 General works
3969.5 Statistics. Election returns
3969.9 Political corruption
Political parties
For National Socialist Party, Nationalsozialistische Deutsche Arbeiterpartei see DD253.2+
3970.A1 General works
3970.A2-Z Special parties, A-Z
1945-
Including West Germany to 1990, West and East Germany to 1990, and Reunified Germany after 1990
3971.A1 Periodicals. Societies. Serials
3971.A12-.A125 Directories. Registers
3971.A127 Dictionaries. Encyclopedias
(3971.A13-.A32) Constitutional history. Constitutional law. Constitutions
see KK4436+
(3971.A34) Treatises
see JN3971.A58
3971.A38A-.A38Z Special topics, A-Z
3971.A38C58 Civil-military relations
Federal and state relations see JN3971.A38S8
Language policy see P119.3+
Military-civil relations see JN3971.A38C58
3971.A38M5 Minorities
3971.A38R343 Regionalism
3971.A38S8 State rights. Federal-state relations. Federal government
Government. Public administration

Germany
1945-
Government. Public administration -- Continued

(3971.A4) Directories. Registers
see JN3971.A1+
3971.A5 History
General works see JN3971.A58
3971.A56A-.A56Z Special topics, A-Z
3971.A56A8 Automation. Electronic data processing
3971.A56C54 Communication systems
Confidential information see JN3971.A56S4
3971.A56C55 Consultants
3971.A56C57 Correspondence
3971.A56C6 Corruption. Political corruption
3971.A56C75 Crisis management
3971.A56D42 Decentralization
3971.A56D45 Decision making
Electronic data processing see JN3971.A56A8
3971.A56E8 Ethics. Political ethics
3971.A56I6 Intelligence service. Espionage
3971.A56I63 Investigations
3971.A56M37 Marketing
3971.A56O35 Office practice
3971.A56O4 Ombudsman
3971.A56P37 Paperwork
3971.A56R4 Records. Public records
3971.A56S4 Secret and confidential information
3971.A56W55 Whistle blowing
(3971.A57) Administrative law
see KK5569+
3971.A58 General works
Executive branch. President. Chancellor
3971.A61 General works
Departments. Ministries
For departments or ministries limited to a particular subject, see the subject
3971.A63 General works
Civil service
(3971.A66) History
see JN3971.A67
3971.A67 General works
3971.A69A-.A69Z Special topics, A-Z
3971.A69A6 Appointments and removals
3971.A69C55 Classification
Dismissal see JN3971.A69A6
3971.A69E87 Examinations

Germany
1945-
Government. Public administration
Executive branch. President. Chancellor
Departments. Ministries
Civil service
Special topics, A-Z -- Continued

3971.A69E9 Executives
3971.A69I6 In-service training. Interns
3971.A69M54 Minorities
3971.A69P35 Part-time employment
3971.A69P44 Personnel management
3971.A69P64 Political activity
3971.A69P7 Promotions
Public relations see JN3971.A69P85
3971.A69P85 Public relations. Propaganda. Government publicity
3971.A69R3 Rating of employees
3971.A69R45 Relocation of employees. Transfers
Removals see JN3971.A69A6
Selection and appointment see JN3971.A69A6
3971.A69T7 Travel
3971.A69W6 Women in the civil service
3971.A69W68 Work sharing
3971.A691 Salaries. Pensions. Retirement
3971.A693 Ministry of the Interior

Legislative branch
For the Bundestag see JN3971.A78
3971.A7 Directories. Registers
3971.A71 General works
(3971.A72-.A75) Organization and procedures. Powers and duties
see KK5310+
3971.A76 Legislative reference bureaus
3971.A77 Federal Council. Bundesrat
Federal Assembly. Bundestag
Directories. Registers see JN3971.A7
3971.A78 General works
3971.A785A-.A785Z Special topics, A-Z
3971.A785B74 Broadcasting of proceedings. Reporting
3971.A785E45 Employees
3971.A785E85 Ethics
(3971.A785L39) Legislative power
see KK5329
(3971.A785L42) Legislative process
see KK5349
Lobbying see JN3971.A785P7

Germany
1945-
Government. Public administration
Legislative branch
Special topics, A-Z -- Continued

3971.A785O6 Opposition
3971.A785P53 Political planning. Public policy
3971.A785P7 Pressure groups. Lobbying
(3971.A785P8) Publication of proceedings
see JN3971.A78B74
(3971.A785R4) Reporters and reporting
see JN3971.A78B74
3971.A785S65 Speaker. Presiding officer. Bundestagspräsident
(3971.A8-.A87) Judiciary
see KK5452
3971.A9 Government property. Public buildings
Political rights. Political participation. Practical politics
3971.A91 General works
3971.A92 Citizenship. Civics
(3971.A93) Naturalization
see KK6044
Elections. Voting. Suffrage. Right to vote
3971.A95 General works
3971.A953A-.A953Z Local results of national elections, A-Z
3971.A956 Election statistics. Election returns
(3971.A96) Election law
see KK5272
3971.A975 Election fraud
Political parties
3971.A979 General works
3971.A98A-.A98Z Special parties, A-Z
e.g.
(3971.A98S4-.A98S5717) Sozialdemokratische Partei Deutschlands
see JN3971.A98S571712+
3971.A98S571712-.A98S6999 Sozialdemokratische Partei Deutschlands
3971.A988 State government (General and comparative)
For local government see JS5301+
(3971.A99-.Z8) By state
see JN4000+
3971.5 German Democratic Republic, 1949-1990 (Table J11 modified)
Political parties
3971.5.A979 General works
3971.5.A98A-.A98Z Special parties, A-Z
e.g.

JN

Germany
German Democratic Republic, 1949-1990
Political parties
Special parties, A-Z -- Continued
Sozialistische Einheitspartei Deutschlands

3971.5.A98S4-.A98S57 Official serials
Alphabetically by author (or title if title entry)
3971.5.A98S58 Official monographs. By date
3971.5.A98S582 Statutes. Constitution. By date
3971.5.A98S6 Congresses. By date
3971.5.A98S63 Zentralkomitee
All publications, by date
3971.5.A98S64-.A98S649 Serials, non-official
3971.5.A98S65 Works about the party. By date
(3971.5.A99-.Z8) By state
see JN4000+
(3972) Reunified Germany, 1990
see JN3971

States
Including provinces and extinct states
For local government see JS5301+

4000-4019 Alsace-Lorraine (Table J9)
4020-4039 Anhalt (Table J9)
4040-4139 Baden (Table J8)
4139.5 Baden-Württemberg (Table J11)
4140-4239 Bavaria (Table J8)
4239.3 Brandenburg (Table J11)
4239.5 Brandenburg (State, 1990-) (Table J11)
4240-4259 Bremen (Table J9)
4260-4279 Brunswick (Table J9)
4279.5 Friesland (Table J11)
4280-4299 Hamburg (Table J9)
4299.5 Hanover (Table J11)
4300-4319 Hesse (Table J9)
4320-4339 Lippe (Table J9)
4339.5 Lower Saxony (Table J11)
4340-4359 Lübeck (Table J9)
4359.5 Mainz (Table J11)
4359.7 Mecklenburg (State, 1990-) (Table J11)
4360-4379 Mecklenburg-Schwerin (Table J9)
4380-4399 Mecklenburg-Strelitz (Table J9)
4399.5 Nassau (Table J11)
4399.7 North Rhine-Westphalia (Table J11)
4400-4419 Oldenburg (Table J9)
4420 Pomerania (Table J11)

Germany
States -- Continued
Prussia
4421 Periodicals. Serials
4424 Directories. Registers
4431 General works
History
Cf. KKB8901+ Constitutional history
By period
4445 To 1850
4451 1850-1918
4461 1918-1949
1949- see JN3971.5
Government. Public administration
(4484) Directories. Registers
see JN4424
General works see JN4431
Executive branch. Crown
4487 General works
4508 Departments. Ministries
For departments dealing with a particular subject, see the subject
Civil service
(4527) Directories. Registers
see JN4424
4533 General works
4548 Salaries. Pensions
Legislative branch
4551 Directories. Registers
4557 General works. History
(4563-4577) Procedure. Legislative powers
see KKB9194.7
4582 Upper house. House of Peers. Herrenhaus
4597 Lower house. House of Representatives. Abgeordnetenhaus
(4607-4613) Judiciary
see KK9149
Political rights. Citizenship. Political participation
4623 General works
(4633-4638) Naturalization
see KKB9188.5
Suffrage
4643 General works
4645 Qualifications
4648 Women's suffrage
Elections. Voting. Right to vote

Germany
States
Prussia
Political rights. Citizenship. Political participation
Elections. Voting. Right to vote -- Continued
4653 General works
(4656-4658) Election law
see KKB9194
4681-4683 Political parties
4681 General works
4683.A-Z Special parties, A-Z
States see JN4000+
4700-4719 Reuss (Elder Line) (Table J9)
4720-4739 Reuss (Younger Line) (Table J9)
4739.3 Rhine Province (Table J11)
4739.5 Rhineland-Palatinate (Table J11)
4739.7 Ruhr Region (Table J11)
4739.8 Saarland (Table J11)
4740-4759 Saxe-Altenburg (Table J9)
4760-4779 Saxe-Meiningen (Table J9)
4820-4839 Saxony (Table J9)
4839.5 Saxony (State, 1990-) (Table J11)
4839.7 Saxony-Anhalt (Table J11)
Saxony, Lower see JN4339.5
4840-4859 Schaumburg-Lippe (Table J9)
4859.5 Schleswig-Holstein (Table J11)
4860-4879 Schwarzburg-Rudolstadt (Table J9)
4880-4899 Schwarzburg-Sondershausen (Table J9)
4900-4909 Thuringia (1920-1952) (Table J10)
4910 Thuringia (1990-) (Table J11)
4915 Waldeck (Table J11)
4916 Westphalia (Table J11)
4920-4939 Württemberg (Table J9)
4944 Würzburg (Table J11)
(4945) Other political divisions
see JN4000+
(4960-4980) States no longer existing in 1871
see JN4000+
Greece
For ancient Greece see JC71+
5001 Periodicals. Societies. Serials
5004 Directories. Registers
Constitutional history. Constitutional law. Constitutions see KKE1+
5016 General works
History

Greece
History -- Continued
By period
5031 Early to 1822
5035 National Assembly at Piadi (1822) to establishment of monarch, 1833
Otto of Bavaria, King of Greece (1833-1862)
5041 General works
(5044) Constitution
see KKE2064.51843
George I (1863-1913)
5051 General works
(5053) Constitution of 1864
see KKE2064.51864
5056 Constantine I (1913-1922)
5057 George II (1922-1933)
Republic, 1924-
(5058) Constitution
see KKE2064.51925
5059 General works
(5060) Contemporary works
see JN5059
5061 Ionian Islands
(5062) General works
see JN5016
General works see JN5016
Government. Public administration
Directories. Registers see JN5004
5064.A-Z Special topics, A-Z
5064.O43 Ombudsman
5064.P83 Public relations. Propaganda. Government publicity
Executive. Crown
5065 General works
5075 Departments. Ministries
For ministries limited to a particular subject, see the subject
Civil service
(5081) Directories. Registers
see JN5004
5093 General works
Legislative branch
5101 Directories. Registers
5107 General works
5116 Senate
5123 House of Representatives. Voulē
(5141-5143) Judiciary
see KKE283+

Greece -- Continued
Political rights. Citizenship. Political participation
5147 General works
Elections. Voting. Suffrage. Right to vote
5165 General works
5166 Election statistics. Election returns
5181 Election fraud. Corrupt practices
5183 Political corruption
Political parties
5185.A1 General works
5185.A2-Z Special parties, A-Z
Prefectures. Nomoi
5190 General works
5191.A-Z By prefecture, A-Z
Subarrange each by Table J12
Italy
For ancient Rome see JC81+
5201 Periodicals. Societies. Serials
5203 Directories. Registers
(5208) Constitutional history. Constitutional law. Constitutions
see KKH2050+
5211 General works
History
By period
Early to French Revolution (ca. 1793)
5231 General works
Special states and regions
5251 Piedmont. Savoy
5256 Liguria. Genoa
5261 Lombardy. Milan
5266 Venice
5271 Emilia. Romagna
Including Modena and Parma
5276 Tuscany. Florence
5281 Rome. Marches. Umbria
5286 Naples. Sicily
5291 Sardinia. Corsica
5299.A-Z Other, A-Z
Nineteenth century (circa 1796-1900)
5345 General works
By period
5348 Napoleonic era, 1796-1814
1814-1870. Risorgimento
5381 General works
5383 1814-1848
5385 1848-1860/1870

Italy
History
By period
Nineteenth century (circa 1796-1900)
By period
1814-1870. Risorgimento -- Continued
Sardinia (Kingdom). House of Savoy
5391 General works
(5395-5401) Constitutional history
see KKH7191+
5405 Executive branch
5411 Legislative branch
(5414) Judiciary
see KKH7184
Other states
5425 Lombardo-Venetian Kingdom
5429 Tuscany
5431 Papal States. Rome
5433 Kingdom of Naples and Sicily
5435.A-Z Other, A-Z
United Italy (1870-). Italian Republic
5441 Periodicals. Serials
5443 Societies
Constitutional history. Constitutional law. Constitutions see KKH1+
5448 General works
History
By period
5449 1870-1922
5450 1922-1945
5451 1945-1994
5452 1994-
5460 Separation of powers. Delegation of powers
(5471) Church and state
see BX1545
5477.A-Z Special topics, A-Z
5477.A8 Automatic data processing. Electronic data processing
Including use of the Internet for the delivery of government services
(5477.D38) Data processing
see JN5477.A8
5477.D4 Decentralization
5477.F43 Federalism
5477.I6 Intelligence service. Espionage
5477.P7 Pressure groups. Lobbying
5477.P83 Publicity

Italy
United Italy (1870-). Italian Republic
Special topics, A-Z -- Continued
5477.R35 Regionalism
5477.S33 Secret and confidential information
Government. Public administration
(5478) Directories. Registers
see JN5203
(5479) General works. History
see JN5448+
Special topics see JN5477.A+
Executive branch
5483 General works
(5489) Powers, prerogatives
see KKH2578
Departments. Ministries
For departments limited to a particular subject, see the subject
5493 General works
5494 Ministry of the Interior
5497 Council of state. Consiglio di Stato
Civil service. Bureaucracy
(5503) Directories. Registers
see JN5203
5511 General works. History
5519.A-Z Special topics, A-Z
5519.A6 Appointments and removals. Patronage
Corrupt practices see JN5641
5519.E87 Examinations
5519.E9 Executives, Government
5519.I6 In-service training
Incentive awards see JN5519.S83
5519.L5 Labor productivity
5519.S83 Suggestion systems. Incentive awards
5519.W6 Women in the civil service
5526 Salaries. Pensions
Legislative branch. Parlamento
5531 Directories. Registers
5535 History
5537 General works
(5539-5540) Parliamentary practice
see KKH2516
Senate
5541 Directories. Registers
5544 General works
Chamber of Deputies

Italy
  United Italy (1870-). Italian Republic
    Government. Public administration
      Legislative branch. Parlamento
        Chamber of Deputies -- Continued
5564 Directories. Registers
5567 General works
(5581-5585) Judiciary
see KKH283+
5589 Government property. Public buildings
    Political rights. Citizenship
5591 General works
5593 Political participation
(5596) Naturalization
see KKH2440
      Elections. Voting. Suffrage. Right to vote
5607 History
        Provinces
Class here works on national elections
For provincial elections see JN5690.A+
For local elections see JS5796.A+
5608.A2 General works
5608.A3-.Z8 By province, A-Z
5608.Z9A-.Z9Z Local, A-Z
Class here works on local results of national elections
5609 Election statistics. Election returns
5611 General works
5615 Women's suffrage. Women's right to vote
(5619-5623) Election law
see KKH2506
5641 Corrupt practices. Political corruption
    Political parties
5651 General works
5657.A-Z Special parties, A-Z
5690.A-Z By region or province, A-Z
Class here works on regional or provincial government
For local government see JS5796.A+
5695 San Marino (Table J11)
5697 Vatican City (Table J11)
5700 Benelux countries (Table J11a)
Netherlands
5701 Periodicals. Societies. Serials
5703 Directories. Registers
(5707) Constitutional history. Constitutional law. Constitutions
see KKM2050+
  History

Netherlands
History -- Continued
5711 General works
By period
Early to 1789/1795
5718 General works
5731 1555 to 1648
5745 1648 to 1795
Nineteenth century
5755 General works
By period
5758 Batavian Republic (1795-1806)
5761 Kingdom of Holland (1806-1810)
5764 French annexation (1810-1815)
5770 Kingdom of Netherlands (1815-1830)
5773 Separation of Belgium
5789 Kingdom of the Netherlands (1830-)
5801 General works
(5803) Compends. Textbooks
see JN5801
Government. Public administration
(5809) General works
see JN5801
5810.A-Z Special topics, A-Z
5810.A8 Automatic data processing. Data processing
5810.C67 Corruption. Political corruption
5810.D43 Decentralization
Electronic data processing see JN5810.A8
5810.P8 Public relations. Propaganda. Government publicity
5810.S4 Secret and confidential information
Executive branch
5813 General works
(5818) Powers, prerogatives
see KKM2578
Departments. Ministries
5828 General works
(5831) Powers and prerogatives
see KKM2602
Individual departments and ministries
5836 Ministry of the Interior
Other departments or ministries
see the subject
5837 Council of State. Raad van State
Civil service
(5841) Directories. Registers
see JN5703

Netherlands
Government. Public administration
Executive branch
Civil service -- Continued
5855 General works
5861 Salaries. Pensions
Legislative branch. Staten-General
5873 Directories. Registers
5881 General works
5883 Lobbying. Pressure groups
Upper House. Eerste Kamer
5887 General works
(5891-5897) Constitution, powers and prerogatives
see KKM2510+
5901 Lower House. Tweede Kamer
(5921-5929) Judiciary
see KKM283+
5933 Government property. Public buildings
Political rights. Citizenship. Political participation
5935 General works
(5941-5945) Naturalization
see KKM2440
Elections. Voting. Suffrage. Right to vote
5951 General works
(5953-5955) Election law
see KKM2506
5971 Political corruption
Political parties
5981 General works
5985.A-Z Special parties, A-Z
5999.A-Z By province, A-Z
For local government see JS5950.A+
Belgium
6101 Periodicals. Societies. Serials
6105 Directories. Registers
History
6114 General works
By period
6135 1830-1893
6155 1893-
6165 General works
6175 Federal-state relations. Central-local relations. Regionalism
Government. Public administration
(6183) General
see JN6165
6184.A-Z Special topics, A-Z

Belgium
Government. Public administration
Special topics, A-Z -- Continued
6184.E4 Electronic data processing
6184.P82 Public relations. Propaganda. Government publicity
Executive branch
6189 General works
(6199) Powers, prerogatives
see KJK2578
6205 Departments. Ministries
For departments or ministries limited to a particular subject, see the subject
Civil service
(6215) Directories. Registers
see JN6105
6223 General works
6235 Salaries. Pensions
Legislative branch. Parlement
6243 Directories. Registers
6247 General works
(6248) Constitution, powers, and prerogatives
see KJK2510+
6249 Lobbying. Pressure groups
6255 Senate
6271 Chamber of Representatives
(6283-6288) Judiciary
see KJK283+
6290 Government property. Public buildings
Political rights. Citizenship. Political participation
6301 General works
(6311-6315) Naturalization
see KJK2440
Elections. Voting. Suffrage. Right to vote
6331 General works
(6335-6339) Election law
see KJK2506
6355 Political corruption
Political parties
6365 General works
6371.A-Z Special parties, A-Z
Local
Provinces to 1830 see JN5999.A+
Provinces after 1830 see JS6020.A+
6380-6399 Luxembourg (Table J9)
6500-6598 Soviet Union. Russia. Former Soviet Republics (Table J8 modified)

Soviet Union. Russia. Former Soviet Republics -- Continued
Government. Public administration
Political parties
6598.A1 General works
6598.A2-Z Special parties, A-Z
e.g.
Kommunisticheskai͡a partii͡a Sovetskogo Soi͡uza
6598.K4 Serials
6598.K5 Congresses. By date
6598.K55A-.K55Z History. By language, A-Z, and date
6598.K7 General works
Konstitut͡sionno-demokraticheskai͡a partii͡a
6598.K9 Serials
6598.K93 Congresses. By date
6598.K95 General works
State, provincial, prefecture government (General and comparative)
(6599.A-Z) Individual republics
see JN6615+
6615 Estonia (Table J11)
6630-6639 Ukraine (Table J10)
6640-6649 Belarus (Table J10)
Caucasus
General see JQ1759
(6650-6659) Armenia
see JQ1759.3
(6660-6669) Azerbaijan
see JQ1759.5
(6670-6679) Georgia
see JQ1759.7
6680-6689 Moldova (Table J10)
6690-6699 Russia (Federation) (Table J10)
For Siberia see JQ1100+
(6700-6719) Finland
see JN7390+
Baltic States
6729 General (Table J11a)
Estonia see JN6615
6730-6739 Latvia (Table J10)
6745 Lithuania (Table J11)
6750-6769 Poland (Table J9)
Scandinavia. Northern Europe
Constitutional history. Constitutional law. Constitutions see KJC530+
7011 General works
History

Scandinavia. Northern Europe
History -- Continued
By period
7021 To 1523
7036 Denmark and Norway (1523-1814)
7041 Norway and Sweden (1814-1905)
7042 1905-
Including the Nordic Council
7051 Executive branch
7056 Legislative branch
7066 Political parties
Denmark
7101 Periodicals. Societies. Serials
7104 Directories. Registers
(7105) Constitutional history. Constitutional law. Constitutions
see KJR2061+
History
7111 General works
By period
7118 To 1814
7155 Kingdom of Denmark, 1814-
7161 General works
Government. Public administration
(7169) General works
see JN7161
7170.A-Z Special topics, A-Z
7170.D42 Decentralization
7170.E4 Electronic data processing
7170.P75 Productivity. Government productivity
7170.P8 Public relations. Propaganda. Government publicity
Executive branch
7178 General works
(7183) Powers and prerogatives
see KJR2578
7191 Departments. Ministries
For departments or ministries limited to a particular subject, see the subject
Civil service
(7207) Directories. Registers
see JN7104
7221 General works
7223 Salaries. Pensions
Legislative branch. Rigsdag
7228 Directories. Registers
7235 General works

Denmark
Government. Public administration
Legislative branch. Rigsdag -- Continued
(7238) Legislative powers and process
see KJR2510+
7241 Lobbying. Pressure groups
7255 Upper House. Landstinget
7270 Lower House. Unicameral legislature. Folketinget
(7275-7289) Judiciary
see KJR283+
7279 Government property. Public buildings
Political rights. Citizenship
7295 General works
7296 Political participation
(7301-7305) Naturalization
see KJR2440
Elections. Voting. Suffrage. Right to vote
7321 General works
(7325-7328) Election law
see KJR2506
7355 Political corruption
Political parties
7365.A1 General works
7365.A2-Z Special parties, A-Z
7367 Faroe Islands
7370-7379 Greenland (Table J10)
7380-7389 Iceland (Table J10)
7390-7399 Finland (Table J10)
Norway
7401 Periodicals. Societies. Serials
7405 Directories. Registers
(7409) Constitutional history. Constitutional law. Constitutions
see KKN2061+
History
7415 General works
By period
7421 To 1814
1814-1905
7431 General works
(7432) Rigsforsamlingen (1814). Eidsvold
see KKN2064.5
(7433) The Grundlow (1814)
see KKN2064.5
7451 1905-
7461 General works

Norway -- Continued
(7471) Language question
see P119.32
Government. Public administration
(7479) General works
see JN7461
7480.A-Z Special topics, A-Z
7480.C67 Corruption. Political corruption
7480.E4 Electronic data processing
7480.P82 Public relations. Propaganda. Government publicity
7480.R43 Records. Public records
Executive branch
7483 General works
(7491) Powers and prerogatives
see KKN2578
7501 Departments. Ministries
For departments or ministries limited to a particular subject, see the subject
Civil service
(7513) Directories. Registers
see JN7405
7525 General works
7528 Salaries. Pensions
Legislative branch. Stortinget
7541 Directories. Registers
7543 General works
(7544) Elections
see JN7651
7548 Ombudsman
7549 Pressure groups. Lobbying
7561 Upper House. Lagting
7581 Lower House. Odelsting
(7601-7605) Judiciary
see KKN283+
7606 Government property. Public buildings
Political rights. Citizenship. Political participation
7615 General works
(7631-7635) Naturalization
see KKN2440
Elections. Voting. Suffrage. Right to vote
7651 General works
7653 Election statistics. Election returns
(7655-7659) Election law
see KKN2506
(7681) Political corruption
see JN7480.C67

Norway -- Continued
Political parties
7691.A1 General works
7691.A2-Z Special parties, A-Z
(7693) Counties
see JS6220
7695 Spitzbergen
Sweden
7721 Periodicals. Societies. Serials
7724 Directories. Registers
Constitutional history. Constitutional law. Constitutions see KKV1+
History
7741 General works
By period
To 1905
7761 General works
(7765) Constitution of 1809
see KKV2064.5
7799 1905-
7825 General works
7835 Central-local government relations
Government. Public administration
(7849) General works
see JN7825
7850.A-Z Special topics, A-Z
Confidential information see JN7850.S4
7850.D43 Decentralization
7850.D45 Decision making
7850.E4 Electronic data processing
7850.P38 Paperwork. Government paperwork
7850.P75 Productivity. Government productivity
7850.P8 Public relations. Propaganda. Government publicity
7850.S4 Secret and confidential information
Executive branch
7853 General works
(7865) Powers and prerogatives
see KKV2578
7869 Royal household
7875 Departments. Ministries
For departments or ministries limited to a particular subject, see the subject
7877 Council of State. Statsradet
Civil service
(7888) Directories. Registers
see JN7724

Sweden
Government. Public administration
Executive branch
Civil service -- Continued
7903 General works
7904 Salaries. Pensions
Legislative branch. Riksdag
7911 Directories. Registers
7913 History
7915 General works
7916 Speaker. Talmannen
7918 Ombudsman
7921 Upper House. Forsta Kammaren
7928 Lower House. Andra Kammaren
(7934-7936) Unicameral Legislature (1971)
see JN7911+
(7938-7941) Judiciary
see KKV283+
7943 Government property. Public buildings
Political rights. Citizenship. Political participation
7945 General works
(7951) Naturalization
see KKV2440
Elections. Voting. Suffrage. Right to vote
7958 General works
7958.2 Election statistics. Election returns
(7959-7963) Election law
see KKV2506
7985 Political corruption
Political parties
7995.A1 General works
7995.A2-Z Special parties, A-Z
(7997) Local
see JS6270+
Spain
8101 Periodicals. Societies. Serials
8103 Directories. Registers
(8107) Constitutional history. Constitutional law. Constitutions
see KKT2050+
8108 Dictionaries. Encyclopedias
History
8111 General
By period
To 1516
8118 General works

Spain
History
By period
To 1516 -- Continued
(8123) Cortes
see JN8298
The old kingdoms
8128 Majorca
8130 Asturias. Leon
8133 Navarre
8137 Aragon
8140 Castile and Leon
8142 Valencia
8145 Kingdom of Spain, 1516-1808
Nineteenth century
8155 General works
8157 Napoleonic era, 1808-1814
(8159) Constitution of 1809
see KKT2064.51809
(8161) Constitution of 1812
see KKT2064.51812
Period of constitutional struggle, 1814-1872
8173 General works
(8174) Constitution of 1837
see KKT2064.51837
(8174.5) Constitution of 1869
see KKT2064.51869
(8179) Contemporary works
see JN8173
8183 Republic of Spain, 1873-1876
Kingdom of Spain, 1876-1931
8195 General works
(8197) Constitution of 1876
see KKT2064.51876
Republic and Franco era, 1931-1975
(8205) Constitution of 1931
see KKT2064.51931
8209 General works
8210 1975-
8221 General works
8230 Civil-military relations
8231 Regionalism. Autonomous communities
Government. Public administration
(8236) General works
see JN8221
8237.A-Z Special topics, A-Z

Spain
Government. Public administration
Special topics, A-Z -- Continued
8237.A87 Automatic data processing. Electronic data processing
Including use of the Internet for the delivery of government services
Corruption see JN8386
8237.D43 Decentralization
Electronic data processing see JN8237.A87
8237.E84 Ethics
Executive branch. Crown
8246 General works
(8251) Powers and prerogatives
see KKT2550+
Departments. Ministries
8258 General works
Individual departments or ministries
8261 Ministry of the Interior
Other departments or ministries, see the subject
8266 Council of state. Consejo de estado
Civil service
(8273) Directories. Registers
see JN8103
8281 General works
8289 Salaries. Pensions
Legislative branch. Cortes
8293 Directories. Registers
8298 General works
8300 Lobbying. Pressure groups
(8305) Powers and prerogatives
see KKT2510+
8309-8311 Upper House. Senado
8309 Directories. Registers
8311 General works
Lower House. Congreso de los Diputados
8319 Directories. Registers
8321 General works
(8335-8338) Judiciary
see KKT283+
8340 Government property. Public buildings
Political rights. Political participation. Practical politics
8341 General works
8343 Citizenship
(8351-8354) Naturalization
see KKT2440
Elections. Voting. Suffrage. Right to vote

Spain
Government. Public administration
Political rights. Political participation. Practical politics
Elections. Voting. Suffrage. Right to vote -- Continued

8371 General works
8372 Women's suffrage. Women's right to vote
(8374-8378) Election law
see KKT2506
8386 Political corruption
Political parties
8395.A2 General works
8395.A3-Z Special parties, A-Z
8398 State, provincial, prefecture government (General and comparative)
8399.A-Z By region, province, or autonomous community, A-Z
Subarrange each by Table J12
Class here works on regional or provincial government
For the old kingdoms see JN8128+
For local government see JS6320.A+

Portugal
8423 Directories. Registers
(8427) Constitutional history. Constitutional law. Constitutions
see KKQ2050+
History
8436 General
By period
8444 To 1640
8461 Kingdom of Portugal, 1640-1807
8465 Napoleonic era, 1807-1826
8499 Kingdom of Portugal, 1826-1910
8502 Republic, 1910-
8509 General works
8514 Civil-military relations
8515 Regionalism
Government. Public administration
(8519) General works
see JN8509
8520.A-Z Special topics, A-Z
8520.E43 Electronic data processing
8520.S43 Secret and confidential information
Executive branch. Crown
8525 General works
(8531) Powers and prerogatives
see KKQ2550+

Portugal
Government. Public administration
Executive branch. Crown -- Continued
8536 Departments. Ministries
For departments or ministries limited to a particular subject, see the subject
Civil service
(8547) Directories. Registers
see JN8423
8557 General works
8559 Salaries. Pensions
Legislative branch. Cortes. Assembleia da República
8565 Directories. Registers
8568 General works
8581 Upper House. Camara dos Pares. Senado
8585 Lower House. Camara dos Deputados
(8595-8599) Judiciary
see KKQ283+
8600 Government property. Public buildings
Political rights. Citizenship. Political participation
8605 General works
(8611-8613) Naturalization
see KKQ2440
Elections. Voting. Suffrage. Right to vote
8623 General works
8624 Women's suffrage. Women's right to vote
(8625-8629) Election law
see KKQ2506
8641 Political corruption
Political parties
8651.A2 General works
8651.A3-Z Special parties, A-Z
8660 State, provincial, district government (General and comparative)
8661 Azores
Switzerland
8701 Periodicals. Societies. Serials
8704 Directories. Registers
(8705-8709) Constitutional history. Constitutional law. Constitutions
see KKW2050+
History
8711 General works
By period
8719 To 1648
1648-1874
8758 General

Switzerland
History
By period
1648-1874 -- Continued
(8759-8761) Constitution of 1848
see KKW2064.51848
(8762) Contemporary works
see JN8758
(8763-8765) Constitution of 1874
see KKW2064.51874
1874-
(8766) Contemporary works
see JN8767
8767 General works
8781 General works
8788 Federalism. Federal-cantonal relations. Regionalism
(8791) Church and state
see BR1033
Language question see P119.3+
8795 Minorities
Government. Public administration
General works see JN8781
8800.A-Z Special topics, A-Z
Government publicity see JN8800.P8
8800.P8 Public relations. Propaganda. Government publicity
Publicity, Government see JN8800.P8
Executive branch
8801 General works
(8809) Powers and prerogatives
see KKW2578
8812 Federal Council. Bundesrat
Civil service
(8825) Directories. Registers
see JN8704
8831 General works
8839 Salaries. Pensions
Legislative branch. Federal Assembly.
Bundesversammlung
8845 Directories. Registers
8850 General works
8852 Pressure groups. Lobbying
(8853) Powers and prerogatives
see KKW2510+
8855 Upper House. Council of States
8862 Lower House. Nationalrat

Switzerland
Government. Public administration -- Continued
(8875-8878) Judiciary
see KKW283+
Political rights. Citizenship. Political participation
8901 General works
(8911-8915) Naturalization
see KKW2440
Elections. Voting. Suffrage. Right to vote
8931 General works
(8935-8939) Election law
see KKW2506
8961 Political corruption
Political parties
8971.A1 General works
8971.A2-Z Special parties, A-Z
Cantonal government
9015 General and comparative
By canton
For local government see JS6421+
9100-9119 Aargau (Table J9)
9120-9139 Appenzell-Ausser Rhoden (Table J9)
9140-9159 Appenzell Inner Rhoden (Table J9)
9160-9179 Baselland (Table J9)
9180-9199 Basel-Stadt (Table J9)
9200-9219 Bern (Table J9)
9220-9239 Fribourg (Table J9)
9240-9259 Geneva (Table J9)
9260-9279 Glarus (Table J9)
9280-9299 Graubunden (Table J9)
9299.5 Jura (Table J11)
9300-9319 Lucerne (Table J9)
9320-9339 Neuchâtel (Table J9)
9340-9359 St. Gall (Table J9)
9360-9379 Schaffhausen (Table J9)
9380-9399 Schwyz (Table J9)
9400-9419 Solothurn (Table J9)
9420-9439 Thurgau (Table J9)
9440-9459 Ticino (Table J9)
9460-9479 Unterwalden nid dem Wald. Nidwalden (Table J9)
9480-9499 Unterwalden ob dem Wald. Obwalden (Table J9)
9500-9519 Uri (Table J9)
9520-9539 Valais (Table J9)
9540-9559 Vaud (Table J9)
9560-9579 Zug (Table J9)
9580-9599 Zurich (Table J9)

Balkan States
For the Balkan States in general see JN97
9600-9609 Bulgaria (Table J10)
9610-9619 Montenegro (Table J10)
9620-9639 Romania (Table J9)
9640-9659 Serbia (Table J9)
9660-9679 Yugoslavia (Table J9)
Class here works on Yugoslavia to 1992 and works on Yugoslavia (i. e. Serbia and Montenegro collectively) after April 27, 1992
9679.A6-Z By republic, province, etc.
(9679.B6) Bosnia and Hercegovina
see JN2203
Croatia see JN2202
(9679.M3) Macedonia
see JN9679.5
Montenegro see JN9610+
Serbia see JN9640+
(9679.S6) Slovenia
see JN2201
9679.5 Macedonia (Table J11)
9680-9689 Albania (Table J10)
Turkey see JQ1800+

Political institutions and public administration (Asia, Africa, Australia, Pacific Area, etc.)

Asia

(1) Periodicals. Societies. Serials
see JQ21.A1

(5) Constitutional history. Constitutional law. Constitutions
see KM

21.A1 Periodicals. Societies. Serials

21.A11-.A19 Directories. Registers

21.A25 Dictionaries. Encyclopedias

(22) Constitutional history. Constitutional law. Constitutions
see KM

24 General works

26 Civil-military relations

29.5 Political corruption

Executive branch

31 General works

32 Civil service

33 Legislative branch

Political rights. Political participation. Practical politics

36 General works

38 Elections. Voting. Suffrage. Right to vote

39 Political parties

Regions

(94) Middle East. Southwest Asia
see JQ1758

(96) Southeast Asia
see JQ750

South Asia

98 General (Table J11a)

India

200-298 General (Table J8 modified)

Government. Public administration

States and union territories

298.8 States and union territories treated collectively

Individual states
see JQ320+

320-339 Assam (Table J9)

360-379 Bengal (Table J9)

(379.4) East Bengal
see JQ630+

379.5 West Bengal (Table J11)

400-419 Bombay (State) (Table J9)

(440-450) Burma
see JQ751

Asia
South Asia
India
States and union territories -- Continued

480-499 Madhya Pradesh. Central Provinces (Table J9)
520-539 Tamil Nadu. Madras (Table J9)
(540-559) Pakistan
see JQ629
560-579 Punjab (Table J9)
600-619 Uttar Pradesh. United Provinces of Agra and Oudh (Table J9)
620.A-Z Other states and union territories, A-Z
620.A66-.A669 Andaman and Nicobar Islands (Table J12)
620.A7-79 Andhra Pradesh (Table J12)
620.A792-7929 Arunāchal Pradesh (Table J12)
620.B52-.B529 Bihar (Table J12)
620.C48-.C489 Chandigarh (Table J12)
620.C52-.C529 Chhattīsgarh (Table J12)
620.D2-.D29 Dadra and Nagar Haveli (Table J12)
620.D225-.D2259 Daman and Diu (Table J12)
620.D4-.D49 Delhi (Table J12)
620.G6-.G69 Goa (Table J12)
620.G8-.G89 Gujarat (Table J12)
620.H3-.H39 Haryana (Table J12)
620.H5-.H59 Himachal Pradesh (Table J12)
Jammu and Kashmir see JQ620.K3+
620.J45-.J459 Jharkhand (Table J12)
620.K2-.K29 Karnataka. Mysore (Table J12)
620.K3-.K39 Kashmir. Jammu and Kashmir (Table J12)
620.K47-.K479 Kerala (Table J12)
620.L32-.L329 Lakshadweep (Table J12)
620.M26-.M269 Maharashtra (Table J12)
620.M29-.M299 Manipur (Table J12)
620.M45-.M459 Meghalaya (Table J12)
620.M58-.M589 Mizoram (Table J12)
(620.M7) Mysore
see JQ620.K2
620.N2-.N29 Nagaland (Table J12)
620.O7-.O79 Orissa (Table J12)
620.P6-.P69 Pondicherry (Table J12)
620.R28-.R289 Rajasthan (Table J12)
620.S48-.S489 Sikkim (Table J12)
620.T82-.T829 Tripura (Table J12)
620.U88-.U889 Uttarakhand (Table J12)

Afghanistan see JQ1760+

Asia
South Asia -- Continued
628 Nepal (Table J11)
628.5 Bhutan (Table J11)
629 Pakistan (Table J11)
630-639 Bangladesh (Table J10)
639.5 Maldives (Table J11)
(640) Brunei
see JQ1064
650-659 Sri Lanka. Ceylon (Table J10)
(660-669) Cyprus
see JQ1811
(670-679) Hong Kong
see JQ1539.5
(710-719) Malaysia. Malaya
see JQ1062
(745) Singapore
see JQ1063
Southeast Asia. Indochina
750 General (Table J11a)
751 Burma. Myanmar (Table J11)
760-779 Indonesia (Table J9 modified)
Government. Public administration
Political parties
Special parties
779.A5114 PDI Perjuangan (Organization). Partai Demokrasi Indonesia-Perjuangan
779.A51145 Partai Amanat Nasional
779.A5115 Partai Bhinneka Tunggal Ika Indonesia. PBI
779.A512 Partai Bulan
779.A513 Partai Demokrasi Indonesia
779.A514 Partai Demokrasi Islam Indonesia
779.A5143 Partai Demokrat
779.A5145 Partai Golkar
779.A5147 Partai Hati Nurani Rakyat
779.A515 Front Nasional. Pengurus Besar
779.A517 Partai Keadilan
779.A518 Partai Keadilan Sejahtera
779.A533 Partai Kebangkitan Bangsa
779.A55 Partai Komunis Indonesia
779.A553 Masyumi (Organization). Partai Masyumi
779.A555 Partai Muslimin Indonesia
779.A558 N.U. (Organization). Partai Nahdlatul Ulama
779.A56 Partai Nasional Indonesia
779.A566 Partai Persatuan Pembangunan

Asia
  Southeast Asia. Indochina
    Indonesia
      Government. Public administration
        Political parties
          Special parties -- Continued
779.A57 Partai Rakyat Demokratik
779.A576 Golongan Karya (Organization). Sekber Golkar
  Cf. JQ779.A5145 Partai Golkar
779.A58 Partai Sarekat Islam. Partai Sjarikat Islam
790 Timor-Leste. East Timor (Table J11)
    Philippines see JQ1250+
800-899 Vietnam (Table J8)
930-939 Cambodia. Kampuchea (Table J10)
950-959 Laos (Table J10)
(960-969) Pondicherry. French India
  see JQ620
(1050-1059) Goa
  see JQ620
(1061) Macau
  see JQ1519.5
    Thailand see JQ1740+
1062 Malaysia. Malaya (Table J11)
1063 Singapore (Table J11)
1064 Brunei (Table J11)
  Central Asia
1070-1089 General (Table J9)
1090 Kazakhstan (Table J11)
1092 Kyrgyzstan (Table J11)
1093 Tajikistan (Table J11)
1094 Turkmenistan (Table J11)
1095 Uzbekistan (Table J11)
1100-1199 Siberia (Russia) (Table J8)
  Philippines
1250-1269 Spanish regime, to 1898 (Table J9)
1300-1399 United States rule, 1898-1946 (Table J8)
1400-1419 Republic, 1946- (Table J9)
  East Asia. Far East
1499 General (Table J11a)
1500-1519 China (Table J9)
  For Macau see JQ1519.5
  For Hong Kong see JQ1539.5
1519.3 Tibetan Government-in-Exile. Central Tibetan Administration-in-Exile (Table J11)
1519.5 Macau (Table J11)

Asia
East Asia. Far East -- Continued
1520-1539 Taiwan (Table J9)
1539.5 Hong Kong (Table J11)
1600-1699 Japan (Table J8)
1720-1729 Korea (Table J10)
Including South Korea
1729.5 North Korea (Table J11)
1730 Mongolia. Outer Mongolia (Table J11)
1740-1749 Thailand (Table J10)
Middle East. Near East. Southwest Asia. Islamic Empire
1758 General (Table J11a)
Caucasus
1759 General (Table J11a)
1759.3 Armenia (Table J11)
1759.5 Azerbaijan (Table J11)
1759.7 Georgia (Republic) (Table J11)
1760-1769 Afghanistan (Table J10)
1780-1789 Iran (Table J10)
1800-1809 Turkey (Table J10)
1811 Cyprus (Table J11)
(1825) Other
see JQ1826+
1826 Syria (Table J11)
1828 Lebanon (Table J11)
1830 Israel. Palestine (Table J11)
Gaza see JQ1830
West Bank (Territory under Israeli occupation, 1967-) see JQ1830
1833 Jordan (Table J11)
Arabian Peninsula. Arabia. Persian Gulf States
1840 General works
1841 Saudi Arabia (Table J11)
1842 Yemen (Table J11)
1843 Oman. Muscat and Oman (Table J11)
1844 United Arab Emirates. Trucial States (Table J11)
1845 Qatar (Table J11)
1846 Bahrain (Table J11)
1848 Kuwait (Table J11)
1849 Iraq (Table J11)
Iran see JQ1780+
1850 Arab countries (Table J11a)
1852 Islamic countries (Table J11a)
Africa
1870-1879 General (Table J10)

	Africa -- Continued
	English-speaking Africa
1880-1899	General (Table J9)
	South Africa. Republic of South Africa
1900-1999	General (Table J8)
(2000-2699)	Provinces. Self-governing territories. Homelands see JQ1999
	Southern Africa. Central Africa
2720	General (Table J11a)
2721	Swaziland (Table J11)
2740	Lesotho. Basutoland (Table J11)
2760	Botswana. Bechuanaland (Table J11)
2780-2789	Rhodesia. Federation of Rhodesia and Nyasaland. British Central African Protectorate (Table J10)
2800-2899	Zambia. Northern Rhodesia (Table J8)
2920-2929	Zimbabwe. Southern Rhodesia (Table J10)
2941	Malawi (Table J11)
	Namibia. Southwest Africa see JQ3540+
	East Africa
2945	General (Table J11a)
2947	Kenya (Table J11)
	Tanganyika see JQ3510+
	Zanzibar see JQ3510+
2951	Uganda (Table J11)
	West Africa
2998	General (Table J11a)
3001	Gambia (Table J11)
	Liberia see JQ3920+
3020-3039	Ghana. Gold Coast (Table J9)
3080-3099	Nigeria (Table J9)
3121	Sierra Leone (Table J11)
(3141-3151)	Atlantic Ocean islands see JQ3982+
	Indian Ocean islands
3158	General (Table J11a)
3159	Maldives (Table J11)
3160-3179	Mauritius (Table J9)
3185	Seychelles (Table J11)
	Comoros see JQ3494
	Réunion see JQ3480+
3188	Kerguelen Islands (Table J11)
	North Africa
3198	General (Table J11a)
	Morocco see JQ3940+
3200-3299	Algeria (Table J8)

Africa
North Africa -- Continued
3320-3339 Tunisia (Table J9)
3340-3349 Libya (Table J10)
Egypt see JQ3800+
Sudan see JQ3981
French-speaking Africa
3349.5 General works
French-speaking West Africa
3350-3369 General (Table J9)
3376 Benin. Dahomey (Table J11)
Togo see JQ3530+
3381 Guinea (Table J11)
3386 Côte d'Ivoire. Ivory Coast (Table J11)
3389 Mali. French Sudan (Table J11)
3391 Mauritania (Table J11)
3394 Niger (Table J11)
3396 Senegal (Table J11)
3398 Burkina Faso. Upper Volta (Table J11)
French-speaking Equatorial Africa
3403 General (Table J11a)
Zaire see JQ3600+
3404 Central African Republic. Ubangi-Shari (Table J11)
3405 Chad (Table J11)
Cameroon see JQ3520+
3406 Congo (Brazzaville). Middle Congo (Table J11)
3407 Gabon (Table J11)
3421 Djibouti. French Territory of the Afars and Issas. French Somaliland (Table J11)
3450-3469 Madagascar. Malagasy Republic (Table J9)
3480-3489 Réunion (Table J10)
3494 Comoros (Table J11)
3495 Mayotte (Table J11)
3500-3509 German East Africa (Table J10)
3510-3519 Tanzania. Tanganyika. Zanzibar (Table J10)
3520-3529 Cameroon (Table J10)
3530-3539 Togo (Table J10)
3540-3549 Namibia. Southwest Africa (Table J10)
3566 Burundi (Table J11)
3567 Rwanda (Table J11)
3580 Italian East Africa (Table J11)
3583 Eritrea (Table J11)
3585 Somalia. Italian Somaliland (Table J11)
Djibouti see JQ3421

	Africa -- Continued
(3590-3599)	Libya see JQ3340+
3600-3619	Zaire. Congo (Democratic Republic). Belgian Congo (Table J9)
3650	Portuguese-speaking Africa (Table J11a)
3651	Angola. Portuguese West Africa (Table J11)
3661	Cape Verde (Table J11)
3671	Mozambique. Portuguese East Africa (Table J11)
3681	Guinea-Bissau. Portuguese Guinea (Table J11)
3685	Sao Tome and Principe (Table J11)
3701	Western Sahara. Spanish Sahara (Table J11)
3702	Equatorial Guinea (Table J11)
3750-3769	Ethiopia. Abyssinia (Table J9)
3800-3899	Egypt. United Arab Republic (Table J8)
3920-3929	Liberia (Table J10)
3940-3949	Morocco (Table J10)
3981	Sudan (Table J11)
	Atlantic Ocean islands
3981.5	General (Table J11a)
3982	Azores (Table J11)
	Bermuda see JL590+
3983	Madeira Islands (Table J11)
3984	Canary Islands (Table J11)
	Cape Verde see JQ3661
3986	Saint Helena (Table J11)
3986.5	Tristan da Cunha (Table J11)
3986.7	Falkland Islands (Table J11)
	Indian Ocean islands see JQ3158+
3995	Australasia (Table J11a)
	Australia
4000-4099	General (Table J8)
4400-4499	Australian Capital Territory (Table J8)
4500-4599	New South Wales (Table J8)
4640-4659	Northern Territory (Table J9)
4700-4799	Queensland (Table J8)
4900-4999	South Australia (Table J8)
5100-5199	Tasmania (Table J8)
5300-5399	Victoria (Table J8)
5500-5599	Western Australia (Table J8)
5800-5899	New Zealand (Table J8)
	Pacific Area. Pacific Ocean islands
5995	General works
6000-6019	Guam (Table J9)

Pacific Area. Pacific Ocean islands -- Continued

(6080-6199) Hawaii
see JK9301+

Samoa. Western Samoa see JQ6651

6220-6239 Samoan Islands. American Samoa (Table J9)

6240 Trust Territory of the Pacific. Micronesia (Federated States) (Table J11)

6241 Marshall Islands (Table J11)

6242 Mariana Islands (Table J11)
Including Northern Marianas

6301 Fiji (Table J11)

6311 Papua New Guinea (Table J11)

6312 Kiribati. Gilbert Islands (Table J11)

6313 Tuvalu. Ellice Islands (Table J11)

6321 Tonga (Table J11)

6340 Cook Islands (Table J11)

6341 Solomon Islands (Table J11)

6345 Tokelau (Table J11)

6400 Vanuatu. New Hebrides (Table J11)

6401 New Caledonia (Table J11)

6431 French Polynesia (Table J11a)

(6500-6519) New Guinea
see JQ6311

6591 Palau (Table J11)

(6601) Solomon Islands
see JQ6341

6651 Samoa. Western Samoa (Table J11)

Local government. Municipal government
Official gazettes, codes, charters
see class K
(3-37) Serial documents
see JS300+
Periodicals. Serials
Class here general periodicals by place of imprint
39 American
40 British
41 Other
42 Societies (International)
43 Museums. Exhibitions
44 Congresses
48 Dictionaries. Encyclopedias
49 Study and teaching. Training of local and municipal employees
50 Theory. Method. Scope. Relations to other subjects
(51) City and central government
see JS113
History
55 General
58 Ancient
61 Medieval
64 Modern to 1800
66 Nineteenth century
67 Twentieth century
68 Twenty-first century
78 General works
(85) Legal works
see K3428+
(91) Social and economic aspects
see HT101+
100 Electronic data processing
Including use of the Internet for the delivery of government services
105 Public relations
113 Federal-city relations. State-local relations. Municipal home rule
Executive branch. Mayor
141 General works
(145) Administration
see JS141
Civil service
148 General works
Study and teaching see JS49
153 Salaries. Pensions. Retirement
163 Public records management
171 Legislative branch

(185-188) Municipal courts
see K2100
211 Political participation. Neighborhood government
Elections. Local elections. Municipal elections
221 General works
(227) Election law
see K3299
231 Political corruption
Local government other than municipal
241 General works
251 Intermediate levels of government. State government. Provincial government. Departmental government
261 County government
271 Village government. Rural public administration
United States
Local and municipal government
300 Periodicals. Serials
(301) Yearbooks
see JS39
Societies
302 National
303.A-.W State, A-W
303.5 Citizens' associations
For individual associations see JS451.A+
304 Congresses
305 Museums. Exhibitions
(308) Collections
see JS331
History
309 General works
By period
Colonial to 1800
311 General works
(315) Local
see JS431+
319 19th century to 1880
323 Recent, 1880-
331 General works
(335) Compends
see JS331
(338) Legal
see KF5304+
(341) Social and economic aspects
see HT123+
Commission government. Municipal government by commission
342 General works

	United States
	Local and municipal government
	Commission government. Municipal government by commission -- Continued
343.A3A-.A3W	By state, A-W
(343.A4-Z)	By city see JS504+
344.A-Z	Other topics, A-Z
	Annexation
344.A5	General works
344.A52A-.A52W	By state, A-W
	City manager
344.C5	General works
344.C52A-.C52W	By state, A-W
	Commission government see JS342+
	Electronic data processing
344.E4	General works
344.E42A-.E42W	By state, A-W
(344.F4)	Federal-city relations see JS348+
(344.P6-.P62)	Police power see KF5399
	Public records management
344.P77	General works
344.P772A-.P772W	By state, A-W
	Public relations
344.P8	General works
344.P82A-.P82W	By state, A-W
	Recall
344.R4	General works
344.R42A-.R42W	By state, A-W
	Telecommunication systems
344.T45	General works
344.T452A-.T452W	By state, A-W
(345)	Pamphlets, lectures, etc. see JS331
346	Juvenile works
	Federal-city relations. State-local relations. Municipal home rule
348	General works
349.A-.W	By state, A-W
(351)	Law see KF5304+
(354)	Incorporation. Charters see KF5313
	Executive branch. Mayor
356	General works

JS

United States
Local and municipal government
Executive branch. Mayor -- Continued
Civil service
358 General works
(359) Study and teaching. Training of local and municipal employees
see JK716+
361 Salaries. Pensions. Retirement
362 Consultants. Government consultants
362.3 Incentive awards. Merit increases. Performance awards
362.5 Minorities. Affirmative action programs
363 Productivity. Labor productivity
364 Selection and appointment. Recruiting. Dismissal
371 Legislative branch. City councils
(381-385) Judiciary. Municipal courts
see subclasses KFA-KFW
388 Government property. Government purchasing
391 Political participation. Neighborhood government
Elections. Local elections. Municipal elections
395 General works
(397) Election law
see KF4916
401 Political corruption
Local government other than municipal
408 General works
State government see JK2403+
411 County government
418 Township government
422 Metropolitan government
425 Rural public administration. Village government
426 Special districts. Public authorities
Local
By region
431 Northeastern States. New England
434 Middle West
437 South. Southern States
440 West
451.A-.W By state, A-W
Under each:
.x *Periodicals. Serials*
.x5 *General works*
Local
By city, see JS504 JS1583
.x8A-.x8Z *By metropolitan area, A-Z*
.x9A-.x9Z *By county, township, parish, A-Z*
For District of Columbia see JK2701+

United States
Local -- Continued
By city

504 A to Akron
Subarrange each by Table J17

505-505.9 Akron, Ohio (Table J16)

506 Akron to Alameda
Subarrange each by Table J17

507-507.9 Alameda, California (Table J16)

509 Alameda to Albany
Subarrange each by Table J17

511-519 Albany, New York (Table J15)

521 Albany to Alexandria
Subarrange each by Table J17

524-524.9 Alexandria, Virginia (Table J16)

525 Alexandria to Allegheny
Subarrange each by Table J17

531-539 Allegheny, Pennsylvania (Table J15)

541 Allegheny to Altoona
Subarrange each by Table J17

545-545.9 Altoona, Pennsylvania (Table J16)

546 Altoona to Annapolis
Subarrange each by Table J17

547-547.9 Annapolis, Maryland (Table J16)

548 Annapolis to Atlanta
Subarrange each by Table J17

551-559 Atlanta, Georgia (Table J15)

561 Atlanta to Auburn
Subarrange each by Table J17

562-562.9 Auburn, New York (Table J16)

563 Auburn to Augusta
Subarrange each by Table J17

565-565.9 Augusta, Georgia (Table J16)

566 Augusta, Maine to Austin
Subarrange each by Table J17

567-567.9 Austin, Texas (Table J16)

568 Austin to Baltimore
Subarrange each by Table J17

571-590 Baltimore, Maryland (Table J14)

591 Baltimore to Bangor
Subarrange each by Table J17

592-592.9 Bangor, Maine (Table J16)

593 Bangor to Berj.
Subarrange each by Table J17

594 Berkeley to Binghamton
Subarrange each by Table J17

595-595.9 Binghamton, New York (Table J16)

United States
Local
By city -- Continued
596 Binghamton to Birmingham
Subarrange each by Table J17
598-598.9 Birmingham, Alabama (Table J16)
599 Birmingham to Boston
Subarrange each by Table J17
601-620 Boston, Massachusetts (Table J14)
621 Boston to Bridgeport
Subarrange each by Table J17
623-623.9 Bridgeport, Connecticut (Table J16)
624 Bridgeport to Brockton
Subarrange each by Table J17
625-625.9 Brockton, Massachusetts (Table J16)
626 Brockton to Brooklyn
Subarrange each by Table J17
631-650 Brooklyn, New York (Table J14)
651 Brooklyn to Brunswick
Subarrange each by Table J17
656-656.9 Brunswick, Georgia (Table J16)
657 Brunswick to Buffalo
Subarrange each by Table J17
661-680 Buffalo, New York (Table J14)
681 Buffalo to Cambridge
Subarrange each by Table J17
683-683.9 Cambridge, Massachusetts (Table J16)
684 Cambridge to Camden
Subarrange each by Table J17
685-685.9 Camden, New Jersey (Table J16)
686 Camden to Canton
Subarrange each by Table J17
687-687.9 Canton, Ohio (Table J16)
688 Canton to Charleston
Subarrange each by Table J17
689-689.9 Charleston, South Carolina (Table J16)
690 Charleston, South Carolina to Charlestown, Massachusetts
Subarrange each by Table J17
693-693.9 Charlestown, Massachusetts (Table J16)
694 Charlestown to Chelsea
Subarrange each by Table J17
697-697.9 Chelsea, Massachusetts (Table J16)
698 Chelsea to Chicago
Subarrange each by Table J17
701-720 Chicago, Illinois (Table J14)

United States
Local
By city -- Continued

721 Chicago, Illinois to Chillicothe, Missouri
Subarrange each by Table J17

725-725.9 Chilicothe, Ohio (Table J16)

726 Chillicothe, Texas to Cincinnati, Iowa
Subarrange each by Table J17

731-750 Cincinnati, Ohio (Table J14)

751 Cincinnati, Ohio to Cleveland, North Carolina
Subarrange each by Table J17

761-780 Cleveland, Ohio (Table J14)

781 Cleveland, Ohio to Cohoes, New York
Subarrange each by Table J17

783-783.9 Cohoes, New York (Table J16)

784 Cohoes to Colorado
Subarrange each by Table J17

785-785.9 Colorado Springs, Colorado (Table J16)

786 Colorado Springs, Colorado to Columbia, South Carolina
Subarrange each by Table J17

787-787.9 Columbia, South Carolina (Table J16)

789 Columbia to Columbus
Subarrange each by Table J17

791-799 Columbus, Ohio (Table J15)

800 Columbus to Covington
Subarrange each by Table J17

801-801.9 Covington, Kentucky (Table J16)

802 Covington to Dallas
Subarrange each by Table J17

803-803.9 Dallas, Texas (Table J16)

804 Dallas to Dayton
Subarrange each by Table J17

805-805.9 Dayton, Ohio (Table J16)

806 Dayton to Decatur
Subarrange each by Table J17

807-807.9 Decatur, Illinois (Table J16)

808 Decatur to Denver
Subarrange each by Table J17

811-819 Denver, Colorado (Table J15)

821 Denver to Des Moines
Subarrange each by Table J17

823-823.9 Des Moines, Iowa (Table J16)

824 Des Moines to Detroit
Subarrange each by Table J17

831-849 Detroit, Michigan (Table J14a)

849.5 Local. By district, ward, etc.

United States
Local
By city -- Continued

850 Detroit to Duluth
Subarrange each by Table J17

851-851.9 Duluth, Minnesota (Table J16)

852 Duluth to Easton
Subarrange each by Table J17

853-853.9 Easton, Pennsylvania (Table J16)

854 Easton to Elizabeth
Subarrange each by Table J17

855-855.9 Elizabeth, New Jersey (Table J16)

856 Elizabeth to Erie
Subarrange each by Table J17

861-861.9 Erie, Pennsylvania (Table J16)

862 Erie to Evansville
Subarrange each by Table J17

865-865.9 Evansville, Indiana (Table J16)

866 Evansville to Fall River
Subarrange each by Table J17

871-879 Fall River, Massachusetts (Table J15)

883 Fall River to Fort Wayne
Subarrange each by Table J17

885-885.9 Fort Wayne, Indiana (Table J16)

886 Fort Wayne to Galveston
Subarrange each by Table J17

888-888.9 Galveston, Texas (Table J16)

889 Galveston to Grand Forks
Subarrange each by Table J17

891-891.9 Grand Forks, North Dakota (Table J16)

892 Grand Forks to Grand Rapids
Subarrange each by Table J17

893-893.9 Grand Rapids, Michigan (Table J16)

894 Grand Rapids to Harrisburg
Subarrange each by Table J17

895-895.9 Harrisburg, Pennsylvania (Table J16)

896 Harrisburg to Hartford
Subarrange each by Table J17

901-909 Hartford, Connecticut (Table J15)

910 Hartford to Haverhill
Subarrange each by Table J17

911-911.9 Haverhill, Massachusetts (Table J16)

912 Haverhill to Hoboken
Subarrange each by Table J17

915-915.9 Hoboken, New Jersey (Table J16)

916 Hoboken to Holyoke
Subarrange each by Table J17

United States
Local
By city -- Continued

921-929 Holyoke, Massachusetts (Table J15)
931 Holyoke to Houston
Subarrange each by Table J17
935-935.9 Houston, Texas (Table J16)
936 Houston to Indianapolis
Subarrange each by Table J17
941-949 Indianapolis, Indiana (Table J15)
953 Indianapolis to Jacksonville, Florida
Subarrange each by Table J17
954-954.9 Jacksonville, Florida (Table J16)
955-955.9 Jacksonville, Illinois (Table J16)
956 Jacksonville to Jefferson
Subarrange each by Table J17
957-957.9 Jefferson City, Missouri (Table J16)
959 Jefferson City to Jersey
Subarrange each by Table J17
961-969 Jersey City, New Jersey (Table J15)
970 Jersey City to Joliet
Subarrange each by Table J17
971-971.9 Joliet, Illinois (Table J16)
972 Joliet to Joplin
Subarrange each by Table J17
973-973.9 Joplin, Missouri (Table J16)
974 Joplin to Kalamazoo
Subarrange each by Table J17
975-975.9 Kalamazoo, Michigan (Table J16)
976 Kalamazoo to Kansas City
Subarrange each by Table J17
979-979.9 Kansas City, Kansas (Table J16)
981-989 Kansas City, Missouri (Table J15)
990 Kansas City to Lancaster
Subarrange each by Table J17
991-991.9 Lancaster, Pennsylvania (Table J16)
992 Lancaster to Lawrence
Subarrange each by Table J17
993-993.9 Lawrence, Massachusetts (Table J16)
994 Lawrence to Lem
Subarrange each by Table J17
995 Len to Lincoln
Subarrange each by Table J17
996-996.9 Lincoln, Nebraska (Table J16)
997 Lincoln to Little Rock
Subarrange each by Table J17
998-998.9 Little Rock, Arkansas (Table J16)

United States
Local
By city -- Continued

999 Little Rock to Los Angeles
Subarrange each by Table J17
1001-1009 Los Angeles, California (Table J15)
1011 Los Angeles to Louisville
Subarrange each by Table J17
1021-1040 Louisville, Kentucky (Table J14)
1041 Louisville to Lowell
Subarrange each by Table J17
1051-1059 Lowell, Massachusetts (Table J15)
1061 Lowell to Lynn
Subarrange each by Table J17
1071-1079 Lynn, Massachusetts (Table J15)
1080 Lynn to McKeesport
Subarrange each by Table J17
1081-1081.9 McKeesport, Pennsylvania (Table J16)
1082 McKeesport to Madison
Subarrange each by Table J17
1083-1083.9 Madison, Wisconsin (Table J16)
1084 Madison to Manchester
Subarrange each by Table J17
1085-1085.9 Manchester, New Hampshire (Table J16)
1086 Manchester to Marquette
Subarrange each by Table J17
1087-1087.9 Marquette, Michigan (Table J16)
1088 Marquette to Memphis
Subarrange each by Table J17
1091-1099 Memphis, Tennessee (Table J15)
1101 Memphis to Middletown
Subarrange each by Table J17
1105-1105.9 Middletown, Connecticut (Table J16)
1106 Middletown to Mill
Subarrange each by Table J17
1108 Mill to Milwaukee
Subarrange each by Table J17
1111-1119 Milwaukee, Wisconsin (Table J15)
1125 Milwaukee to Minneapolis
Subarrange each by Table J17
1131-1150 Minneapolis, Minnesota (Table J14)
1151 Minneapolis to Mobile
Subarrange each by Table J17
1155-1155.9 Mobile, Alabama (Table J16)
1156 Mobile to Montgomery
Subarrange each by Table J17
1157-1157.9 Montgomery, Alabama (Table J16)

United States
Local
By city -- Continued

1159 Montgomery to Nashville
Subarrange each by Table J17
1161-1169 Nashville, Tennessee (Table J15)
1185 Nashville to New Bedford, Indiana
Subarrange each by Table J17
1193-1193.9 New Bedford, Massachusetts (Table J16)
1194 New Bedford, New Jersey to New Haven, Connecticut
Subarrange each by Table J17
1195-1195.9 New Haven, Connecticut (Table J16)
1198 New Haven to New Orleans
Subarrange each by Table J17
1201-1209 New Orleans, Louisiana (Table J15)
1211 New Orleans to New York
Subarrange each by Table J17
1221-1240 New York, New York (Table J14)
1241 New York to Newark
Subarrange each by Table J17
1242-1242.9 Newark, New Jersey (Table J16)
1243 Newark to Norfolk
Subarrange each by Table J17
1245-1245.9 Norfolk, Virginia (Table J16)
1246 Norfolk to North
Subarrange each by Table J17
1247 North Adams to Oakland
Subarrange each by Table J17
1248-1248.9 Oakland, California (Table J16)
1249 Oakland to Omaha
Subarrange each by Table J17
1251-1251.9 Omaha, Nebraska (Table J16)
1252 Omaha to Paterson
Subarrange each by Table J17
1253-1253.9 Paterson, New Jersey (Table J16)
1254 Paterson to Pawtucket
Subarrange each by Table J17
1255-1255.9 Pawtucket, Rhode Island (Table J16)
1256 Pawtucket to Peoria
Subarrange each by Table J17
1258-1258.9 Peoria, Illinois (Table J16)
1259 Peoria to Philadelphia
Subarrange each by Table J17
1261-1280 Philadelphia, Pennsylvania (Table J14)
1281 Philadelphia, Pennsylvania to Pittsburgh, New Hampshire
Subarrange each by Table J17

United States
Local
By city -- Continued

1291-1310 Pittsburgh, Pennsylvania (Table J14)
1311 Pittsburgh, Pennsylvania to Pittsfield, Massachusetts
Subarrange each by Table J17
1312-1312.9 Pittsfield, Massachusetts (Table J16)
1313 Pittsfield, Michigan to Portland, Iowa
Subarrange each by Table J17
1315-1315.9 Portland, Maine (Table J16)
1316 Portland, Michigan to Portland, North Dakota
Subarrange each by Table J17
1318-1318.9 Portland, Oregon (Table J16)
1319 Portland, Pennsylvania to Providence, Pennsylvania
Subarrange each by Table J17
1321-1329 Providence, Rhode Island (Table J15)
1330 Providence, South Carolina to Quincy, Florida
Subarrange each by Table J17
1331-1331.9 Quincy, Illinois (Table J16)
1332 Quincy, Indiana to Reading, Ohio
Subarrange each by Table J17
1335-1335.9 Reading, Pennsylvania (Table J16)
1339 Reading, Vermont to Richmond, Vermont
Subarrange each by Table J17
1341-1349 Richmond, Virginia (Table J15)
1351 Richmond, Virginia to Rochester
Subarrange each by Table J17
1361-1369 Rochester, New York (Table J15)
1370 Rochester to Rockland
Subarrange each by Table J17
1371-1371.9 Rockland, Maine (Table J16)
1372 Rockland to Saginaw
Subarrange each by Table J17
1373-1373.9 Saginaw, Michigan (Table J16)
1374 Saginaw to St. Joseph
Subarrange each by Table J17
1376-1376.9 St. Joseph, Missouri (Table J16)
1377 St. Joseph to St. Louis
Subarrange each by Table J17
1381-1400 St. Louis, Missouri (Table J14)
1401 St. Louis to St. Paul
Subarrange each by Table J17
1411-1419 St. Paul, Minnesota (Table J15)
1420 St. Paul to Salem
Subarrange each by Table J17
1421-1421.9 Salem, Massachusetts (Table J16)

United States
Local
By city -- Continued

1422 Salem to Salt Lake
Subarrange each by Table J17
1423-1423.9 Salt Lake City, Utah (Table J16)
1424 Salt Lake City to San Antonio
Subarrange each by Table J17
1425-1425.9 San Antonio, Texas (Table J16)
1426 San Antonio to San Diego
Subarrange each by Table J17
1427-1427.9 San Diego, California (Table J16)
1428 San Diego to San Francisco
Subarrange each by Table J17
1431-1449 San Francisco, California (Table J14a)
1449.5 Local. By district, ward, etc.
1450 San Francisco to Savannah
Subarrange each by Table J17
1451-1451.9 Savannah, Georgia (Table J16)
1452 Savannah to Scranton
Subarrange each by Table J17
1453-1453.9 Scranton, Pennsylvania (Table J16)
1454 Scranton to Seattle
Subarrange each by Table J17
1455-1455.9 Seattle, Washington (Table J16)
1456 Seattle to Shz
Subarrange each by Table J17
1457 Si to Somerville
Subarrange each by Table J17
1458-1458.9 Somerville, Massachusetts (Table J16)
1459 Somerville to Springfield
Subarrange each by Table J17
1460-1460.9 Springfield, Illinois (Table J16)
1461 Springfield, Kentucky to Springfield, Maine
Subarrange each by Table J17
1462-1462.9 Springfield, Massachusetts (Table J16)
1464-1464.9 Springfield, Missouri (Table J16)
1466 Springfield to Steubenville
Subarrange each by Table J17
1467-1467.9 Steubenville, Ohio (Table J16)
1468 Steubenville to Superior
Subarrange each by Table J17
1469-1469.9 Superior, Wisconsin (Table J16)
1470 Superior to Syracuse
Subarrange each by Table J17
1471-1479 Syracuse, New York (Table J15)

United States
Local
By city -- Continued

1480 Syracuse to Tacoma
Subarrange each by Table J17

1481-1481.9 Tacoma, Washington (Table J16)

1482 Tacoma to Taunton
Subarrange each by Table J17

1485-1485.9 Taunton, Massachusetts (Table J16)

1486 Taunton to Terre Haute
Subarrange each by Table J17

1487-1487.9 Terre Haute, Indiana (Table J16)

1488 Terre Haute to Toledo
Subarrange each by Table J17

1491-1499 Toledo, Ohio (Table J15)

1500 Toledo to Topeka
Subarrange each by Table J17

1501-1501.9 Topeka, Kansas (Table J16)

1502 Topeka to Trenton
Subarrange each by Table J17

1503-1503.9 Trenton, New Jersey (Table J16)

1504 Trenton to Troy
Subarrange each by Table J17

1505-1505.9 Troy, New York (Table J16)

1507 Troy to Utica
Subarrange each by Table J17

1508-1508.9 Utica, New York (Table J16)

1509 Utica to Washington
Subarrange each by Table J17

(1511-1530) Washington, District of Columbia
see JK2701+

1531 Washington to Waterbury
Subarrange each by Table J17

1535-1535.9 Waterbury, Connecticut (Table J16)

1536 Waterbury to Wheeling
Subarrange each by Table J17

1538-1538.9 Wheeling, West Virginia (Table J16)

1539 Wheeling to Wichita
Subarrange each by Table J17

1540-1540.9 Wichita, Kansas (Table J16)

1541 Wichita to Wilkes-Barre
Subarrange each by Table J17

1543-1543.9 Wilkes-Barre, Pennsylvania (Table J16)

1544 Wilkes-Barre to Wilmington
Subarrange each by Table J17

1545-1545.9 Wilmington, Delaware (Table J16)

United States
Local
By city -- Continued
1546 Wilmington to Winston
Subarrange each by Table J17
1547-1547.9 Winston-Salem, North Carolina (Table J16)
1548 Winston to Wom
Subarrange each by Table J17
1549 Won to Worcester
Subarrange each by Table J17
1551-1559 Worcester, Massachusetts (Table J15)
1561 Worcester to Yonkers
Subarrange each by Table J17
1563-1563.9 Yonkers, New York (Table J16)
1564 Yonkers to Youngstown
Subarrange each by Table J17
1565-1565.9 Youngstown, Ohio (Table J16)
1566 Youngstown to Ypsilanti
Subarrange each by Table J17
1568-1568.9 Ypsilanti, Michigan (Table J16)
1579 Ypsilanti to Zanesville
Subarrange each by Table J17
1581-1581.9 Zanesville, Ohio (Table J16)
1583 Zanesville to Zz
Subarrange each by Table J17
Canada
1701-1719 General (Table J14a)
1721.A-Z Local. By province, A-Z
Subarrange each by Table J17
Local. By city
1726 A
Subarrange each by Table J17
1728 B
Subarrange each by Table J17
1731-1731.9 Calgary (Table J16)
1733 Calgary to Charlottetown
Subarrange each by Table J17
1734-1734.9 Charlottetown (Table J16)
1737 Charlottetown to Dawson
Subarrange each by Table J17
1738-1738.9 Dawson (Table J16)
1741 Dawson to Edmonton
Subarrange each by Table J17
1742-1742.9 Edmonton (Table J16)
1743 Edmonton to Fredericton
Subarrange each by Table J17
1744-1744.9 Fredericton (Table J16)

Canada
Local. By city -- Continued

1747 Fredericton to Halifax
Subarrange each by Table J17
1749-1749.9 Halifax (Table J16)
1750 Halifax to Hamilton
Subarrange each by Table J17
1751-1751.9 Hamilton (Table J16)
1756 Hamilton to London
Subarrange each by Table J17
1757-1757.9 London (Table J16)
1760 London to Montreal
Subarrange each by Table J17
1761-1761.9 Montreal (Table J16)
1762 Montreal to Moosejaw
Subarrange each by Table J17
1763-1763.9 Moosejaw (Table J16)
1765 Moosejaw to Ottawa
Subarrange each by Table J17
1766-1766.9 Ottawa (Table J16)
1770 Ottawa to Quebec
Subarrange each by Table J17
1771-1771.9 Québec (Table J16)
1773 Québec to Regina
Subarrange each by Table J17
1775-1775.9 Regina (Table J16)
1776 Regina to St. John
Subarrange each by Table J17
1779-1779.9 St. John (Table J16)
1780 St. John to Saskatoon
Subarrange each by Table J17
1781-1781.9 Saskatoon (Table J16)
1784 Saskatoon to Sydney
Subarrange each by Table J17
1785-1785.9 Sydney (Table J16)
1788 Sydney to Toronto
Subarrange each by Table J17
1789-1789.9 Toronto (Table J16)
1790 Toronto to Vancouver
Subarrange each by Table J17
1791-1791.9 Vancouver (Table J16)
1792 Vancouver to Victoria
Subarrange each by Table J17
1793-1793.9 Victoria (Table J16)
1795 Victoria to Winnipeg
Subarrange each by Table J17
1797-1797.9 Winnipeg (Table J16)

Canada
Local. By city -- Continued
1800 Winnipeg to Z
Subarrange each by Table J17
(1811-1819) Newfoundland
see JS1721
1830 Bermuda
West Indies. Caribbean Area
1840 General works
1841 Bahamas
1851-1858 British West Indies. English-speaking Caribbean (Table J15a)
Cuba see JS2001+
Haiti see JS2051+
Dominican Republic see JS2055+
1861-1869 Jamaica (Table J15)
Puerto Rico see JS2021+
Virgin Islands of the United States see JS2058+
British West Indies. English-speaking Caribbean see JS1851+
1869.5 Barbados
Leeward Islands
1870 General works
1871 Anguilla
1871.5 Antigua and Barbuda
1872 Montserrat
1873 Saint Kitts and Nevis
Windward Islands
1874 General works
1875 Dominica
1876 Grenada
1877 Saint Lucia
1877.5 Saint Vincent and the Grenadines
1878 Trinidad and Tobago
Danish West Indies see JS2058+
Netherlands Antilles. Dutch West Indies
1911 General works
1913 Aruba
1915 Bonaire
1918 Curaçao
1920 Saba
1921 Saint Eustatius
1922 Saint Martin
French West Indies
1941 General works
1942 Guadeloupe
1943 Martinique

West Indies. Caribbean Area -- Continued
2001-2020 Cuba (Table J14)
2021-2040 Puerto Rico (Table J14)
2051-2051.9 Haiti (Table J16)
2055-2055.9 Dominican Republic (Table J16)
2058-2058.9 Virgin Islands of the United States (Table J16)
2061 Latin America
Mexico
2101-2119 General (Table J14a)
2119.5.A-Z Local. By state, A-Z
Local. By city, A-Z
2120 A to M
2121-2140 Mexico City (Table J14)
2143 M to Z
Central America
2145 General works
2151-2159 Belize (Table J15)
2161-2169 Costa Rica (Table J15)
2171-2179 Guatemala (Table J15)
2181-2189 Honduras (Table J15)
2191-2199 El Salvador (Table J15)
2201-2209 Nicaragua (Table J15)
2211-2219 Panama (Table J15)
South America
2300 General works
Argentina
2301-2319 General (Table J14a)
2325.A-Z Local. By province, A-Z
2328.A-Z Local. By city, A-Z
2351-2370 Bolivia (Table J14)
Brazil
2401-2419 General (Table J14a)
2423.A-Z Local. By state, etc., A-Z
2425.A-Z Local. By city, A-Z
Chile
2451-2469 General (Table J14a)
2475.A-Z Local. By province, etc., A-Z
2478.A-Z Local. By city, A-Z
2501-2520 Colombia (Table J14)
2551-2570 Ecuador (Table J14)
Guianas
2573 Guyana
2575 Suriname. Dutch Guiana
2577 French Guiana
2601-2620 Paraguay (Table J14)
Peru
2651-2669 General (Table J14a)

South America
Peru -- Continued
2675.A-Z Local. By region or province, etc., A-Z
2678.A-Z Local. By city, A-Z
2701-2720 Uruguay (Table J14)
Venezuela
2751-2769 General (Table J14a)
2775.A-Z Local. By state, etc., A-Z
2778.A-Z Local. By city, A-Z
Europe
3000 General
Including European Union countries discussed collectively
Local government other than municipal
3000.2 General works
3000.25 Intermediate levels of government. State government. Provincial government. Regional government
3000.3 European Community countries
3000.7 Eastern Europe
Great Britain. England
3001 Periodicals. Societies. Serials
(3003) Annuals
see JS3001
3008 Congresses
3011 Museums. Exhibitions
(3013-3020) Collections
see JS3025+
History
3025 General works
3029 Early to 1066
3041 Norman Conquest to William and Mary (1066-1689)
3051 1689 to 1835
3065 Nineteenth century
3095 Twentieth century
3111 General works
(3113) Compends, textbooks, etc.
see JS3111
(3115-3125) Municipal government
see JS3111
Federal-city relations. Central-local government relations. Municipal home rule
(3134) Law
see KD4765
3137 General works
(3141) Local taxation
see HJ9425+
3152.A-Z Other topics, A-Z
3152.E4 Electronic data processing

Europe
Great Britain. England
Other topics, A-Z -- Continued
3152.L5 Limits, Territorial. Local and administrative divisions. Administrative and political divisions
Executive branch. Mayor
3158 General works
Civil service
(3169) Law
see KD4805+
3173 General works
3175 Salaries. Pensions. Retirement
3185 Legislative branch. City councils
3200 Government property. Government purchasing
3209 Political participation
Elections. Local elections. Municipal elections
3215 General works
(3218) Election law
see KD4347
3225 Political corruption
Local government other than municipal
3251 General works
3260 County government
3265 Boroughs
3270 District government
3275 Parish government
3325.A-Z Local. By county, shire, etc., A-Z
Local. By city
3331 Avon to Birmingham
Subarrange each by Table J17
3341-3360 Birmingham (Table J14)
3365 Birmingham to Bradford
Subarrange each by Table J17
3371-3379 Bradford (Table J15)
3385 Bradford to Bristol
Subarrange each by Table J17
3401-3420 Bristol (Table J14)
3425 Bristol to Hull
Subarrange each by Table J17
3451-3459 Hull (Table J15)
3465 Hull to Liverpool
Subarrange each by Table J17
3481-3500 Liverpool (Table J14)
London
3551 Periodicals. Societies. Serials
3553 Directories. Registers

Europe
Great Britain. England
Local. By city
London -- Continued

(3557) Laws, ordinances, etc.
see KD8866+
History
3559 General works
3562 Early to 1699
3566 18th century
3571 19th century
3600 20th century
3605 General works
3611 Central-local government relations. Municipal home rule
3613 Relations to the City of London
Greater London Council. London County Council
3624 Directories. Registers
3625 General works
Corporation of the City of London
3658 General works
3661 Lord Mayor
3663 Aldermen
Civil Service
3668 General works
3674 Salaries. Pensions. Retirement
3675 Civil service examinations
3681 Political participation
3693 Elections
3705 Political corruption
3711 Local. By borough, parish, etc.
3731-3750 Manchester (Table J14)
3758-3758.9 Newcastel-under-Lyme (Table J16)
3759-3759.9 Newcastel-upon-Tyne (Table J16)
3781-3789 Norwich (Table J15)
3801-3820 Nottingham (Table J14)
3841-3860 Portsmouth (Table J14)
3865 Portsmouth to Rochester
Subarrange each by Table J17
3875-3875.9 Rochester (Table J16)
3880 Rochester to Salford
Subarrange each by Table J17
3891-3899 Salford (Table J15)
3911-3930 Sheffield (Table J14)
3930.5 Sheffield to Sunderland
Subarrange each by Table J17
3931-3939 Sunderland (Table J15)

Europe
Great Britain. England
Local. By city -- Continued
3940 Sunderland to West Ham
Subarrange each by Table J17
3961-3969 West Ham (Table J15)
3970 West Ham to York
Subarrange each by Table J17
3971-3979 York (Table J15)
Wales
4001-4019 General (Table J14a)
Local
4025.A-Z By county, shire, etc., A-Z
By city
4030 A - Cardiff
Subarrange each by Table J17
4031-4039 Cardiff (Table J15)
4045-4045.9 Merthyr-Tydfil (Table J16)
4051-4051.9 Swansea (Table J16)
Scotland
4101-4190 General (Table J13)
4206.A-Z By county, shire, etc., A-Z
By city
4211-4219 Aberdeen (Table J15)
4225-4225.9 Dundee (Table J16)
4231-4250 Edinburgh (Table J14)
4261-4280 Glasgow (Table J14)
4290.A-Z Other cities, A-Z
4295-4295.9 Northern Ireland (Table J16)
Ireland. Irish Republic
4301-4390 General (Table J13)
(4403) Northern Ireland
see JS4295
4411.A-Z Local. By county, shire, etc., A-Z
Local. By city
4441-4449 Dublin (Table J15)
4461-4469 Limerick (Table J15)
4490.A-Z Other cities, A-Z
Austria
4501-4590 General (Table J13)
4605.A-Z Local. By state, etc., A-Z
Local. By city
4607 A - Vienna
Subarrange each by Table J17
4631-4650 Vienna (Table J14)
4655 Vienna - Z
Subarrange each by Table J17

Europe -- Continued
Hungary
4661-4680 General (Table J14)
4682.A-Z Local. By county, etc., A-Z
Local. By city
4685 A - Budapest
Subarrange each by Table J17
4686-4694 Budapest (Table J15)
4696 Budapest - Z
Subarrange each by Table J17
Czechoslovakia. Czech Republic. Bohemia
4721-4740 General (Table J14)
4742.A-Z Local. By region, province, etc., A-Z
Subarrange each by Table J17
Local. By city
4745 A - Prague
Subarrange each by Table J17
4746-4754 Prague (Table J15)
4756 Prague - Z
Subarrange each by Table J17
4760-4760.9 Slovakia (Table J16)
4770-4770.9 Leichtenstein (Table J16)
France
4801 Periodicals. Societies. Serials
4803 Directories. Registers
4807 Museums. Exhibitions
History
General works see JS4881
By period
Ancien Régime (To 1789)
4821 General works
Provincial government
4842 Administrative and political divisions
4843 Intendants
4845.A-Z Local. By province, etc., A-Z
4851 1789-1900
4874 Twentieth century
4881 General works
4895 Central-local government relations. Municipal home rule
Local government other than municipal
4901 General works
4902 Regional government
Départmental government
4903 General works
4905 Prefect. Commissaire de la République
4907 Conseil-Général
4912 Arrondissements

Europe
France
Local government other than municipal
Départmental government -- Continued
4917 Cantons
4922 Communes
For municipalities see JS5000+
Municipal government specifically
(4931-4944) General works
see JS4821+
4947 Executive branch. Mayor
4953 Municipal council
4965 Government property. Government purchasing
4965.5.A-Z Other topics, A-Z
4965.5.B6 Boundaries
4966 Political participation
4975 Elections. Local elections. Municipal elections
4981 Political corruption
4990.A-Z Local. By region, A-Z
4991.A-Z Local. By department, A-Z
Under each:

.xA1-.xA4	*Periodicals. Serials*
.xA5	*General works*
.xA6-.xZ	*Local. By arrondissement, commune, etc., A-Z*

For Seine (Dept.) see JS5101+
Local. By city
5000 A - Bordeaux (Aquitaine)
Subarrange each by Table J17
5001-5009 Bordeaux (Aquitaine) (Table J15)
5015 Bordeaux (Aquitaine) to Lille
Subarrange each by Table J17
5021-5029 Lille (Table J15)
5035 Lille to Lyons
Subarrange each by Table J17
5041-5049 Lyons (Table J15)
5061-5069 Marseilles (Table J15)
5075 Marseilles to Paris
Subarrange each by Table J17
5101-5190 Paris (Table J13)
Including Départment of the Seine
5205 Paris to Toulouse
Subarrange each by Table J17
5241-5249 Toulouse (Table J15)
5250 Toulouse to Z
Subarrange each by Table J17
Germany

Europe
Germany -- Continued
5301 Periodicals. Societies. Serials
5303 Directories. Registers
5305 Congresses
5307 Museums. Exhibitions
History
5321 General works
By period
5324 To 1800
5371 Nineteenth century
5390 Twentieth century
5395 General works
For municipal government see JS5431+
Central-local government relations. Municipal home rule
5409 General works
(5411) Law
see KK5876+
Local government other than municipal
5415 General works
5417 Provinz. Provincial government
5419 Regierungsbezirk
5421 Kreis. Landkreis. Stadtkreis. Ämter
5425 Gemeinde
Municipal government
5431 General works
5437 Executive branch. Mayor
5441 City councils. Stadtverordnetenersammlung
5445 Government property. Government purchasing
5448 Political participation
Elections. Local elections. Municipal elections
(5457) Election law
see KK5295
5459 General works
5463 Political corruption
5471.A-Z Local. By state or province, A-Z
Under each:
.xA1-.xA4 *Periodicals. Serials*
.xA5 *General works*
.xA6-.xZ *Local. By Regierungsbezirk, Kreis, Ämter, etc., A-Z*
For government at the state or province level see JN4000+
5472-5472.9 German Democratic Republic (1949-1990) (Table J16)
Class here works on the government of the Bezirke and Kreise of the former East Germany

Europe
Germany -- Continued
For works on the government of the cities located in East Germany see JS5474+
Local. By city

5474-5474.9 Aachen (Aix-la-Chapelle) (Table J16)
5475 Aachen to Altona
Subarrange each by Table J17
5476-5476.9 Altona (Table J16)
5477 Altona to Barmen
Subarrange each by Table J17
5478 Barmen to Berlin
Subarrange each by Table J17
5481-5500 Berlin (Table J14)
5501 Berlin to Bielefeld
Subarrange each by Table J17
5502-5502.9 Bielefeld (Table J16)
5503 Bielefeld to Bonn
Subarrange each by Table J17
5506-5506.9 Bonn (Table J16)
5507 Bonn to Bremen
Subarrange each by Table J17
5508-5508.9 Bremen (Table J16)
5509 Bremen to Breslau
Subarrange each by Table J17
5511-5519 Breslau (Table J15)
5520 Breslau to Charlottenburg
Subarrange each by Table J17
5521-5521.9 Charlottenburg (Table J16)
5522 Charlottenburg to Chemnitz
Subarrange each by Table J17
5523-5523.9 Chemnitz (Table J16)
5524 Chemnitz to Cologne
Subarrange each by Table J17
5525-5525.9 Cologne (Table J16)
5526 Cologne to Crefeld
Subarrange each by Table J17
5527-5527.9 Crefeld (Table J16)
5528 Crefeld to Danzig
Subarrange each by Table J17
5529-5529.9 Danzig (Table J16)
5530 Danzig to Dresden
Subarrange each by Table J17
5531-5539 Dresden (Table J15)
5541 Dresden to Düsseldorf
Subarrange each by Table J17
5543-5543.9 Düsseldorf (Table J16)

Europe
Germany
Local. By city -- Continued

5545 Düsseldorf to Essen
Subarrange each by Table J17

5546-5546.9 Essen (Table J16)

5547 Essen to Frankfurt a. M.
Subarrange each by Table J17

5548-5548.9 Frankfurt a. M. (Table J16)

5549 Frankfurt a. M. to Hamburg
Subarrange each by Table J17

5551-5559 Hamburg (Table J15)

5560 Hamburg to Kiel
Subarrange each by Table J17

5561-5561.9 Kiel (Table J16)

5562 Kiel to Königsberg i. Pr.
Subarrange each by Table J17

5563-5563.9 Königsberg i. Pr. (Table J16)

5564 Königsberg i. Pr. to Leipzig
Subarrange each by Table J17

5565-5565.9 Leipzig (Table J16)

5566 Leipzig to Lübeck
Subarrange each by Table J17

5567-5567.9 Lübeck (Table J16)

5568 Lübeck to Magdeburg
Subarrange each by Table J17

5569-5569.9 Magdeburg (Table J16)

5570 Magdeburg to Munich
Subarrange each by Table J17

5571-5579 Munich (Table J15)

5581 Munich to Nuremberg
Subarrange each by Table J17

5585-5585.9 Nuremberg (Table J16)

5586 Nuremberg to Posen
Subarrange each by Table J17

5587-5587.9 Posen (Table J16)

5588 Posen to Rostock
Subarrange each by Table J17

5589-5589.9 Rostock (Table J16)

5590 Rostock to Stettin
Subarrange each by Table J17

5591-5591.9 Stettin (Table J16)

5592 Stettin to Strassburg i. E.
Subarrange each by Table J17

5593-5593.9 Strassburg i. E. (Table J16)

5594 Strassburg i. E. to Stuttgart
Subarrange each by Table J17

Europe
Germany
Local. By city -- Continued
5595-5595.9 Stuttgart (Table J16)
5596 Stuttgart to Wiesbaden
Subarrange each by Table J17
5597-5597.9 Wiesbaden (Table J16)
5598 Wiesbaden to Z
Subarrange each by Table J17
Greece
5601-5619 General (Table J14a)
Local
5621-5629 Athens (Table J15)
5638.A-Z Other cities, regions, provinces, etc., A-Z
Subarrange each by Table J17
Italy
5701-5790 General (Table J13)
5796.A-Z Local. By region, province, A-Z
For government of the individual regions or provinces at the regional or provincial level see JN5690.A+
Local. By city
5811-5819 Florence (Table J15)
5831-5839 Milan (Table J15)
5851-5859 Naples (Table J15)
5871-5879 Rome (Table J15)
5881-5889 Trieste (Table J15)
5891-5899 Turin (Table J15)
5911-5919 Venice (Table J15)
5925.A-Z Other cities, A-Z
Subarrange each by Table J17
5927-5927.9 Malta (Table J16)
Benelux Countries. Low Countries
5928 General works
Netherlands
5931-5949 General (Table J14a)
5950.A-Z Local. By province, A-Z
Local. By city
5961-5969 Amsterdam (Table J15)
5981-5989 The Hague (Table J15)
5995-5995.9 Rotterdam (Table J16)
5998.A-Z Other cities, A-Z
Subarrange each by Table J17
Belgium
6001-6019 General (Table J14a)
6020.A-Z Local. By province, etc., A-Z
Local. By city
6021-6029 Antwerp (Table J15)

Europe
Benelux Countries. Low Countries
Belgium
Local. By city -- Continued
6031-6039 Brussels (Table J15)
6043-6043.9 Ghent (Table J16)
6047-6047.9 Liege (Table J16)
6048.A-Z Other cities, A-Z
Subarrange each by Table J17
6049-6049.9 Luxembourg (Table J16)
Russia. Soviet Union. Former Soviet republics
For individual cities, other than Moscow and St. Petersburg, see the successor states to the Soviet Union
6051-6069 General (Table J14a)
6081-6089 Moscow (Table J15)
6101-6109 St. Petersburg. Leningrad. Petrograd (Table J15)
Soviet Central Asia see JS7261+
Siberia see JS7281+
(6112) Armenia
see JS7437
(6113) Azerbaijan
see JS7438
6114-6114.9 Belarus (Table J16)
(6115) Georgia
see JS7439
6116-6116.9 Moldova (Table J16)
6117-6117.9 Russia (Federation) (Table J16)
6118-6118.9 Ukraine (Table J16)
Autonomous republics of the former Russian S.F.S.R. see JS6117+
Finland see JS6291+
6130.2-.29 Estonia (Table J16a modified)
6130.2.A1 Periodicals. Societies. Serials
6130.2.A12 Directories. Registers
(6130.2.A3) Laws. Ordinances. Codes
see class K
Elections. Local elections. Municipal elections
(6130.27.A7-.A8) Election law
see class K
(6130.27.A73) This number not used
(6130.27.A75) This number not used
6130.273 General works
6130.275 Statistics. Election returns
6130.3-.39 Latvia (Table J16a modified)
6130.3.A1 Periodicals. Societies. Serials
6130.3.A12 Directories. Registers

	Europe
	Latvia -- Continued
(6130.3.A3)	Laws. Ordinances. Codes
	see class K
	Elections. Local elections. Municipal elections
(6130.37.A7-.A8)	Election law
	see class K
(6130.37.A73)	This number not used
(6130.37.A75)	This number not used
6130.373	General works
6130.375	Statistics. Election returns
6130.5-.59	Lithuania (Table J16a modified)
6130.5.A1	Periodicals. Societies. Serials
6130.5.A12	Directories. Registers
(6130.5.A3)	Laws. Ordinances. Codes
	see class K
	Elections. Local elections. Municipal elections
(6130.57.A7-.A8)	Election law
	see class K
(6130.57.A73)	This number not used
(6130.57.A75)	This number not used
6130.573	General works
6130.575	Statistics. Election returns
6131-6139	Poland (Table J15)
	Scandinavia
6141-6148	General (Table J15a)
	Denmark
6151-6169	General (Table J14a)
	Local
6170.A-Z	By region, province, county, etc., A-Z
	By city
6171-6179	Copenhagen (Table J15)
6185.A-Z	Other, A-Z
	Subarrange each by Table J17
6187-6187.9	Greenland (Table J16)
6189-6189.9	Iceland (Table J16)
	Norway
6201-6219	General (Table J14a)
	Local
6220.A-Z	By region, province, county, etc., A-Z
	By city
6221-6229	Oslo. Kristiania (Table J15)
6235.A-Z	Other, A-Z
	Subarrange each by Table J17
	Sweden
6251-6269	General (Table J14a)
	Local

Europe
Scandinavia
Sweden
Local -- Continued
6270.A-Z By region, province, county, etc., A-Z
By city
6271-6279 Stockholm (Table J15)
6285.A-Z Other, A-Z
Subarrange each by Table J17
6291-6299 Finland (Table J15)
Spain
6301-6319 General (Table J14a)
Local
6320.A-Z By region, province, etc., A-Z
By city
6321-6329 Madrid (Table J15)
6335.A-Z Other, A-Z
Subarrange each by Table J17
Portugal
6341-6359 General (Table J14a)
Local
6360.A-Z By region, district, etc., A-Z
By city
6361-6369 Lisbon (Table J15)
6375.A-Z Other, A-Z
Subarrange each by Table J17
Switzerland
6401-6419 General (Table J14a)
Local. By canton
For government of the individual cantons at the canton level see JN9100+
6421-6429 Aargau (Table J15)
6441-6449 Appenzell Ausserrhoden (Table J15)
6461-6469 Appenzell Innerrhoden (Table J15)
6481-6489 Baselland (Table J15)
6491-6499 Basel-Stadt (Table J15)
6501-6509 Basel (City) (Table J15)
6511-6519 Bern (Table J15)
6521-6529 Bern (City) (Table J15)
6531-6539 Fribourg (Table J15)
6541-6549 Fribourg (City) (Table J15)
6551-6559 Geneva (Table J15)
6561-6569 Geneva (City) (Table J15)
6571-6579 Glarus (Table J15)
6591-6599 Grisons (Graubunden) (Table J15)
6611-6619 Lucerne (Table J15)
6621-6629 Lucerne (City) (Table J15)

Europe
Switzerland
Local. By canton -- Continued
6631-6639 Neuchâtel (Table J15)
6641-6649 Neuchâtel (City) (Table J15)
6651-6659 St. Gall (Table J15)
6661-6669 St. Gall (City) (Table J15)
6671-6679 Schaffhausen (Table J15)
6681-6689 Schaffhausen (City) (Table J15)
6691-6699 Schwyz (Table J15)
6711-6719 Solothurn (Table J15)
6721-6729 Solothurn (City) (Table J15)
6731-6739 Thurgau (Table J15)
6751-6759 Ticino (Table J15)
6771-6779 Unterwalden (Table J15)
6791-6799 Uri (Table J15)
6811-6819 Valais (Wallis) (Table J15)
6821-6829 Vaud (Table J15)
6831-6839 Lausanne (City) (Table J15)
6851-6859 Zug (Table J15)
6871-6879 Zurich (Table J15)
6881-6889 Zurich (City) (Table J15)
Balkan States
6899.5 General works
6900-6900.9 Albania (Table J16)
6901-6909 Bulgaria (Table J15)
6921-6929 Romania (Table J15)
6931-6939 Serbia (Table J15)
6941-6949 Yugoslavia (Table J15 modified)
(6949.A-Z) Local
see the individual republics
6949.2-.29 Bosnia and Hercegovina (Table J16a modified)
6949.2.A1 Periodicals. Societies. Serials
6949.2.A12 Directories. Registers
(6949.2.A3) Laws, ordinances, codes
see class K
Elections. Local elections. Municipal elections
(6949.27.A7-.A8) Election law
see class K
(6949.27.A73) This number not used
(6949.27.A75) This number not used
6949.273 General works
6949.275 Statistics. Election returns
6949.5-.59 Croatia (Table J16a modified)
6949.5.A1 Periodicals. Societies. Serials
6949.5.A12 Directories. Registers

Europe
Balkan States
Croatia -- Continued
(6949.5.A3) Laws, ordinances, codes
see class K
Elections. Local elections. Municipal elections
(6949.57.A7-.A8) Election law
see class K
(6949.57.A73) This number not used
(6949.57.A75) This number not used
6949.573 General works
6949.575 Statistics. Election returns
6949.7-.79 Macedonia (Republic) (Table J16a modified)
6949.7.A1 Periodicals. Societies. Serials
6949.7.A12 Directories. Registers
(6949.7.A3) Laws, ordinances, codes
see class K
Elections. Local elections. Municipal elections
(6949.77.A7-.A8) Election law
see class K
(6949.77.A73) This number not used
(6949.77.A75) This number not used
6949.773 General works
6949.775 Statistics. Election returns
Serbia see JS6931+
6949.8-.89 Slovenia (Table J16a modified)
6949.8.A1 Periodicals. Societies. Serials
6949.8.A12 Directories. Registers
(6949.8.A3) Laws, ordinances, codes
see class K
Elections. Local elections. Municipal elections
(6949.87.A7-.A8) Election law
see class K
(6949.87.A73) This number not used
(6949.87.A75) This number not used
6949.873 General works
6949.875 Statistics. Election returns
Asia
6950 General works
6951-6959 Turkey (Table J15)
Middle East. Southwest Asia see JS7435+
South Asia
6970 General works
India
7001-7019 General (Table J14a)
7025.A-Z Local. By state, union territory, etc., A-Z
Local. By city

Asia
South Asia
India
Local. By city -- Continued
7030 A - Bombay
Subarrange each by Table J17
7031-7039 Bombay (Table J15)
7040 Bombay - Calcutta
Subarrange each by Table J17
7051-7059 Calcutta (Table J15)
7065 Calcutta - Madras
Subarrange each by Table J17
7081-7089 Madras (Table J15)
7090 Madras - Z
Subarrange each by Table J17
Afghanistan see JS7441+
Nepal see JS7180+
7090.5-.59 Bhutan (Table J16a modified)
7090.5.A1 Periodicals. Societies. Serials
7090.5.A12 Directories. Registers
(7090.5.A3) Laws, ordinances, codes
see class K
Elections. Local elections. Municipal elections
(7090.57.A7-.A8) Election law
see class K
(7090.57.A73) This number not used
(7090.57.A75) This number not used
7090.573 General works
7090.575 Statistics. Election returns
7091-7099 Pakistan (Table J15)
7100-7100.9 Bangladesh (Table J16)
7111-7119 Burma. Myanmar (Table J15)
7121-7129 Sri Lanka. Ceylon (Table J15)
(7135) Local
see JS7129
Southeast Asia. Indochina
7139 General works
(7141-7149) Hong Kong
see JS7367
Burma (Myanmar) see JS7111+
Sri Lanka see JS7121+
7150-7150.9 Cambodia. Kampuchea (Table J16)
7151-7151.9 Laos (Table J16)
7152-7152.9 Vietnam (Table J16)
7153-7153.9 Thailand (Table J16)
7161-7169 Malaysia. Malaya (Table J15)
7171-7179 Singapore (Table J15)

Asia
South Asia
Southeast Asia. Indochina -- Continued
7180-7180.9 Nepal (Table J16)
7185-7185.9 Brunei (Table J16)
Indonesia
7191-7198 General (Table J15a)
7205.A-Z Local. By province, district, etc., A-Z
7206.A-Z Local. By city, A-Z
Subarrange each by Table J17
7207-7207.9 Timor-Leste. East Timor (Table J16)
Philippines see JS7301+
(7225) Vietnam
see JS7152
Central Asia
7261 General works
7265-7265.9 Kazakhstan (Table J16)
7267-7267.9 Kyrgyzstan (Table J16)
7271-7271.9 Tajikistan (Table J16)
7275-7275.9 Uzbekistan (Table J16)
7281-7289 Siberia (Russia) (Table J15)
Including Siberian republics and autonomous areas
(7295) Local
see JS7289
Philippines
7301-7308 General (Table J15a)
Local
7321-7329 Manila (Table J15)
7335.A-Z Other, A-Z
Subarrange each by Table J17
East Asia. Far East
7350 General works
China
For Hong Kong see JS7367+
7351-7358 General (Table J15)
7365.A-Z Local, A-Z
Subarrange each by Table J17
7365.5-.59 Macau (Table J16a modified)
7365.5.A1 Periodicals. Societies. Serials
7365.5.A12 Directories. Registers
(7365.5.A3) Laws, ordinances, codes
see class K
Elections. Local elections. Municipal elections
(7365.57.A7-.A8) Election law
see class K
(7365.57.A73) This number not used
(7365.57.A75) This number not used

Asia
East Asia. Far East
Macau
Elections. Local elections. Municipal elections -- Continued
7365.573 General works
7365.575 Statistics. Election returns
7366-7366.9 Taiwan (Table J16)
7367-7367.9 Hong Kong (Table J16)
Japan
7371-7378 General (Table J15a)
7384.A-Z Local. By prefecture, etc., A-Z
7385.A-Z Local. By city, A-Z
Subarrange each by Table J17
7391-7399 Korea (Table J15)
Including South Korea
7400-7400.9 North Korea (Table J16)
7400.95-.959 Mongolia. Outer Mongolia (Table J16a modified)
7400.95.A1 Periodicals. Societies. Serials
7400.95.A12 Directories. Registers
(7400.95.A3) Laws, ordinances, codes
see class K
Elections. Local elections. Municipal elections
(7400.957.A7-.A8) Election law
see class K
(7400.957.A73) This number not used
(7400.957.A75) This number not used
7400.9573 General works
7400.9575 Statistics. Election returns
(7401-7415) Thailand
see JS7150
Middle East. Near East. Southwest Asia. Islamic Empire
7435 General works
Caucasus
7436 General works
7437-7437.9 Armenia (Table J16)
7438-7438.9 Azerbaijan (Table J16)
7439-7439.9 Georgia (Republic) (Table J16)
Turkey see JS6951+
Afghanistan
7441-7449 General (Table J15)
(7455) Local
see JS7449
Iran
7461-7469 General (Table J15)
(7475) Local
see JS7469

Asia
Middle East. Near East. Southwest Asia. Islamic Empire -- Continued

(7499) Other
see JS7500+

7500-7500.9 Cyprus (Table J16)
7501-7501.9 Syria (Table J16)
7501.95-.959 Lebanon (Table J16a modified)
7501.95.A1 Periodicals. Societies. Serials
7501.95.A12 Directories. Registers
(7501.95.A3) Laws, ordinances, codes
see class K

Elections. Local elections. Municipal elections
(7501.957.A7-.A8) Election law
see class K

(7501.957.A73) This number not used
(7501.957.A75) This number not used
7501.9573 General works
7501.9575 Statistics. Election returns
7502-7502.9 Israel. Palestine (Table J16)
7503-7503.9 Jordan (Table J16)

Arabian Peninsula. Arabia. Persian Gulf States
7504 General works
7506-7506.9 Saudi Arabia (Table J16)
7506.92-.929 Qatar (Table J16a modified)
7506.92.A1 Periodicals. Societies. Serials
7506.92.A12 Directories. Registers
(7506.92.A3) Laws, ordinances, codes
see class K

Elections. Local elections. Municipal elections
(7506.927.A7-.A8) Election law
see class K

(7506.927.A73) This number not used
(7506.927.A75) This number not used
7506.9273 General works
7506.9275 Statistics. Election returns
7506.93-.939 Yemen (Table J16a modified)
7506.93.A1 Periodicals. Societies. Serials
7506.93.A12 Directories. Registers
(7506.93.A3) Laws, ordinances, codes
see class K

Elections. Local elections. Municipal elections
(7506.937.A7-.A8) Election law
see class K

(7506.937.A73) This number not used
(7506.937.A75) This number not used
7506.9373 General works

Asia
Middle East. Near East. Southwest Asia. Islamic Empire
Arabian Peninsula. Arabia. Persian Gulf States
Yemen
Elections. Local elections. Municipal elections -- Continued
7506.9375 Statistics. Election returns
7506.95-.959 Oman. Muscat and Oman (Table J16a modified)
7506.95.A1 Periodicals. Societies. Serials
7506.95.A12 Directories. Registers
(7506.95.A3) Laws, ordinances, codes
see class K
Elections. Local elections. Municipal elections
(7506.957.A7-.A8) Election law
see class K
(7506.957.A73) This number not used
(7506.957.A75) This number not used
7506.9573 General works
7506.9575 Statistics. Election returns
7506.97-.979 United Arab Emirates. Trucial States (Table J16a modified)
7506.97.A1 Periodicals. Societies. Serials
7506.97.A12 Directories. Registers
(7506.97.A3) Laws, ordinances, codes
see class K
Elections. Local elections. Municipal elections
(7506.977.A7-.A8) Election law
see class K
(7506.977.A73) This number not used
(7506.977.A75) This number not used
7506.9773 General works
7506.9775 Statistics. Election returns
7507-7507.9 Bahrain (Table J16)
7508-7508.9 Kuwait (Table J16)
7509-7509.9 Iraq (Table J16)
Iran see JS7461+
7510 Arab countries
7520 Islamic countries
Africa
7525 General works
English-speaking Africa
7528 General works
South Africa
7531-7539 General (Table J15)
(7551-7635) Local
see JS7539
Southern Africa. Central Africa

Africa
English-speaking Africa
Southern Africa. Central Africa -- Continued
7637 General works
7638-7638.9 Botswana. Bechuanaland (Table J16)
7639-7639.9 Lesotho. Basutoland (Table J16)
7640-7640.9 Swaziland (Table J16)
7641-7641.9 Rhodesia. Federation of Rhodesia and Nyasaland. British Central African Protectorate (Table J16)
7642-7642.9 Zambia. Northern Rhodesia (Table J16)
7643-7643.9 Zimbabwe. Southern Rhodesia (Table J16)
7644-7644.9 Malawi (Table J16)
7645-7645.9 Namibia. Southwest Africa (Table J16)
East Africa
7647 General works
7648-7648.9 Kenya (Table J16)
Tanganyika see JS7697+
Zanzibar see JS7697+
7649-7649.9 Uganda (Table J16)
West Africa
7653 General works
7654-7654.9 Gambia (Table J16)
Liberia see JS7799+
7655-7655.9 Ghana. Gold Coast (Table J16)
7656-7656.9 Nigeria (Table J16)
7657-7657.9 Sierra Leone (Table J16)
7660 French-speaking Africa
North Africa
7660.5 General works
Morocco see JS7809+
7661-7669 Algeria (Table J15)
7670-7670.9 Tunisia (Table J16)
Egypt see JS7761+
Sudan see JS7819+
7670.95-.959 Libya (Table J16a modified)
7670.95.A1 Periodicals. Societies. Serials
7670.95.A12 Directories. Registers
(7670.95.A3) Laws, ordinances, codes
see class K
Elections. Local elections. Municipal elections
(7670.957.A7-.A8) Election law
see class K
(7670.957.A73) This number not used
(7670.957.A75) This number not used
7670.9573 General works
7670.9575 Statistics. Election returns
French-speaking West Africa

Africa
French-speaking West Africa -- Continued
7671 General works
7672-7672.9 Benin. Dahomey (Table J16)
7672.95-.959 Togo (Table J16a modified)
7672.95.A1 Periodicals. Societies. Serials
7672.95.A12 Directories. Registers
(7672.95.A3) Laws, ordinances, codes
see class K
Elections. Local elections. Municipal elections
(7672.957.A7-.A8) Election law
see class K
(7672.957.A73) This number not used
(7672.957.A75) This number not used
7672.9573 General works
7672.9575 Statistics. Election returns
7673-7673.9 Guinea (Table J16)
7674-7674.9 Côte d'Ivoire. Ivory Coast (Table J16)
7675-7675.9 Mali. French Sudan (Table J16)
7676-7676.9 Mauritania (Table J16)
7677-7677.9 Niger (Table J16)
7678-7678.9 Senegal (Table J16)
7679-7679.9 Burkina Faso. Upper Volta (Table J16)
French-speaking Equatorial Africa
7681 General works
Zaire see JS7715+
7682-7682.9 Central African Republic. Ubangi-Shari (Table J16)
7683-7683.9 Chad (Table J16)
Cameroon see JS7692+
7684-7684.9 Congo (Brazzaville). Middle Congo (Table J16)
7685-7685.9 Gabon (Table J16)
7687-7687.9 Djibouti. French Territory of the Afars and Issas. French Somaliland (Table J16)
7688-7688.9 Madagascar. Malagasy Republic (Table J16)
7690-7690.9 German East Africa (Table J16)
7692-7692.9 Cameroon (Table J16)
7694-7694.9 Burundi (Table J16)
7695-7695.9 Rwanda (Table J16)
(7696) Namibia
see JS7645
7697-7697.9 Tanzania. Tanganyika. Zanzibar (Table J16)
(7698) Togo
see JS7672.95
7703-7703.9 Italian East Africa (Table J16)
(7705) Libya
see JS7670.95
7707-7707.9 Somalia. Italian Somaliland (Table J16)

Africa -- Continued
Djibouti see JS7687+
7715-7715.9 Zaire. Congo (Democratic Republic). Belgian Congo (Table J16)
7723-7723.9 Angola. Portuguese West Africa (Table J16)
7725-7725.9 Cape Verde (Table J16)
7727-7727.9 Guinea-Bissau. Portuguese Guinea (Table J16)
7729-7729.9 Mozambique. Portuguese East Africa (Table J16)
7731-7731.9 Sao Tome and Principe (Table J16)
7735-7735.9 Spanish West Africa (Table J16)
7736-7736.9 Equatorial Guinea (Table J16)
7755-7755.9 Ethiopia. Abyssinia (Table J16)
Egypt. United Arab Republic
7761-7769 General (Table J15)
(7781-7790) Local
see JS7769
7799-7799.9 Liberia (Table J16)
7809-7809.9 Morocco (Table J16)
7819-7819.9 Sudan (Table J16)
Atlantic Ocean islands
7820-7820.9 Azores (Table J16)
7821-7821.9 Bermuda (Table J16)
7822-7822.9 Madeira Islands (Table J16)
7823-7823.9 Canary Islands (Table J16)
Cape Verde see JS7725+
7825-7825.9 Saint Helena (Table J16)
7826-7826.9 Tristan da Cunha (Table J16)
7827-7827.9 Falkland Islands (Table J16)
Indian Ocean islands
7899-7899.9 General works (Table J16 modified)
(7899.9.A-Z) Local, A-Z
see JS7900+
7900-7900.9 Maldives (Table J16)
7901-7901.9 Seychelles (Table J16)
7902-7902.9 Comoros (Table J16)
7904-7904.9 Mauritius (Table J16)
7905-7905.9 Réunion (Table J16)
7906-7906.9 Kerguelen Islands (Table J16)
Australia
8001-8090 General (Table J13)
Local. By state
8131-8139 Australian Capital Territory (Table J15)
8141-8149 New South Wales (Table J15)
8150-8150.9 North Australia. Northern Territory (Table J16)
8151-8159 Queensland (Table J15)
8161-8169 South Australia (Table J15)
8171-8179 Tasmania (Table J15)

Australia
Local. By state -- Continued
8181-8189 Victoria (Table J15)
8191-8199 Western Australia (Table J15)
Local. By city
8241-8249 Adelaide (Table J15)
8253 Adelaide to Brisbane
Subarrange each by Table J17
8261-8269 Brisbane (Table J15)
8273 Brisbane to Hobart
Subarrange each by Table J17
8275-8275.9 Hobart (Table J16)
8278 Hobart to Melbourne
Subarrange each by Table J17
8281-8289 Melbourne (Table J15)
8293 Melbourne to Perth
Subarrange each by Table J17
8295-8295.9 Perth (Table J16)
8298 Perth to Sydney
Subarrange each by Table J17
8301-8309 Sydney (Table J15)
8310 Sydney to Z
Subarrange each by Table J17
New Zealand
8331-8349 General (Table J14a)
8350.A-Z Local. By territorial local authority, regional authority, district, etc., A-Z
Local. By city
8351-8359 Auckland (Table J15)
8371-8379 Christchurch (Table J15)
8391-8399 Wellington (Table J15)
Pacific Area. Pacific Ocean islands
(8401-8408) Hawaii
see JS451
8450 General works
(8455) By island
see JS8460+
8460-8460.9 Melanesia (Table J16)
8462-8462.9 Trust Territory of the Pacific. Micronesia (Federated States) (Table J16)
8463-8463.9 Marshall Islands (Table J16)
8464-8464.9 Mariana Islands (Table J16)
Including Northern Marianas
8465-8465.9 Palau (Table J16)
8466-8466.9 Guam (Table J16)
8467-8467.9 Papua New Guinea (Table J16)
8468-8468.9 Kiribati. Gilbert Islands (Table J16)

Pacific Area. Pacific Ocean islands -- Continued
8469-8469.9 Tuvalu. Ellice Islands (Table J16)
8470-8470.9 Solomon Islands (Table J16)
8471-8471.9 New Caledonia (Table J16)
8472-8472.9 Vanuatu. New Hebrides (Table J16)
8473-8473.9 Fiji (Table J16)
8474-84749 Tonga (Table J16)
8475-8475.9 Cook Islands (Table J16)
Samoan Islands
8480 General works
8481-8481.9 American Samoa (Table J16)
8482-8482.9 Samoa. Western Samoa (Table J16)
8490-8490.9 French Polynesia (Table J16)
Arctic regions
8495 General works
8496-8496.9 Greenland (Table J16)
8499-8499.9 Antarctica (Table J16)
8500 Developing countries

Colonies and colonization
Periodicals. Serials
Class here general periodicals by place of imprint
1 American
2 British
3 Dutch
4 French
5 German
6 Italian
7 Spanish
9 Other
Societies
For periodical publications with distinctive titles and not limited to proceedings or transactions see JV1+
10 International
11 American
12 British
13 Dutch
14 French
15 German
16 Italian
17 Spanish
19 Other
21 Congresses
22 Dictionaries. Encyclopedias
23 Museums. Exhibitions
(31-37) Documents
see JV500+
51 Theory. Philosophy
Study and teaching
55 General works
57.A-Z By region or country, A-Z
60 Biography
For individual biography and collective biography by country see JV500+
History
61 General works
By period
Ancient
71 General
Special countries
75 Egypt
81 Phoenicia
85 Carthage
93 Greece
98 Rome
Modern

History
By period
Modern -- Continued
105 General
121 Medieval to 1500
125 15th-16th century
131 17th century
135 18th century
141 19th century to 1870
145 1870 to 1900
151 20th century
152 21st century
185 General works
By region, hemisphere, continent
201 Tropics
America. Western hemisphere
221 General works
226 North America
231 South America. Latin America
Eastern hemisphere
236 General works
241 Asia and Pacific Area
246 Africa
Relations with indigenous peoples
305 General works
(308) Administration of colonies
see JV412
321 Colonization and Christianity
331 Colonization and education
341 Colonization and economics
Cf. JV420 Economic policy
(365) Colonial companies
see HF481+
(373) Penal colonies
see HV8935+
(406-407) Law
see K3375
Administration. Colonial administration
412 General works
420 Economic policy
Executive
Including Viceroy, governor
431 General works
443 Civil service
461 Legislative bodies
Including Colonial assemblies
Colonizing nations

	Colonizing nations -- Continued
500-597	United States (Table J18)
1000-1097	Great Britain (Table J18)
1800-1897	France (Table J18)
2000-2097	Germany (Table J18)
2200-2297	Italy (Table J18)
2500-2597	Netherlands. Holland (Table J18)
2800-2897	Belgium (Table J18)
3000-3097	Russia. Soviet Union (Table J18)
3300-3397	Denmark (Table J18)
3500-3597	Sweden (Table J18)
4000-4097	Spain (Table J18)
4200-4297	Portugal (Table J18)
5200-5297	Japan (Table J18)
5300-5397	Australia (Table J18)

Emigration and immigration. International migration
Cf. HB1951+ Population geography
Periodicals. Serials
Class here general periodicals by place of imprint
6001 American
6002 English
6003 French
6004 German
6005 Italian
6006 Other
6008 Societies
6011 Congresses
6012 Dictionaries. Encyclopedias
6013 Psychological aspects
6013.5 Study and teaching. Research
Statistics
6019 Collections of statistics
6020 Theory. Statistical methods
History
6021 General
By period
6026 To 1800
6029 19th century
6032 20th century
6033 21st century
6035 General works
6038 Government policy
(6045-6049) Law
see K3275
Emigration
(6061-6081) History
see JV6021+
6091 General works
Causes of emigration
6098 Economic
6101 Social
6104 Political
6107 Religious
Effects of emigration
6118 Economic
6121 Social
6124 Political
(6135-6149) Emigration to and from special regions or countries
see JV6350+
Immigration
History see JV6021+

Immigration -- Continued
6201 General works
(6214) Immigration and labor. Foreign workers
see HD6300
6217 Economic aspects
6217.5 Return migration
Social aspects
6225 General works
(6228) Illiteracy
see LC149+
(6231) Crime
see HV6181
6255 Political aspects
(6268) Inspection and registration
see K3275
6271 Government policy
(6325-6337) Services for immigrants. Social work with immigrants
see HV4005+
6342 Assimilation of immigrants
6344 Children
6346 Refugees
6347 Women immigrants
(6348) By ethnic group
see classes D, E, F
America. Western Hemisphere
6350 General works
North America
6351 General works
United States
Periodicals see JV6001
Manuals, guides for immigrants see JV6543+
6403 Societies
For immigrant relief societies see HV4010+
For societies at the state level see JV6905+
6405 Congresses
Documents
(6409-6416) Federal documents
see JV6435
(6419) State documents
see JV6905+
(6421-6429) Laws. Regulations
see KF4801+
6435 Emigration
Immigration
History
6450 General

America. Western Hemisphere
North America
United States
Immigration
History -- Continued
6451 Early to 1880
6453 1880-1900
6455 1900-2000
6456 2000-
6461 Statistics
6465 General works
6471 Economic aspects
(6473) Immigration and labor. Foreign workers
see HD8081
6475 Social aspects
6477 Political aspects
(6479) Medical aspects
see RA448.5.I44
Immigration policy. Government policy
(6481) Documents
see JV6483
6483 General works
6484 Ellis Island Immigration Station. Ellis Island Museum
(6485) Inspection and registration
see KF4840
6487 Fees. Poll tax
Cf. HJ4930 Taxation
(6491-6495) Regulation and control
see KF4801+ Law, JV6483 Government policy
(6501-6509) Restriction and exclusion
see JV6483
(6525-6533) Services for immigrants. Social work with immigrants
see HV4010+
(6535) Padrone system
see HV4871+
Handbooks, manuals, etc. for immigrants
6543 General works
6545.A-Z Manuals in foreign languages. By language, A-Z
Local
By section
6554 New England. Northeastern States
6556 Middle States. Middle Atlantic States
6559 Southern States
6565 West
6567 Middle West
6569 Northwestern States

America. Western Hemisphere
North America
United States
Local
By section -- Continued
6571 Pacific States
By state see JV6905+
Local see JV6905+
Special groups of immigrants
6600 Children
6601 Refugees
6602 Women immigrants
(6606) Occupational groups
see HD8039
(6611-6895) By race or ethnic origin
see E184.A1+
By state
6905-6907 Alabama (Table J19)
6908-6910 Alaska (Table J19)
6912-6914 Arizona (Table J19)
6916-6918 Arkansas (Table J19)
California
6920 General (Table J19a)
6923 San Francisco (Table J19a)
6926.A-Z Other local, A-Z
6928-6930 Colorado (Table J19)
6932-6934 Connecticut (Table J19)
6936-6938 Delaware (Table J19)
6940-6942 District of Columbia (Table J19)
6944-6946 Florida (Table J19)
6947-6949 Georgia (Table J19)
6950.5-.7 Hawaii (Table J19)
6951-6953 Idaho (Table J19)
Illinois
6954 General (Table J19a)
6957 Chicago (Table J19a)
6960.A-Z Other local, A-Z
6965-6967 Indiana (Table J19)
6968-6970 Iowa (Table J19)
6972-6974 Kansas (Table J19)
6975-6977 Kentucky (Table J19)
Louisiana
6979 General (Table J19a)
6982 New Orleans (Table J19a)
6985.A-Z Other local, A-Z
6987-6989 Maine (Table J19)

America. Western Hemisphere
North America
United States
By state -- Continued
Maryland
6991 General (Table J19a)
6994 Baltimore (Table J19a)
6997.A-Z Other local, A-Z
Massachusetts
7001 General (Table J19a)
7004 Boston (Table J19a)
7007.A-Z Other local, A-Z
7009-7011 Michigan (Table J19)
7012-7014 Minnesota (Table J19)
7016-7018 Mississippi (Table J19)
7019-7021 Missouri (Table J19)
7023-7025 Montana (Table J19)
7027-7029 Nebraska (Table J19)
7031-7033 Nevada (Table J19)
7034-7036 New Hampshire (Table J19)
7037-7039 New Jersey (Table J19)
7041-7043 New Mexico (Table J19)
New York
7045 General (Table J19a)
New York City
7048.A2 Societies
7048.A3-Z General works
7050.A-Z Individual boroughs, A-Z
7051.A-Z Other local, A-Z
7053-7055 North Carolina (Table J19)
7057-7059 North Dakota (Table J19)
7061-7063 Ohio (Table J19)
7065-7067 Oklahoma (Table J19)
7070-7072 Oregon (Table J19)
Pennsylvania
7075 General (Table J19a)
7078 Philadelphia (Table J19a)
7081.A-Z Other local, A-Z
7083-7085 Rhode Island (Table J19)
7087-7089 South Carolina (Table J19)
7091-7093 South Dakota (Table J19)
7095-7097 Tennessee (Table J19)
7098-7100 Texas (Table J19)
7102-7104 Utah (Table J19)
7106-7108 Vermont (Table J19)
7109-7111 Virginia (Table J19)

America. Western Hemisphere
North America
United States
By state -- Continued
7114-7116 Washington (Table J19)
7117-7119 West Virginia (Table J19)
7121-7123 Wisconsin (Table J19)
7125-7127 Wyoming (Table J19)
Canada, Latin America, etc.
7200-7295 Canada (Table J20)
7310-7319 Bermuda (Table J21)
Mexico see JV7400+
Central America see JV7412+
West Indies. Caribbean Area
7320-7329 General (Table J21)
7329.3 Bahamas
Cuba see JV7370+
Haiti see JV7393
7329.5 Jamaica
Dominican Republic see JV7395
Puerto Rico see JV7380+
Virgin Islands of the United States see JV7397
British West Indies. English-speaking Caribbean
7330-7339 General (Table J21)
7341 Barbados
Guyana see JV7499.3
Leeward Islands
7341.5 General works
7341.6 Anguilla
7341.7 Antigua and Barbuda
7341.8 Montserrat
7341.9 Saint Kitts and Nevis
Windward Islands
7345 General works
7345.3 Dominica
7345.4 Grenada
7345.5 Saint Lucia
7345.6 Saint Vincent and the Grenadines
7352 Trinidad and Tobago
(7353) Danish West Indies
see JV7397
Netherlands Antilles. Dutch West Indies
7356 General works
7356.2 Aruba
7356.3 Bonaire
7356.4 Curaçao

America. Western Hemisphere
Canada, Latin America, etc.
West Indies. Caribbean Area
Netherlands Antilles. Dutch West Indies -- Continued

7356.5 Saba
7356.6 Saint Eustatius
7356.7 Saint Martin
Suriname see JV7499.5
French West Indies
7359 General works
French Guyana see JV7499.7
7360 Guadeloupe
7361 Martinique
7370-7379 Cuba (Table J21)
7380-7389 Puerto Rico (Table J21)
7393 Haiti
7395 Dominican Republic
7397 Virgin Islands of the United States
Latin America
7398 General works
7400-7409 Mexico (Table J21)
Central America
7412 General works
7412.5 Belize. British Honduras
7413 Costa Rica
7416 Guatemala
7419 Honduras
7423 El Salvador
7426 Nicaragua
7429 Panama
7432 Panama Canal Zone
South America
7433 General works
7436 Southern Cone of South America
7440-7449 Argentina (Table J21)
7450-7459 Bolivia (Table J21)
7460-7469 Brazil (Table J21)
7470-7479 Chile (Table J21)
7480-7489 Colombia (Table J21)
7490-7499 Ecuador (Table J21)
Guianas
7499.2 General works
7499.3 Guyana. British Guiana
7499.5 Suriname. Dutch Guiana
7499.7 French Guiana
7500-7509 Paraguay (Table J21)

America. Western Hemisphere
Canada, Latin America, etc.
Latin America
South America -- Continued
7510-7519 Peru (Table J21)
7520-7529 Uruguay (Table J21)
7530-7539 Venezuela (Table J21)
Europe
7590 General works
Including European Union countries discussed collectively
7595 European Community countries
7597 Eastern Europe
7600-7695 Great Britain. England (Table J20)
7700-7709 Scotland (Table J21)
7709.5 Northern Ireland
7710-7719 Ireland. Irish Republic (Table J21)
7720-7729 Wales (Table J21)
7800-7895 Austria (Table J20)
7899.15 Czechoslovakia. Czech Republic
7899.2 Slovakia
7899.3 Hungary
7899.5 Liechtenstein
7900-7995 France (Table J20)
8000-8095 Germany (Table J20)
8110-8119 Greece (Table J21)
8130-8139 Italy (Table J21)
8141 Malta
Benelux countries. Low countries
8149 General works
8150-8159 Netherlands (Table J21)
8160-8169 Belgium (Table J21)
8175 Luxembourg
8180-8189 Russia. Soviet Union. Former Soviet republics (Table J21)
8190 Russia (Federation)
8191 Estonia
8192 Finland
Baltic States
8192.5 General works
Estonia see JV8191
8193 Latvia
8194 Lithuania
8195 Poland
8195.2 Belarus
8195.5 Moldova
8196 Ukraine
Scandinavia

Europe
Scandinavia -- Continued
8198 General works
8200-8209 Denmark (Table J21)
8209.5 Iceland
8210-8219 Norway (Table J21)
8220-8229 Sweden (Table J21)
8250-8259 Spain (Table J21)
8259.5 Andorra
8259.7 Gibraltar
8260-8269 Portugal (Table J21)
8280-8289 Switzerland (Table J21)
Balkan States
8295 General works
8296 Albania
8300-8309 Bulgaria (Table J21)
8320-8329 Romania (Table J21)
8330-8339 Yugoslavia. Serbia (Table J21)
8339.2 Slovenia
8339.4 Croatia
8339.5 Bosnia and Hercegovina
8339.7 Macedonia (Republic)
Greece see JV8110+
(8340-8349) Turkey
see JV8745
Asia
8490 General works
8500-8509 India (Table J21)
8510 Nepal
(8515-8635) Former colonies in Asia
see JV8500+
8685 Philippines
8700-8709 China (Table J21)
For Hong Kong see JV8758
8710-8719 Taiwan (Table J21)
8720-8729 Japan (Table J21)
Middle East. Near East
8739 General works
Caucasus
8739.5 General works
8739.6 Armenia
8739.7 Azerbaijan
8739.8 Georgia (Republic)
8741 Iran
8745 Turkey
8746 Cyprus

Asia
Middle East. Near East -- Continued
8747 Syria
8748 Lebanon
8749 Israel. Palestine
8749.5 Jordan
Arabian Peninsula. Arabia. Persian Gulf States
8750 General works
8750.3 Saudi Arabia
8750.5 Yemen (Yemen Arab Republic)
8750.55 Yemen (People's Democratic Republic). Southern Yemen. Aden (Colony and Protectorate)
8750.6 Oman. Muscat and Oman
8750.65 United Arab Emirates. Trucial States
8750.7 Qatar
8750.75 Bahrain
8750.8 Kuwait
8751 Iraq
Iran see JV8741
Central Asia
8751.15 General works
8751.2 Kazakhstan
8751.3 Kyrgyzstan
8751.4 Tajikistan
8751.5 Turkmenistan
8751.6 Uzbekistan
South Asia
8752 General works
8752.3 Afghanistan
8752.5 Burma. Myanmar
8752.7 Sri Lanka. Ceylon
Nepal see JV8510
India see JV8500+
8752.8 Bhutan
8753 Pakistan
8753.5 Bangladesh
Southeast Asia. Indochina
Including French Indochina
8753.7 General works
Burma (Myanmar) see JV8752.5
8754 Cambodia. Kampuchea
8754.3 Laos
8754.5 Vietnam
8754.7 Thailand
8755 Malaysia. Malaya
8755.5 Singapore

Asia
Southeast Asia. Indochina -- Continued
8755.7 Brunei
8756 Indonesia
Philippines see JV8685
East Asia. Far East
8756.5 General works
Japan see JV8720+
8757 Korea
Including South Korea
8757.5 North Korea
China see JV8700+
8757.7 Macau
Taiwan see JV8710+
8758 Hong Kong
8759 Mongolia
8760 Arab countries (Collective)
8762 Islamic countries
Africa
8790 General works
8800-8895 South Africa. Republic of South Africa (Table J20)
(8900-8969) Provinces, cities, etc.
see JV8800+
(8975) Former British colonies
see JV8800+
North Africa
8977 General works
8978 Morocco
8980 Algeria
8981 Tunisia
8983 Libya
8989 Egypt. United Arab Republic
8991 Sudan
(8995) Former French colonies
see JV8977+
Northeast Africa
8996 General works
8996.5 Eritrea
8997 Ethiopia
8998 Somalia
8998.5 Djibouti. French Territory of the Afars and Issas
Southeast Africa
Including East Africa
8998.7 General works
8999 Kenya
9001 Uganda

Africa

Southeast Africa -- Continued

9001.5 Rwanda

9001.7 Burundi

9002 Tanzania. Tanganyika. Zanzibar

9003 Mozambique

9004 Madagascar. Malagasy Republic

(9005) Former German colonies

see JV9001.5 Rwanda JV9001.7 Burundi; JV9007.5 Namibia; JV9018 Cameroon; JV9020.7 Togo

Southern Africa

9006 General works

South Africa see JV8800+

9006.15 Rhodesia

Including Zimbabwe (Southern Rhodesia)

9006.3 Zambia. Northern Rhodesia

9006.7 Lesotho. Basutoland

9007 Swaziland

9007.2 Botswana. Bechuanaland

9007.3 Malawi. Nyasaland

9007.5 Namibia. Southwest Africa

(9009) Former Italian Colonies

see JV8983 Libya; JV8998 Somalia

Central Africa. Equatorial Africa

9010 General works

9011 Angola

9015 Zaire. Congo (Democratic Republic)

9015.3 Equatorial Guinea

9015.5 Sao Tome and Principe

9015.7 French-speaking Equatorial Africa

9016 Gabon

9016.5 Congo (Brazzaville). Middle Congo

9016.8 Central African Republic. Ubangi-Shari

9017 Chad

9018 Cameroon

(9019) Former Portuguese colonies

see JV9003 Mozambique; JV9010 Angola; JV9015.5 Sao Tome and Principe; JV9024 Guinea-Bissau

West Africa. West Coast

9020 General works

9020.15 Sahel

9020.3 French-speaking West Africa

9020.5 Benin. Dahomey

9020.7 Togo

9020.8 Niger

9021 Côte d'Ivoire. Ivory Coast

	Africa
	West Africa. West Coast -- Continued
9021.2	Guinea
9021.4	Mali
9021.6	Burkina Faso. Upper Volta
9021.7	Senegal
9021.8	Mauritania
9022	Nigeria
9022.3	Ghana
9023	Sierra Leone
9023.5	Gambia
9023.6	Liberia
9024	Guinea-Bissau. Portuguese Guinea
9024.5	Spanish Sahara
(9025)	Independent African States see JV8790+
	Atlantic Ocean islands
9029	General works
	Iceland see JV8209.5
9030	Azores
	Bermuda see JV7310+
9031	Madeira Islands
9032	Canary Islands
9033	Cape Verde
9034	Saint Helena
9035	Tristan da Cunha
9036	Falkland Islands
	Indian Ocean islands
9040	General works
9041	Maldives
9042	Seychelles
9043	Comoros
9045	Mauritius
9046	Réunion
9047	Kerguelen Islands
	Australia
9100-9195	General (Table J20)
(9200-9299)	States, cities, etc. see JV9100+
9260-9269	New Zealand (Table J21)
	Pacific Area. Pacific Ocean islands
9290	General works
(9300-9445)	Former colonies see JV9290+
9446	Melanesia
9447	Trust Territory of the Pacific. Micronesia (Federated States)

Pacific Area. Pacific Ocean islands -- Continued
9448 Marshall Islands
9449 Mariana Islands
9450 Palau
(9451) Hawaii
see JV6950.5+
9452 Guam
9453 Papua New Guinea
9455 Kiribati. Gilbert Islands
9456 Tuvalu. Ellice Islands
9457 Solomon Islands
9458 New Caledonia
9459 Vanuatu. New Hebrides
9460 Fiji
9461 Tonga
9462 Cook Islands
Samoan Islands
9465 General works
9466 American Samoa
9467 Samoa. Western Samoa
9470 French Polynesia
Arctic regions
9472 General works
9473 Greenland
9475 Antarctica
9480 Developing countries

International law
Subclass JX was used at the Library of Congress until 1997. In 1997, it was replaced by two new subclasses, JZ, International relations, and KZ, Law of nations. All JX numbers are now coded as obsolete and shown in parentheses. See references have been made where possible to the corresponding numbers in subclasses JZ and KZ.
For international law, see subclass KZ
For international relations, see subclass JZ
Periodicals
International law, see K1+
International relations, see JZ5.5+
(1) American and English
(3) French and Belgian
(5) German
(7) Italian
(9) Spanish, Portuguese and Latin American
(18) Other
Yearbooks
For Annuaire de la vie internationale, see KZ6125
For Annuaire de l'Institut de droit international, see KZ24.I47
(21) General works
see KZ21; JZ21
Societies
see KZ24+ JZ24+
(24) International
(27) American
(31) English
(32) French, etc.
(33) German
(34) Italian
(35) Spanish, etc.
(38) Other
Congresses and conferences
For intergovernmental congresses and conferences, see KZ60+ for congresses and conferences in international relations, see JZ43.A+ for nongovernmental conferences on international law, see KZ1240
(41) General works. Organization. History
(54.A-Z) Special congresses. By name, A-Z
Collections. Documents. Cases
see KZ63+ JZ63+
General. Selections, sources, etc.
Polyglot editions
(63) Early
(64) Recent
(65) Latin

Collections. Documents. Cases
General. Selections, sources, etc. -- Continued
(68) English
(71) Dutch
(74) French, etc.
(77) German
(81) Italian
(84) Spanish, etc.
(91.A-Z) Other, A-Z
(97) Pamphlets, lectures, etc.
Diplomatic relations (Universal collections)
(101) Latin (and polyglot)
(103) English
(105) French
(107) German
(109) Italian
(111) Spanish
(115) Other
Treaties (General collections)
For collections of treaties of one particular country with other countries, see KZ235.3+ and list of countries beginning at KZ351+ (subdivision (6) under each country)
For collections of arbitration treaties, see KZ183.2
(118) Ancient
see JX2001
To 1700
(120) Latin (and polyglot)
Subarranged by title or editor
(121) English
Subarranged by title or editor
(122) French
Subarranged by title or editor
(123) German
Subarranged by title or editor
(124) Italian
Subarranged by title or editor
(125) Spanish
Subarranged by title or editor
(128.A-Z) Other, A-Z
Subarranged by title or editor
1700-1789
(130) Latin (and polyglot)
Subarranged by title or editor
(131) English
Subarranged by title or editor
(132) French
Subarranged by title or editor

Collections. Documents. Cases
Treaties (General collections)
1700-1789 -- Continued

(133) German
Subarranged by title or editor

(134) Italian
Subarranged by title or editor

(135) Spanish
Subarranged by title or editor

(138.A-Z) Other, A-Z
Subarranged by title or editor

1789-1815

(140) Latin (and polyglot)
Subarranged by title or editor

(141) English
Subarranged by title or editor

(142) French
Subarranged by title or editor

(143) German
Subarranged by title or editor

(144) Italian
Subarranged by title or editor

(145) Spanish
Subarranged by title or editor

(148.A-Z) Other, A-Z
Subarranged by title or editor

1815-1860

(150) Latin (and polyglot)
Subarranged by title or editor

(151) English
Subarranged by title or editor

(152) French
Subarranged by title or editor

(153) German
Subarranged by title or editor

(155) Spanish
Subarranged by title or editor

(158.A-Z) Other, A-Z
Subarranged by title or editor

1860-1900

(160) Latin (and polyglot)
Subarranged by title or editor

(161) English
Subarranged by title or editor

(162) French
Subarranged by title or editor

Collections. Documents. Cases
Treaties (General collections)
1860-1900 -- Continued

(163) German
Subarranged by title or editor

(164) Italian
Subarranged by title or editor

(165) Spanish
Subarranged by title or editor

(168.A-Z) Other, A-Z
Subarranged by title or editor

1900-

(170) Latin (and polyglot)
Subarranged by title or editor

(171) English
Subarranged by title or editor

(172) French
Subarranged by title or editor

(173) German
Subarranged by title or editor

(174) Italian
Subarranged by title or editor

(175) Spanish
Subarranged by title or editor

(178.A-Z) Other, A-Z
Subarranged by title or editor

1920-

(180) Treaty series of intergovernmental organizations
see KZ170+

(181) By language

Topical treaties

(181.53) Boundary treaties. By region or country
see KZ176+

(181.6) Treaties of arbitration investigation, mediation, reconcilation and compulsory adjudication
see KZ183+

(182) Treaties of peace
see KZ184+

(191) Separate treaties
see the subject or the country
For boundary treaties and treaties of peace, see classes D-F; KZ176+ KZ184+
For arbitration treaties, see KZ183+
For extradition treaties, see subclass K
For tariff treaties see HF1721+

Collections. By country

Note: In order to preserve the original JX integral numbers for the source materials of these old collections, the original form division tables have been revised only slightly. The numbers 1-4 in Table I, and the Cutters .A1-.A5A-Z in Table II, are applied in for the non-legal collections that are traditionally classed in Class J. The second set of numbers, 5-10 in Table I, and the Cutters .A55-.A9-Z in Table II, are used in KZ for legal materials that are traditionally classed in Class K. Countries that have been assigned a 10 number span, are subarranged by Table I; such countries that have been assigned 1 numbers, are subarranged by Table II

(220.52) General works

see KZ221+ JZ221+

(221-230) America (Table JX2)

United States

(231) General collections

Foreign relations and diplomatic correspondence

Secretary of state

(232) Report

Including bureau reports and documents

Diplomatic correspondence

Class here general collections, routine correspondence

(233.A1-.A4) Serial (in chronological order of series)

(233.A5-.A59) Special (not limited to special countries)

(233.A6-Z) Relations with particular countries

(234.A1) President's messages and other executive documents

Legislative documents

Senate

(234.A2) Collected

(234.A3) Special. By date

House

(234.A4) Collected

(234.A5) Special. By date

(234.A8-Z) Other documents

Treaties and conventions

(235) Separate treaties. By date

(235.9) Series

Main official series, .A3 by number

(236) Collections. By date of first volume (or if period covered)

(237) Digests of decisions, opinions, etc.

Including United States Attorney-general's opinions on international law questions

(238.A-Z) Cases, claims, etc. By name, A-Z

(238.A2) Collections

(238.A4-.A7) Alabama claims

JX

Collections. By country
United States
Cases, claims, etc. By name, A-Z
Alabama claims -- Continued
(238.A4) Documents, correspondence, etc. prior to Treaty of Washington. By date
Treaty of Washington see JX235+
(238.A42) The Arbitration. Correspondence, etc.
The American case
(238.A43-.A47) Collections. General statement, and other documents (American editions)
(238.A48-.A49) Foreign editions
Special documents
(238.A5) 1872 dated
Chronologically
(a) American official edition
(b)-(x) Foreign editions and translations
(238.A51) 1872 undated
(238.A53) After 1872
The British case
(238.A54-.A57) Collections (English editions)
(238.A58-.A59) Foreign editions
Special documents
(238.A6) 1872 dated
(238.A61) 1872 updated
(238.A63) After 1872
The Tribunal
(238.A64) Collections
(238.A65) Documents prior to the award
(238.A66) Decision and award
(238.A67) Other
(238.A687) United States Court of Commissioners, 1874
United States Court of Commissioners, 1882
(238.A69) Proceedings
(238.A692) Rules, opinions (etc.), 1882-1885
(238.A695) Separate documents. By date
(238.A7) Semiofficial and nonofficial. By date
Mixed Commission on British and American claims under Article XII of the Treaty of Washington, 1871
British claims
(238.A8) Memorials, briefs, decisions
(238.A8a) Testimony
American claims
(238.A81) Memorials, briefs, decisions
(238.A81a) Testimony
(238.A83) List of claims
(238.A85) Other documents, and nonofficial matter. By date

Collections. By country
United States
Cases, claims, etc. By name, A-Z -- Continued
(238.A9-Z) Other cases. By country or name
(238.F4-.F77) French and American claims
(238.F6-.F7) Claims originating 1860-1871
Including Mexican intervention 1860-1866, Franco-German war, 1870-1871
(238.F72-.F75) French spoliation claims
Including spoliations prior to July, 1801 (treaties and awards, etc. under conventions of 1803; 1831; treaty with Spain, 1819; etc.)
(238.F72) General collections
United States
(238.F73) Documents. By date
(238.F74A-.F74Z) Special claims. By name
(238.F743-.F746) French documents
(238.F75) Nonofficial (pamphlets, etc.). By date
(238.F77A-.F77Z) Other special, A-Z
(238.F8-.F9) Fur seal arbitration
(238.N6-.N69) Northeastern fisheries
(238.P5-.P6) Pious Fund cases
(238.S7-.S8) Spanish treaty claims
To include all Spanish claims
(239) Other cases. By date
(245.A-.W) States, A-W
e. g.
(245.T4) Texas (Republic)
Confederate States diplomatic documents, etc.
see KFZ8601+
Other countries
(351-360) Canada (Table JX2)
(355.9.A3) Treaty series. By number
(361-370) Mexico (Table JX2)
(371-380) Central America (Table JX2)
(381-390) Belize (Table JX2)
(391-400) Costa Rica (Table JX2)
(401-410) Guatemala (Table JX2)
(411-420) Honduras (Table JX2)
(421-430) Nicaragua (Table JX2)
(431-440) Panama (Table JX2)
(441-450) El Salvador (Table JX2)
West Indies
(451-460) Cuba (Table JX2)
(461-470) Haiti (Table JX2)
(471-480) Dominican Republic (Table JX2)
(483) Puerto Rico (Table JX1)

Collections. By country
Other countries
West Indies -- Continued

(484) U.S. Virgin Islands (Table JX1)
British West Indies
(485) General
(486.A-Z) Local, A-Z
Danish West Indies
(491) General
(492.A-Z) Local, A-Z
Dutch West Indies
(493) General
(493.A-Z) Local, A-Z
French West Indies
(495) General
(496.A-Z) Local, A-Z
(501-510) South America (Table JX2)
(511-520) Argentina (Table JX2)
(521-530) Bolivia (Table JX2)
(531-540) Brazil (Table JX2)
(541-550) Chile (Table JX2)
(551-560) Colombia (Table JX2)
(561-570) Ecuador (Table JX2)
(571) Guyana (Table JX1)
(574) Suriname (Table JX1)
(577) French Guiana (Table JX1)
(581-590) Paraguay (Table JX2)
(591-600) Peru (Table JX2)
(611-620) Venezuela (Table JX2)
(621-630) Europe (Table JX2)
(631-640) Great Britain (Table JX2)
(671-680) Austria-Hungary (Table JX2)
Czechoslovakia
(680.C9) Collections and serial documents
(680.C92) Treaties and conventions
(680.C93) Cases, claims, etc.
(681-690) France (Table JX2)
(691-700) Germany (Table JX2)
(701-710) Greece (Table JX2)
(711-720) Italy (Table JX2)
(721-730) Netherlands (Table JX2)
(731-740) Belgium (Table JX2)
(741-750) Holland (Table JX2)
(751-760) Russia. Soviet Union (Table JX2)
(761-770) Scandinavia (Table JX2)
(771-780) Denmark (Table JX2)
Iceland see JX899.I3

Collections. By country
Other countries
Europe
Scandinavia -- Continued
(791-800) Norway (Table JX2)
(801-810) Sweden (Table JX2)
(811-820) Spain (Table JX2)
(821-830) Portugal (Table JX2)
Turkey and Balkan States
(841-850) Turkey (Table JX2)
Albania
(850.A4) Collections and serial documents
(850.A5) Treaties and conventions
(850.A6) Cases, claims, etc.
(851-860) Bulgaria (Table JX2)
(861-870) Montenegro (Table JX2)
(871-880) Romania (Table JX2)
(881-890) Yugoslavia. Serbia (Table JX2)
Other European
(893) Luxembourg (Table JX1)
(895) Monaco (Table JX1)
(899.A-Z) Other, A-Z
Subarrange each in the following order: (1) Collections and serial documents; (2) Treaties and conventions; (3) Cases, claims, etc.
e. g.
(899.I3) Iceland
(899.S3) San Marino
Asia
(900) General works
(901-910) Philippines (Table JX2)
British possessions
(911-920) India (Table JX2)
(920.5.A-Z) Other special, A-Z
Subarrange each in the following order: (1) Collections and serial documents; (2) Treaties and conventions; (3) Cases, claims, etc.
(921-930) China (Table JX2)
(931-940) Dutch East Indies. Indonesia (Table JX2)
French possessions
(943) General and Indo-China (Table JX1)
(945.A-Z) Local, A-Z
Subarrange each in the following order: (1) Collections and serial documents; (2) Treaties and conventions; (3) Cases, claims, etc.
German possessions
(947) General

Collections. By country
Other countries
Asia
German possessions -- Continued
(948.A-Z) Local, A-Z
(951-960) Japan (Table JX2)
(961-970) Korea (Table JX2)
(970.15) Korea (Democratic People's Republic) (Table JX1)
(970.5) Pakistan (Table JX1)
(971-980) Iran (Table JX2)
(981-990) Russia in Asia. Soviet Union in Asia (Table JX2)
(991-1000) Thailand (Table JX2)
(1001-1010) Turkey in Asia (Table JX2)
(1015.A-Z) Other, A-Z
Subarrange each in the following order: (1) Collections and serial documents; (2) Treaties and conventions; (3) Cases, claims, etc.
e.g.
(1015.A72) League of Arab States
(1015.U5) United Arab Republic
(1021-1030) Africa (Table JX2)
(1031-1039) Egypt (Table JX2a)
British Africa and South Africa
(1040) General works (Table JX1)
(1041) Cape of Good Hope (Table JX1)
(1042) Natal (Table JX1)
(1043) Orange Free State (Table JX1)
(1044) South African Republic (Table JX1)
(1045) Transvaal (Table JX1)
(1046) Zimbabwe (Table JX1)
(1050.A-Z) Other, A-Z
French possessions
(1059) General
(1060.A-Z) Local, A-Z
German possessions
(1069) General
(1070.A-Z) Local, A-Z
Italian possessions
(1079) General
(1080.A-Z) Local, A-Z
(1085) Zaire (Table JX1)
Portuguese possessions
(1089) General
(1090.A-Z) Local, A-Z
Spanish possessions
(1099) General
(1100.A-Z) Local, A-Z

Collections. By country
Other countries
Africa -- Continued
(1101-1110) Ethiopia (Table JX2)
(1121-1130) Liberia (Table JX2)
(1131-1140) Morocco (Table JX2)
(1145.A-Z) Other, A-Z
(1161-1170) Australia (Table JX2)
(1171-1179) New Zealand (Table JX2a)
Pacific islands
(1180) General works (Table JX1)
American
(1181) Hawaii (Table JX1)
Philippines see JX901+
(1182.A-Z) Other, A-Z
Subarrange each in the following order: (1) Collections and serial documents; (2) Treaties and conventions; (3) Cases, claims, etc.
British
(1184) General
(1185.A-Z) Local, A-Z
French
(1187) General
(1188.A-Z) Local, A-Z
German
(1191) General
(1192.A-Z) Local, A-Z
(1195.A-Z) Other, A-Z
Subarrange each in the following order: (1) Collections and serial documents; (2) Treaties and conventions; (3) Cases, claims, etc.
(1215.22) Digests of cases, e. g. Snow, Wharton, Moore, etc.
see KZ200.5; KZ221+
(1226) Dictionaries
see KZ1161; JZ1161
Theory, scope, relations, sources
see KZ1255+
(1245) General
(1246) General special
Including sanctions: compulsion, enforcement in public international law (Power to enforce treaties, etc.)
(1247) Relation to other disciplines and topics
see JZ1249+ KZ1249+
(1248) Relation to municipal law
(1249-1253) Relation to the social sciences
(1250) Relation to political science
(1251) Relation to sociology

Theory, scope, relations, sources
Relations to other disciplines and topics -- Continued
(1252) Relation to economics
(1253) Relation to history
(1255) Other
Codification of International law
see KZ1287+
(1261) Collections. Congresses. Societies
see KZ1287.A+
Codes
see KZ1289+
(1265) Official. By date (issued by official bodies as documents, etc.)
(1268) Nonofficial. By editor
Including Field, Bluntschli, etc.
Treatises and other general works
see KZ1292+
(1270) Early, to 1860
Recent
(1271) American and English
(1273) French and Belgian
(1275) German
(1277) Italian
(1279) Spanish, Portuguese, and Latin American
(1280.A-Z) Other, A-Z
e. g.
(1280.R8) Russian
(1281) Addresses, essays, lectures
(1283) Special topics
(1287) Procedure
see JX1901+
Study and teaching
see KZ1237+ JZ1237+
(1291) General works
(1293.A-Z) By region or country, A-Z
see KZ1238.A+
(1295.A-Z) By school, A-Z
(1297) Outlines. Syllabi
(1299) Quizzes and examination questions
Textbooks, compends see JX2001+
Foreign relations
see subclass JZ
History of international relations and the development of international law
(1305) Comprehensive works
e. g. Laurent

Foreign relations
History of international relations and the development of international law -- Continued
(1308) Treatises. Textbooks
e. g. Nys, E. Etudes
(1311) Addresses, essays, lectures
By period
Ancient
see KZ1327.5+
(1314.32) Medieval
see KZ1329+
Modern
(1315) Comprehensive works
see KZ1329+
(1318) Balance of power
see JZ1313
(1319) Balkan question
(1321) Far Eastern question
see JZ1720+
By period
Peace of Westphalia to the Treaty of Utrecht (1648-1713)
see KZ1329+ JZ1335+
(1325) General
(1328) Peace of Westphalia
(1331) Spanish succession
(1333) Addresses, essays, lectures
Treaty of Utrecht to the French Revolution (1713-1789)
see KZ1334+ JZ1335+
(1335) General
(1336) Treaty of Paris, 1763
see KZ1336+
(1338.A-Z) Special. By subject, A-Z
e. g. League of the Neutrals
(1341) Contemporary works
French Revolution to the Congress of Vienna (1789-1815)
see KZ1345+ JZ1345+
(1345) General
(1346) Congress of Rastatt
(1347) Treaty of Ghent
(1349) Holy Alliance
(1351) Congress of Vienna
(1352.A-Z) Other, A-Z
(1353) Contemporary works

Foreign relations
History of international relations and the development of international law
By period
Modern
By period -- Continued
Congress of Vienna to the American Civil War (1815-1861)
see KZ1355; JZ1352+
(1358) General
(1361) Congress of Troppau (1820)
(1363) Congress of Laibach (1821)
(1365) Congress of Verona (1822)
(1366) Congress of Panama
(1367) Treaty of Paris (1856)
Class here publications of the English Maritime League
Including works on the Declaration of Paris
(1369) Contemporary works
American Civil War to the First Conference on the Hague (1861-1899)
see KZ1373+ JZ1373+
General
(1375) Geneva Conference, 1864, etc.
see KZ6440+
(1377) St. Petersburg Convention, 1868
(1379) London Conference, 1871
(1381) Brussels Conference, 1875
(1383) Berlin Conference, 1878
(1385) Congo Conference, 1884-1885
(1386.A-Z) Other, A-Z
(1387) Contemporary works
Twentieth century
see JZ1391+ JZ1394+
(1391) General
(1392) World War I
(1392.5) World War II
(1393.A-Z) Other special. By subject, A-Z
(1393.A8) Atlantic Union
(1393.B74) British Honduras question
(1393.C65) Conference on Security and Cooperation in Europe
see KZ6030
(1393.D46) Detente
see JZ5600
(1393.D8) Drago doctrine
(1393.E8) Exterritoriality
see KZ3678

Foreign relations
History of international relations and the development of international law
By period
Modern
Twentieth century
Other special. By subject, A-Z -- Continued

(1393.I53) Indian Ocean Region
see KZ4110.I64
(1393.I8) Italo-Ethiopian War, 1935-1936
(1393.K6) Korean War, 1950-1953
(1393.L3) Latin America
see KZ4116+
London Declaration (Laws of naval war), 1909
see KZ6545+
(1393.M43) Mediterranean Region
see KZ4110.M44
(1393.N54) Nonalignment
(1393.N57) North Atlantic Region
see KZ4110.A+
North Atlantic Treaty Organization (NATO). North Atlantic Assembly
see KZ5925+
(1393.N58-.N62) Official serials
(1393.N63) Official monographs. By date of publication
(1393.N67A-.N67Z) General works
(1393.P3) Pacific islands
see KZ4730+
(1393.R4) Rhine River and Valley
(1393.R8) Russo-Japanese War, 1904-1905
(1393.S5) Sino-Japanese War, 1937-1945
see KZ6795.S55
(1393.S6) South African War, 1899-1902
(1393.S63) South Atlantic Region
see KZ4110.A+
(1393.S65) Spanish Civil War, 1936-1939
(1393.S8) Straits question
see KZ3760+
Strategic Arms Limitation Talks see JX1974.75
(1393.W2) Warsaw Pact Organization
see KZ5965+
(1395) Contemporary works

Interoceanic canals
Class here diplomatic history only
see KZ3710+ JZ3710+
(1398-1398.8) Panama Canal (and Isthmian canals in general)
see KZ3712.2+ JZ3715+

Foreign relations
Interoceanic canals
Panama Canal (and Isthmian canals in general) -- Continued
(1398) General
(1398.2) Early to 1876/1879
(1398.3) French companies (1876/1879 - ca. 1903)
United States
(1398.5) Documents
(1398.6) Clayton-Bulwer Treaty, 1850
(1398.7) Hay-Pauncefote Treaties, 1901-1902
Panama Canal Treaties, 1977
(1398.72) Text of treaties. By date of publication
(1398.73) General works
(1398.8) Nonofficial
(1400) Nicaragua Canal
see KZ3720; JZ3720
(1401) Other American Isthmian canal projects
(1403) Suez Canal
see KZ3730; JZ3730
Foreign relations. By country
see JZ1464+ KZ4112+
(1404) America
see JZ1464+
United States
see JZ1467+
(1405) Collections
(1406) History of international law in the United States
History of foreign relations, diplomatic questions, etc.
(1407) General
see JZ1469+
By period
(1411) Colonial to 1776
(1412) 1776-1800/1815
(1413) 1800/1815-1861
(1414) 1861-1880
Including Trent affair
(1415) 1880-1900
(1416) 1900-1945
(1417) 1945-
Special topics
see JZ1482+
Boundary questions
see class E
(1421) Eastern policy
see JZ1484

Foreign relations. By country
United States
Special topics -- Continued
(1423) Great Lakes
see JZ1485
Monroe Doctrine
Class here works on general theory only
(1425) General works
see JZ1482
(1426) Philippine annexation, etc. Spanish-American War
see JZ1478
Panama Canal
see KZ3712.2+ JZ3715+
(1427.A-Z) Other topics, A-Z
(1427.E5) Embargo
(1427.M5) Military influence
(1428.A-Z) Relations with special countries, A-Z
see JZ1515+
Confederate States
(1429) General
(1430) Contemporary. By date
(1431.A-Z) Special topics. By subject, A-Z
Other countries
see JZ1464+
(1515) Canada. British America (Table JX3)
(1515.5) Latin America
(1516) Mexico (Table JX3)
Central America
(1517) General works
(1517.5) Belize (Table JX3)
(1518) Costa Rica (Table JX3)
(1519) Guatemala (Table JX3)
(1520) Honduras (Table JX3)
(1521) Nicaragua (Table JX3)
(1522) Panama (Table JX3)
(1522.5) Panama Canal (Table JX3)
(1523) El Salvador (Table JX3)
West Indies
(1524) General works
(1524.5) Bahamas (Table JX3)
(1525) Cuba (Table JX3)
(1526) Haiti (Table JX3)
(1526.5) Dominican Republic (Table JX3)
(1527) Jamaica (Table JX3)
(1528) Puerto Rico (Table JX3)
(1528.5) U.S. Virgin Islands (Table JX3)
(1529.A-Z) Other, A-Z

Foreign relations. By country
Other countries -- Continued
South America
(1530) General works
(1531) Argentina (Table JX3)
(1532) Bolivia (Table JX3)
(1533) Brazil (Table JX3)
(1534) Chile (Table JX3)
(1535) Colombia (Table JX3)
(1536) Ecuador (Table JX3)
Guianas
(1537) General works
(1537.1) Guyana (Table JX3)
(1537.3) Suriname (Table JX3)
(1537.5) French Guiana (Table JX3)
(1538) Paraguay (Table JX3)
(1539) Peru (Table JX3)
(1540) Uruguay (Table JX3)
(1541) Venezuela (Table JX3)
Europe
(1542) General works
European communities see KJE5105+
Great Britain. England
(1543) General (Table JX3)
(1545) Scotland (Table JX3)
(1546) Ireland (Table JX3)
(1547) Austria (Table JX3)
(1547.3) Czechoslovakia (Table JX3)
(1548) France (Table JX3)
(1548.3) Monaco (Table JX3)
Germany
(1549) General works
(1549.Z7A2) International relations of the German states to one another
(1549.3) Danzig
(1549.5) Saar
(1550) Greece (Table JX3)
(1550.5) Hungary (Table JX3)
Italy
(1551) General works
(1552) Papacy. States of the Church. Vatican (City) (Table JX3)
Yugoslavia see JX1564.5
(1552.5) Latvia (Table JX3)
(1553) Belgium (Table JX3)
(1554) Holland (and Netherlands in general) (Table JX3)
(1554.5) Luxembourg (Table JX3)

Foreign relations. By country
Other countries
Europe -- Continued
Russia. Soviet Union
(1555) General (Table JX3)
(1555.7) Poland (Table JX3)
(1555.8) Ukraine (Table JX3)
(1555.9) White Russia (Table JX3)
Scandinavia
(1556) General works
(1557) Denmark (Table JX3)
(1558) Iceland (Table JX3)
(1559) Norway (Table JX3)
(1560) Sweden (Table JX3)
(1562) Portugal (Table JX3)
(1563) Switzerland (Table JX3)
Turkey and the Balkan states
(1564) Bulgaria (Table JX3)
(1564.5) Yugoslavia (Table JX3)
(1565) Montenegro (Table JX3)
(1566) Romania (Table JX3)
(1567) Serbia (Table JX3)
(1568) Turkey and Islamic countries in general (Table JX3)
Including capitulations
Asia
(1569) General works
(1570) China (Table JX3)
India
(1571) General (Table JX3)
(1571.5.A-Z) Other British possessions, A-Z
Indochina
(1572) General works
(1573) French Indochina (Table JX3)
Indonesia
(1574) General (Table JX3)
(1575) Dutch East Indies. Indonesia (Table JX3)
(1576) Philippines (Table JX3)
(1577) Japan (Table JX3)
(1577.5) Korea (Table JX3)
(1578) Iran (Table JX3)
(1579) Soviet Union in Asia (Table JX3)
(1579.5) Thailand (Table JX3)
(1579.7) Taiwan (Table JX3)
(1580) Turkey in Asia (Table JX3)
(1581.A-Z) Other divisions of Asia, A-Z
Africa
(1582) General works

Foreign relations. By country
Other countries
Europe
Africa -- Continued
(1583) Egypt (Table JX3)
(1584.A-Z) British possessions, A-Z
(1584.S7) South Africa
(1584.T8) Transvaal
(1585.A-Z) French possessions, A-Z
(1586.A-Z) German possessions, A-Z
(1586.5.A-Z) Italian possessions, A-Z
(1586.7) Zaire (Table JX3)
(1587.A-Z) Portuguese possessions, A-Z
(1587.5.A-Z) Spanish possessions, A-Z
(1588.A-Z) Other divisions of Africa. Native states, A-Z
Morocco
(1588.M5) Collections
General works. History
(1588.M55) To 1800
(1588.M6) 1800-
(1588.M65) Contemporary works. By date
(1588.M7A-.M7Z) Special topics, A-Z
(1588.M8) Relations with special countries
Australia and New Zealand
(1589) General (Table JX3)
(1590) New South Wales
(1591) New Zealand (Table JX3)
(1592) North Australia. Northern Territory
(1593) Queensland
(1594) South Australia
(1595) Tasmania
(1596) Victoria
(1597) Western Australia
(1598.A-Z) Pacific islands, A-Z
Diplomacy. The Diplomatic Service
see JZ1400+
For the laws governing the diplomatic service, including powers, diplomatic privileges and immunities, diplomatic gifts, codes, etc., see the appropriate jurisdiction in class K subclasses, e. g. KF5113, The Foreign Service of the United States
(1621) Periodicals
see K1+ JZ5.5+
(1625) Yearbooks, etc.
Class here general works only
(1628) Societies
(1631) Collections
Class here general works only

Diplomacy. The Diplomatic Service -- Continued
(1632) Codes
see class K subclasses for appropriate country
(1634) Study and teaching. Schools
History. Treatises. General works
(1635) Comprehensive
By period
(1638) Ancient
Medieval (to 1600)
(1641) Treatises
(1643) Contemporary works
Modern
(1648) Comprehensive works
By period
17th century
(1651) Histories
(1652) Contemporary works, etc.
18th century
(1654) Histories
(1655) Contemporary works, etc.
19th century
(1658) Histories
(1659) Contemporary works, etc.
20th century
(1661) Histories
(1662) Contemporary works, etc.
(1664) Addresses, pamphlets, etc.
The Diplomatic Service
Appointment
(1665) Cases, documents, sources
(1666) Treatises
Credentials
(1668) Cases, documents, sources
(1669) Treatises
(1670) Unauthorized negotiations
Including works on their criminal aspects
Powers and privileges. Immunities
(1671) Cases, documents, sources
(1672) Treatises
Duties. Functions
(1674) General works
(1675) To the home government
(1676) To the foreign government
(1677) Diplomatic language, style, etc.
Ceremonials. Precedence
(1678) Cases, documents, sources
(1679) Treatises

Diplomacy. The Diplomatic Service
The Diplomatic Service -- Continued
Dress
(1681) Cases, documents, sources
(1682) Treatises
(1683.A-Z) Other topics, A-Z
(1683.F6) Foreign interests
(1683.G5) Gifts
(1683.P7) Protection of foreign missions
Organization. Administration
(1684) General works
Department of foreign affairs. The minister of state or foreign affairs
(1686) Cases, documents, sources
(1687) Treatises
Ambassadors, plenipotentiaries, envoys, etc.
(1691) Cases, documents, sources
(1692) Treatises
Special
Consuls. Consular service
see JZ1444+
For consular laws (codes) governing the consular service, including privileges and immunities, consular jurisdiction, etc., see the appropriate jurisdiction in class K subclasses, e. g. KK5445+ Germany
For consular courts and procedure, see the appropriate jurisdiction in class K subclasses, e. g. KK3693, Germany
(1694) General works
History
(1695) Cases, documents, sources
(1696) Treatises
(1698.A-Z) Special topics, A-Z
Subarrange each in the following order: (1) Treatises; (2) Cases, etc.
(1698.A4) Administration of estates
(1698.J8) Jurisdiction
(1698.P7) Police
(1698.P8) Privileges and immunities
(1698.T8) Trade and the consular service
(1699) Other
By region or country
see JZ1464+
United States
(1705-1706) General (Table JX6)
(1725.A-.W) States, A-W
(1729-1730) Canada (Table JX6)

Diplomacy. The Diplomatic Service
By region or country -- Continued
(1731-1732) Mexico (Table JX6)
Central America
(1733-1734) General
(1735-1736) Belize and Honduras (Table JX6)
(1737-1738) Costa Rica (Table JX6)
(1739) Guatemala (Table JX4)
Honduras see JX1735+
(1741) Nicaragua (Table JX4)
(1742-1743) Panama (Table JX6)
(1743.5) Panama Canal (Table JX4)
(1744) El Salvador (Table JX4)
West Indies
(1745) General works
(1749-1750) Cuba (Table JX6)
(1751) Haiti (Table JX4)
(1752) Dominican Republic (Table JX4)
(1753) Jamaica (Table JX4)
(1755-1756) Puerto Rico (Table JX6)
(1756.5) U.S. Virgin Islands (Table JX4)
(1757.A-Z) Other, A-Z
Subrrange each by Table JX5
South America
(1758) General works
(1759-1760) Argentina (Table JX6)
(1761-1762) Bolivia (Table JX6)
(1763-1764) Brazil (Table JX6)
(1765-1766) Chile (Table JX6)
(1767-1768) Colombia (Table JX6)
(1769-1770) Ecuador (Table JX6)
Guianas
(1771) General works
(1772) Guyana (Table JX4)
(1772.5) Suriname (Table JX4)
(1772.7) French Guiana (Table JX4)
(1773-1774) Paraguay (Table JX6)
(1775-1776) Peru (Table JX6)
(1777-1778) Uruguay (Table JX6)
(1779-1780) Venezuela (Table JX6)
Europe
(1781) General works
Great Britain. England
(1783-1784) General (Table JX6)
(1787-1788) Scotland (Table JX6)
(1789-1790) Ireland (Table JX6)
(1791-1792) Austria-Hungary (Table JX6)

Diplomacy. The Diplomatic Service
By region or country
Europe -- Continued
(1792.5) Czechoslovakia (Table JX4)
(1793-1794) France (Table JX6)
(1794.5) Monaco (Table JX4)
(1795-1796) Germany (Table JX6)
(1797-1798) Greece (Table JX6)
(1798.5) Hungary (Table JX4)
Italy
(1799-1800) General (Table JX6)
(1801-1802) Papacy. States of the Church. Vatican (City) (Table JX6)
Yugoslavia see JX1828.5
(1802.5) Latvia
see JX1808.5
(1802.7) Malta (Table JX4)
Netherlands
(1803-1804) Belgium (Table JX6)
(1805-1806) Holland (and Netherlands in General) (Table JX6)
(1806.5) Luxembourg (Table JX4)
Soviet Union. Russia
(1807-1808) General (Table JX6)
(1808.2) Estonia (Table JX4)
(1808.3) Finland (Table JX4)
(1808.5) Latvia (Table JX4)
(1808.6) Lithuania (Table JX4)
(1808.7) Poland (Table JX4)
Scandinavia
(1809-1810) General (Table JX6)
Denmark
(1811-1812) General (Table JX6)
(1813-1814) Iceland (Table JX6)
(1815-1816) Norway (Table JX6)
(1817-1818) Sweden (Table JX6)
(1819-1820) Spain (Table JX6)
(1821-1822) Portugal (Table JX6)
(1823-1824) Switzerland (Table JX6)
Turkey (and Balkan states)
(1825-1826) General (Table JX6)
(1826.5) Albania (Table JX4)
(1827-1828) Bulgaria (Table JX6)
(1828.5) Yugoslavia (Table JX4)
(1829) Montenegro (Table JX4)
(1831-1832) Romania (Table JX6)
(1833-1834) Serbia (Table JX6)
Yugoslavia see JX1828.5

Diplomacy. The Diplomatic Service
By region or country -- Continued
Asia
(1835) General works
(1837-1838) China (Table JX6)
(1838.5) Taiwan (Table JX4)
(1839-1840) India (Table JX6)
Indochina
(1841-1842) General (Table JX6)
(1843-1844) French Indochina (Table JX6)
Indonesia
(1845) General works (Table JX4)
(1847-1848) Dutch East Indies. Indonesia (Republic) (Table JX6)
(1849-1850) Philippines (Table JX6)
(1851-1852) Japan (Table JX6)
(1853-1854) Iran (Table JX6)
(1855-1856) Soviet Union in Asia (Table JX6)
(1857-1858) Turkey in Asia (Table JX6)
(1859.A-Z) Other divisions of Asia, A-Z
Subrrange each by Table JX5
Africa
(1861) General works
(1865.A-Z) British possessions, A-Z
Subrrange each by Table JX5
(1867.A-Z) French possessions, A-Z
Subrrange each by Table JX5
(1869.A-Z) German possessions, A-Z
Subrrange each by Table JX5
(1870.A-Z) Italian possessions, A-Z
Subrrange each by Table JX5
(1871.A-Z) Portuguese possessions, A-Z
Subrrange each by Table JX5
(1872.A-Z) Spanish possessions, A-Z
Subrrange each by Table JX5
(1873.A-Z) Other divisions, A-Z
Subrrange each by Table JX5
e.g.
(1873.L4-.L6) Liberia (Table JX5)
(1873.S5-.S7) South African Republic (Table JX5)
(1875-1876) Australia and New Zealand (Table JX6)
Pacific islands
(1891) General works
(1893) Hawaii (Table JX4)
(1894.A-Z) Others, A-Z
Subrrange each by Table JX5
(1896) Agents of foreign principals

International arbitration, organization, etc.
see KZ4850+ JZ4835+
Periodicals
(1901) English and American
(1902) French and Belgian
(1903) Other
(1904) Annuals
(1904.5) Study and teaching. Research
(1905) Handbooks, manuals, etc.
Societies, institutions, etc., for the promotion of peace
see JZ5514+
For publication on special subjects, see the subject
(1905.5) Directories
International
Carnegie endowment for International peace
(1906.A1-.A3) Serial publications, collections, etc.
(1906.A5) Charter, etc.
(1906.A6) Announcements, circulars, etc.
(1906.A63-.A65) United States public documents
(1906.A63) Collections. By earliest date
(1906.A65) Separate documents. By date
(1906.A7-Z) History
(1906.Z5) Pamphlets
(1907.A-Z) Other, A-Z
(1908.A-Z) Local. By country, A-Z
(1909) Celebrations, festivals, "Peace day",
see JZ5537
Congresses and conferences
see JZ5527+
(1910) General works. Organization. History
International
see KZ6015+
The Hague Conferences
see KZ6015+
(1912) Collections
Including official reports of 1st and 2d conferences
1st Conference (1899)
Official publications
(1913.A1) Preliminary correspondence, etc.
(1913.A13) Acts, proceedings
(1913.A16) Rules, etc.
(1913.A2A-.A2Z) Official publications by countries taking part, A-Z
Subarrange each in the following order: (1) Preliminary (Correspondence, etc.); (2) Acts, proceedings (Reports of delegates); (3) Other (Announcements, etc.)
e.g.

International arbitration, organization, etc.
Congresses and conferences
International
The Hague Conferences
1st Conference (1899)
Official publications by countries taking part, A-Z -- Continued
Great Britain
(1913.A2G6) Preliminary
(1913.A2G8) Other
(1913.A3-.A4) 2d Conference (1907)
Official publications
(1913.A31) Preliminary correspondence, etc.
(1913.A33) Acts, proceedings
(1913.A36) Rules, etc.
(1913.A4A-.A4Z) Official publications by countries taking part, A-Z
Subarrange each in the following order: (1) Preliminary (Correspondence, etc.); (2) Acts, proceedings (Reports of delegates); (3) Other (Announcements, etc.)
Nonofficial works on the conferences
(1916) Texts (partial), analyses, commentaries, and other general works
(1918) Popular works
(1919) General special
Special, by subject
see the subject
Permanent Court of Arbitration
see KZ6170+
Documents
(1925.A2) Preliminary (Treaties, etc.), by date of issue
(1925.A5) Sessions
(1925.C2) Cases
For special, see the subject or country e. g. KZ238.P5, The Pious fund case, United States vs. Mexico
For collections see KZ201+
(1928) General works. Legal, etc.
Other international congresses
see JZ5527+
(1930.A-Z) Congresses with permanent organization. By name, A-Z
Subarrange each in the following order: (1) Acts, proceedings; (2) History
(1931) Other. By date
National congresses
United States
see JZ5531.A+

International arbitration, organization, etc.
Congresses and conferences
National congresses
United States -- Continued
(1932.A-Z) Permanent. By name, A-Z
(1933) Other. By date
(1935.A-Z) Other countries, A-Z
Subarrange each in the following order: (1) By name; (2) By date
see JZ5532.A+
(1936) Exhibitions. Museums
see JZ5536
(1936.5) Celebrations, festivals, "Peace day," etc.
see JZ5537
History and other general works
Including popular ethical "peace literature"
see JZ5544+
(1937) Collections
Including digests
(1938) Comprehensive
By period
(1941) Ancient
(1942) Medieval
Modern
(1944) General works
(1945) 17th century
(1946) 18th century
19th century
International arbitration, world peace, etc.
(1948) Treatises
(1949) Popular works
(1950) International organization
20th century
International arbitration, world peace, etc.
(1952) Treatises
(1953) Popular works
(1953.5) Juvenile literature
(1954) International organization
(1961.A-Z) By region or country, A-Z
see JZ5584.A+
(1961.A3) America
(1962.A-Z) Biography, A-Z
see JZ5540+
(1962.A2) Collected

International arbitration, organization, etc. -- Continued
(1964) Illustrative material. Fiction, etc.
Including imaginary wars (works written to show the horrors of war)
Imaginary wars may also be classed as follows: (1) Works illustrating tactical problems: class U; (2) Works showing weakness of national defense: class U; (3) Works illustrating world politics: D445; (4) Works chiefly notable as literature: class P; (5) General tactical works: U313
see JZ5535
Works on diverse concepts and aspects of the subject see JZ6405.A+
(1964.3) Labor and war
(1964.4) Moving pictures and peace
see JZ5577.5
(1964.5) Press and peace movements
see JZ5577.5
(1964.7) Radio broadcasting and peace
see JZ5577.5
(1965) Woman and peace movements
see JZ5578+
(1965.5) Youth and peace movements
see JZ5579
(1966) Theory, Philosophy
see U21+
Special topics
(1968) Compromisory clause
(1970) Compulsory arbitration
Courts of international arbitration
see KZ6165+
(1971) General works
(1971.5) Permanent Court of International Justice
see KZ6260+
(1971.6) International Court of Justice
see KZ6272+
Disarmament. Arms control
see KZ5598.2+
(1974) General works
Conference on the limitation of armament, Washington, D.C., 1921-1922
see KZ5615.C63, JZ5615.A+
(1974.5) General works
Documents
(1974.5.A15) Collections of preliminary documents
(1974.5.A2) 1st-3d plenary sessions
(1974.5.A3) Proposal of the United States for the limitation of naval armament

International arbitration, organization, etc.
Special topics
Disarmament. Arms control
Conference on the limitation of armament, Washington, D.C., 1921-1922
Documents -- Continued
(1974.5.A5) Address of the President at concluding session
(1974.5.A6A-.A6Z) Documents. By country, A-Z
(1974.5.A7A-.A7Z) Special missions. By country, A-Z
(1974.5.A9-Z) Works. By author (or title), A-Z
Nuclear weapons
(1974.7) General works
(1974.73) Nuclear nonproliferation
see KZ5670+
Nuclear-weapon-free-zones
(1974.735) General works
see KZ5687
(1974.74.A-Z) By region or country, A-Z
see KZ5729.2+
(1974.74.L38) Latin America
(1974.75) Strategic Arms Limitation Talks I, 1969. Strategic Arms Limitation Talks II, 1979
see KZ5660+ KZ5662+
(1974.76) Strategic Arms Reduction Talks
see KZ5647+ KZ5650
(1974.8) Nuclear crisis control
see KZ5800
League of nations
see KZ4853+
(1975.A1) Periodicals. Societies. Yearbooks
Documents
see JZ4895+
Collected sets
(1975.A2) By "Official number"
(1975.A25) By "Sales number"
Including Series of League of Nations Publications
(1975.A3) Official journal
see KZ4860.5
(1975.A37) Monthly summary
Texts of the covenant
see KZ4877.3.A2
(1975.A39) English. By date
(1975.A392A-.A392Z) Other languages, A-Z
(1975.A393) Amendments to the covenant. By date
(1975.A395) Proposed amendments. By date
(1975.A397) Reports on application of the covenant. By date
Assembly

International arbitration, organization, etc.
Special topics
League of nations
Documents
Assembly -- Continued
Records (Actes)
see JZ4895
Committees
(1975.A42) General works
(1975.A422) Index to the records
Including Plenary meetings and committees
(1975.A423) Plenary meetings
(1975.A425) Journal
(1975.A43) Special reports of Assembly meetings. By date
(1975.A433) List of delegates
see JZ4870.2
(1975.A435) Guide officiel. Official guide
(1975.A437) Miscellaneous documents. By date
(1975.A438) Rules of procedure. By date
see KZ4892
(1975.A439A-.A439Z) Reports of national delegates or delegations. By country, A-Z
Council. Documents
see JZ4910
(1975.A44) Procès-verbaux. Minutes
Report on the work of the League
(1975.A4415) English edition
(1975.A4416) French edition
(1975.A45) Special reports of Council meetings. By date
(1975.A455) Miscellaneous documents. By date
(1975.A46A-.A46Z) Council reports of special representatives. By country, A-Z
(1975.A465) Rules of procedure. By date
Secretariat. Secretary-General
see KZ4894+
(1975.A488) Serials
(1975.A49) Nonserial documents. By date
(1975.A5-Z) General works
(1975.5.A-JZ1975.5.Z) League of Nations in relation to individual countries, A-Z
see KZ4885
(1975.5.A2) Collective
(1975.6) Sanctions
Including economic and military
see KZ6375

International arbitration, organization, etc.
Special topics
League of Nations -- Continued
(1975.7) Geneva protocol
Including protocol for the pacific settlement of international disputes
see KZ6040
High Commission for Refugees
see JZ4887.5.N35
(1975.8.A1) General works
(1975.8.A3-Z) By country
e. g.
(1975.8.G3) Refugees from Germany
(1975.9) Miscellaneous
Class here drama, juvenile works, cartoons, women's work, etc.
see JZ4871
United Nations
see KZ4935+ JZ4935+
(1976) Genesis of the United Nations
Including preliminary congresses in general
see KZ4985+ JZ4986+
(1976.3) Dumbarton Oaks Conversations, 1944
(1976.4) San Francisco Conference, 1945
(1976.5) Preparatory Commission of the United Nations
(1976.8.A-Z) Ratification of the United Nations Charter. By country, A-Z
United Nations, 1946-
(1977.A1) Periodicals. Societies, etc.
Documents
Texts of the charter
see KZ4991.A2; KZ4991.A3+
(1977.A15) English. By date
(1977.A16.A-Z) Other languages, A-Z
Collected set
(1977.A2) English edition
(1977.A212) French edition
(1977.A213) Spanish edition
(1977.A22) Journal
Bulletin
(1977.A3) English edition
(1977.A314) French edition
(1977.A315) Spanish edition
(1977.A3155.A-Z) Resolutions. By editor or compiler, A-Z
see JZ5010+

International arbitration, organization, etc.
Special topics
United Nations
United Nations, 1946-
Documents -- Continued
Secretariat. Secretary-General
Including subordinate departments, committees, and library
see JZ5008; KZ5085+
(1977.A316-.A359) Serials
Arranged alphabetically by subheading
(1977.A36) Nonserial documents. By date
(1977.A362.A-Z) Nonofficial publications. By author, A-Z
(1977.A365) Administrative Tribunal
see KZ5274
General handbooks, manuals, etc.
see JZ4970
(1977.A37.A-Z) Serial. By title, A-Z
(1977.A38) Nonserial. By date
(1977.A39) Other documents. By date
Including advisory groups, committees, etc., of the United Nations
see JZ5010+
General Assembly
(1977.A4) General works
see KZ5006.2
Official records
see JZ5010.2+
(1977.A41) English edition
(1977.A417) French edition
(1977.A418) Spanish edition
Journal
(1977.A42) English edition
(1977.A422) French edition
(1977.A423-.A46) Other serials
(1977.A47) Nonserial documents of individual sessions. By date
(1977.A48) Reports of national delegations accredited to the General Assembly
Subarrange by country, A-Z, using two successive Cutter numbers for serials and nonserials (by date)
(1977.A49) Miscellaneous documents. By date
(1977.A495.A-Z) Nonofficial publications. By author, A-Z
Security Council
(1977.A5) General works
see KZ5036

International arbitration, organization, etc.
Special topics
United Nations
United Nations, 1946-
Documents
Security Council -- Continued

(1977.A51) Journal
(1977.A515) Official records
see JZ5030
(1977.A52) Report to the General Assembly
(1977.A54) Nonserial documents of meetings. By date
(1977.A59) Miscellaneous documents. By date
(1977.A593.A-Z) Nonofficial publications. By author, A-Z
(1977.A595) Selected documents. By compiler
(1977.A6-.Z7) General works
(1977.Z8) Popular and juvenile works
United Nations in relation to regional organizations
(1977.18.A2) General
(1977.18.A3-Z) By organization, A-Z
(1977.2.A-Z) United Nations in relation to individual countries, A-Z
e.g.
see JZ4995+
(1977.2.A1) Collective
see JZ4995
(1977.25) Relations with non-member nations
see JZ5002.A+
(1977.3) United Nations in relation to learned societies, universities, etc.
Class cooperation in special projects with the project
(1977.3.A2) General works
(1977.3.A3-JZ1977.3.Z) By society, university, etc.
(1977.8.A-JZ1977.8.Z) Special topics, A-Z
(1977.8.D6) Documentation
see JZ5010+
Employees
see KZ5270+
(1977.8.F5) Finance
see KZ5274.5
(1977.8.H4) Headquarters
see KZ4999
(1977.8.L35) Languages. Translating
see KZ4999.5
(1977.8.M4) Membership
see KZ4996+

International arbitration, organization, etc.
Special topics
United Nations
United Nations, 1946-
Special topics, A-Z -- Continued

(1977.8.O35) Officials and employees
see KZ5270+

(1977.8.P7) Police force
see KZ6374+

(1977.8.P8) Postal administration
see KZ5275

(1977.8.S3) Sanctions
see KZ6373

(1977.8.T4) Technical assistance

Translating
see KZ4999.5

(1977.8.T7) Treaty-making power
see KZ4992.2

(1977.8.V4) Veto

(1977.8.V6) Voting
see KZ5004

(1979) Regional organization. Regionalism
see KZ1273; JZ5330+

(1981.A-Z) Other, A-Z
e. g.

(1981.A35) Air force (International)

(1981.B65) Boundary disputes

(1981.N8) Nullity

(1981.P3) Papacy

(1981.P7) Police, International
see KZ6374+

(1981.T45) Terrorism
see class K

Arbitration treaties

(1985) General collections
see KZ183.2

(1987-1987.Z) United States

(1987) General works

(1987.A1-.Z3) Collections

Treaties with several countries collectively

(1987.A4) Documents. By date of signature (or if better known, date of ratification)

(1987.A42.A-Z) General works

(1987.A5-Z) Separate treaties. By country, A-Z

(1988.A-Z) Other countries, A-Z (Collections)

International arbitration, organization, etc.
Arbitration treaties -- Continued
(1989) Other treaties (to which United States is not a party, by date (year and month)
see KZ182.5.A+
International courts
(1990.A2) General works
see KZ6250
(1990.A3-Z) Individual courts
(1990.C2) Cartago, Costa Rica. Corte de justicia centroamericana
see the region
Hague. Permanent Court of Arbitration
see KZ6170+
Hague. Permanent Court of International Justice
see KZ6260+
(1991) General collections
Under each:
.A2-.A28 *Collections of cases of the Hague Permanent Court of Arbitration, chronologically*
.A3-.Z *Other collections. By editor, A-Z*
For collections, by country, and particular cases, see JX200+ subdivision 8 and 9, under each country
Arbitration cases
(1995) International unions, bureaus, "conventions," congresses
International law
Treatises (History and theory)
Ancient
see KZ1327.5+
(2001) Collections. Sources. Documents
(2005) General works
Oriental states
(2008) General works
(2009.A-Z) Special, A-Z
e. g. Assyro-Babylonian Empire; Egypt; Hebrews; Phoenicia
Greece
(2011) General works
(2014.A-Z) Special topics, A-Z
(2014.R5) Rhodian law
see KL4101+
(2014.T7) Treaties
Roman
see KJA3320+
(2021) General works
Special topics
(2025) Jus feciale

International law
Treatises (History and theory)
Ancient
Roman
Special topics -- Continued
(2027) Jus gentium
(2029) Jus sacrum
(2035.A-Z) Other, A-Z
Medieval (To circa 1500)
see KZ1329+
(2041) General works
Consulate of the sea see K1163.C6
Laws of Oléron see K1163.O4
(2051.A-Z) Other special topics, A-Z
Laws of Trani see K1163.T7
(2055) Islamic countries
see JX1568
(2060.A-Z) Individual publicists, A-Z
(2060.T4) Saint Thomas Aquinas
Modern
see KZ2071+
1500-1713
(2061) General works
(2066) Special topics
(2069) Treatises on the "Jus naturae et gentium"
Individual publicists
Class here collected works and works of general theoretical character only (including compends)
(2070-2071) Alonso de la Vera Cruz (Table JX8)
(2072-2073) Ayala (Table JX8)
(2075-2076) Bodin (Table JX8)
(2081-2082) Brunus (Table JX8)
(2083) Brunus to Cumberland
(2084-2085) Cumberland (Table JX8)
(2086) Cumberland to Gentilisk
(2087-2088) Gentilis (Table JX8)
(2091-2099) Grotius (Table JX7)
(2103-2104) Hobbes (Table JX8)
(2107) Hobbes-Leibnitz
(2109-2110) Leibnitz (Table JX8)
(2112-2113) Loccenius (Table JX8)
(2115-2116) Machiavelli (Table JX8)
(2117) Machiavelli to Molloy
(2118-2119) Malloy (Table JX8)
(2125-2126) Peckius (Table JX8)
(2131-2139) Pufendorf (Table JX7)
(2141-2142) Rachel (Table JX8)

International law
Treatises (History and theory)
Modern
1500-1713
Individual publicists -- Continued
(2144-2145) Santerna (Table JX8)
(2147-2148) Selden (Table JX8)
(2155-2156) Suárez (Table JX8)
(2157) Suárez to Victoria
(2158-2159) Vitoria (Table JX8)
(2161-2169) Wicquefort (Table JX7)
(2181-2182) Zouch (Table JX8)
18th century
see KZ2206+
(2206) General works
(2215) Special topics
English publicists
(2220) A to Bentham
(2221-2222) Bentham (Table JX8)
(2223) Bentham to Fulbeck
(2225-2226) Fulbeck (Table JX8)
(2227) Fulbeck to Rutherforth
(2231-2232) Rutherforth (Table JX8)
(2233) Rutherforth to Z
Dutch publicists
(2242) A to Bynkershoek
(2243-2244) Bynkershoek (Table JX8)
(2245) Bynershoek to Z
French publicists
(2260) A to Mably
(2261-2262) Mably (Table JX8)
(2266) Mably to Montesquieu
(2271-2272) Montesquieu (Table JX8)
(2273) Montesquieu to Neyron
(2274-2275) Neyron (Table JX8)
(2276) Neyron to Z
German publicists
(2303-2304) Achenwall (Table JX8)
(2305) Achenwall to Glafey
(2305.E5) Eggers
(2306-2307) Glafey (Table JX8)
(2308) Glafey to Günther
(2311-2312) Günther (Table JX8)
(2313) Günther to Heineccius
(2314-2315) Heineccius (Heinecke) (Table JX8)
(2316) Heineccius to Kant
(2321-2322) Kant (Table JX8)

International law
Treatises (History and theory)
Modern
18th century
German publicists -- Continued
(2323) Kant to Martens
(2323.K7) Köhler, H.
(2324-2325) Martens, G.F. von
see JX2814+
(2326) Martens to Moser
(2328-2329) Moser, F.C. (Table JX8)
(2332-2333) Moser, J.J. (Table JX8)
(2334) Moser to Ompteda
(2335-2336) Ompteda (Table JX8)
(2339) Ompteda to Thomasius
(2339.R7) Römer, C.H. von
(2344-2345) Thomasius (Table JX8)
(2346) Thomasius to Wolff
(2346.W2) Weidler
(2346.W3) Wenck
(2347-2348) Wolff, C. von (Table JX8)
(2349) Wolff to Z
(2349.Z3) Zechin
Italian publicists
(2370) A to Azuni
(2371-2372) Azuni (Table JX8)
(2373) Azuni to Lampredi
(2374-2375) Lampredi (Table JX8)
(2379) Lampredi to Z
(2388.A-Z) Spanish and Portuguese publicists, A-Z
(2388.M8) Muriel, Domingo (Morelli)
(2388.05) Olmeda y Leon
(2388.07) Ortega y Cotes
Scandinavian publicists
(2391) A to Hübner
Eggers see JX2305.E5
(2393-2394) Hübner (Table JX8)
(2395) Hübner to Z
Swiss publicists
(2400) A to Burlamaqui
(2401-2402) Burlamaqui (Table JX8)
(2406) Burlamaqui to Vattel
e.g.
(2406.F4) Félice, F.B.
(2411-2419) Vattel (Table JX7)
(2420) Vattel to Z
(2435.A-Z) Other. By country, A-Z

International law
Treatises (History and theory)
Modern
18th century
Other. By country, A-Z -- Continued
(2435.P7) Polish
19th century
see KZ2441+
(2441) General works
(2446) Special topics
American publicists
(2451) A to Davis, C.
(2451.B6) Bowen, H.W.
(2455-2456) Davis, C.K. (Table JX8)
(2458-2459) Davis, G. B. (Table JX8)
(2460) Davis, G. B., to Field
(2460.D7) Duane
(2464-2465) Field, D.D. (Table JX8)
(2467-2468) Gallaudet (Table JX8)
(2469) Gallaudet to Halleck
(2469.G2) Gardner
(2469.G4) Glenn
(2475-2476) Halleck (Table JX8)
(2478-2479) Kent (Table JX8)
(2480) Kent to Lawrence, W.B.
(2481-2482) Lawrence, W.B. (Table JX8)
(2483) Lawrence to Snow
(2483.L6) Lieber
(2483.P7) Pomeroy
(2483.S3) Schuyler
(2486-2487) Snow (Table JX8)
(2489-2490) Story (Table JX8)
(2492-2493) Wharton (Table JX8)
(2495-2496) Wheaton (Table JX8)
(2498-2499) Woolsey (Table JX8)
(2500) Woolsey to Z
(2502.A-Z) Dutch publicists, A-Z
(2502.A-Z) Dutch publicists, A-Z
English publicists
(2503) A to Amos
(2505-2506) Amos (Table JX8)
(2507) Amos to Creasy
(2514-2515) Creasy (Table JX8)
(2523) Creasy to Hall
(2523.G6) Griffith, W.
(2524-2525) Hall, W.E. (Table JX8)
(2527-2528) Hertslet (Table JX8)

International law
Treatises (History and theory)
Modern
19th century
English publicists -- Continued

(2529) Hertslet to Holland
(2531-2532) Holland (Table JX8)
(2533) Holland to Hosack
(2538-2539) Hosack (Table JX8)
(2540) Hosack to Lawrence
(2542-2543) Lawrence, T.J. (Table JX8)
(2545-2546) Levi (Table JX8)
(2548-2549) Lorimer (Table JX8)
(2550) Lorimer to Mackintosh
(2552-2553) Mackintosh (Table JX8)
(2554) Mackintosh to Maine
(2555-2556) Maine, Sir Henry (Table JX8)
(2558-2559) Manning (Table JX8)
(2564) Manning to Phillimore
(2564.M5) Miller, William G.
(2565-2566) Phillimore (Table JX8)
(2567) Phillimore to Polson
(2572-2573) Polson (Table JX8)
(2574) Polson to Stowell
(2578-2579) Stowell (Table JX8)
(2580) Stowell to Twiss
(2582-2583) Twiss (Table JX8)
(2584) Twiss to Ward
(2584.W3) Walker
(2585-2586) Ward, Robert Plumer (Table JX8)
(2588-2589) Westlake (Table JX8)
(2590) Westlake to Wildman
(2592-2593) Wildman (Table JX8)
(2594) Wildman to Z

French and Belgian publicists

(2607) A to Bonfils
(2608-2609) Bonfils (Table JX8)
(2613) Bonfils to Cauchy
(2613.B8) Bry, Georges
(2614-2615) Cauchy (Table JX8)
(2616) Cauchy to Cussy
(2616.C4) Chrétien
(2624-2625) Cussy (Table JX8)
(2626) Cussy to Despagnet
(2641-2642) Despagnet (Table JX8)
(2643) Despagnet to Fauchille
(2651-2652) Fauchille (Table JX8)

International law
Treatises (History and theory)
Modern
19th century
French and Belgian publicists -- Continued

(2656) Fauchille to Féraud
(2658-2659) Féraud-Giraud (Table JX8)
(2660) Féraud to Funck
(2668-2669) Funck-Bretano (Table JX8)
(2671-2672) Garden, Guillaume de, comte (Table JX8)
(2673) Garden to Laveleye
(2673.G2) Gérard de Rayneval
(2673.G4) Gondon
(2687-2688) Laveleye (Table JX8)
(2701) Laveleye to Nys
(2701.L3) Leseur
(2701.M3) Michel, C.L.S.
(2702-2703) Nys (Table JX8)
(2704) Nys to Piédelièvre
(2714-2715) Piédelièvre (Table JX8)
(2716) Piédelièvre to Pradier
(2725-2726) Pradie-Fodéré (Table JX8)
(2728-2729) Proudhon (Table JX8)
(2730) Proudhon to Renault
(2735-2736) Renault (Table JX8)
(2737) Renault to Rivier
(2739-2740) Rivier (Table JX8)
(2742-2743) Rolin-Jacquemnyns (Table JX8)
(2745-2746) Rouard de Card (Table JX8)
(2747) Rouard to Sorel
(2751-2752) Sorel (Table JX8)
(2753) Sorel to Z

German and Austrian publicists

(2774) A to Bluntschli
(2775-2776) Bluntschli (Table JX8)
(2778-2779) Bulmerincq (Table JX8)
(2781-2782) Gagern (Table JX8)
(2783) Gagern to Gz
(2783.G3) Gareis
(2786) H to Heffter
(2786.H3) Hartmann
(2787-2788) Heffter (Table JX8)
(2789) Heffter to Holtzendorff
(2789.H3) Heilborn
(2791-2792) Holtzendorff (Table JX8)
(2793) Holtzendorff to Kaltenborn
(2797-2798) Kaltenborn von Strachau (Table JX8)

International law
Treatises (History and theory)
Modern
19th century
German and Austrian publicists -- Continued

(2799) Kaltenborn to Kamptz
(2801-2802) Kamptz (Table JX8)
(2804-2805) Klüber (Table JX8)
(2806) Klüber to Lasson
(2811-2812) Lasson, Adolf (Table JX8)
(2814-2815) Martens, G.F. von (Table JX8)
(2817-2818) Neumann (Table JX8)
(2819) Neumann to Oppenheim
(2821-2822) Oppenheim, H.B. (Table JX8)
(2824) Oppenheim to Saafeld
(2824.P7) Pölitz
(2824.Q3) Quaritsch
(2824.R3) Resch
(2826-2827) Saafeld (Table JX8)
(2828) Saafeld to Savigny
(2831-2832) Savigny (Table JX8)
(2833) Savigny to Schmalz
(2834-2835) Schmalz (Table JX8)
(2836) Schmalz to Schulze
(2836.S4) Schmelzing
(2838-2839) Schulze (Table JX8)
(2841-2842) Stoerk (Table JX8)
(2843) Stoerk to Z
(2843.U6) Ullmann

Greek publicists

(2844) A to Saripoulos
(2845-2846) Saripoulos (Table JX8)
(2847) Saripoulos to Z

Italian publicists

(2857) A to Carnazza
(2858-2859) Carnazza-Amari (Table JX8)
(2860) Carnazza to Casanova
(2862-2863) Casanova (Table JX8)
(2865-2866) Celli (Table JX8)
(2868-2869) Contuzzi (Table JX8)
(2870) Contuzzi to Del Bon
(2872-2873) Del Bon (Table JX8)
(2875-2876) Esperson (Table JX8)
(2878-2879) Ferrero Gola (Table JX8)
(2881-2882) Fiore (Table JX8)
(2883) Fiore to Grasso
(2887-2888) Grasso (Table JX8)

International law
Treatises (History and theory)
Modern
19th century
Italian publicists -- Continued
(2889) Grasso to Macri
(2894-2895) Macri (Table JX8)
(2897-2898) Mamiani (Table JX8)
(2899) Mamiani to Morello
(2904-2905) Morello (Table JX8)
(2910) Morello to Pertile
(2910.O7) Olivi, Luigi
(2914-2915) Pertile (Table JX8)
(2917-2918) Pierantoni (Table JX8)
(2919) Pierantoni to Sandonà
(2924-2925) Sandonà
(2926) Sandonà to Schiattarella
(2928-2829) Schiattarella (Table JX8)
(2930) Schiattarella to Z
Russian publicists
(2940) A to Bergholm
(2941-2942) Bergholm (Table JX8)
(2943) Bergholm to Martens
Bulmerincq see JX2778+
(2951-2952) Martens, F.F. (Table JX8)
(2953) Martens to Z
Scandinavian publicists
(2954) A to Matzen
(2955-2956) Matzen (Table JX8)
(2957) Matzen to Tetens
(2961-2962) Tetens (Table JX8)
(2963) Tetens to Z
Spanish, Portuguese, and Latin-American publicists
(2966) A to Alcorta
(2967-2968) Alcorta (Table JX8)
(2969) Alcorta to Arenal
(2975-2976) Arenal (Table JX8)
(2977) Arenal to Bello
(2978-2979) Bello (Table JX8)
(2980) Bello to Calvo
(2980.C3) Calcaño
(2984-2985) Calvo (Table JX8)
(2986) Calvo to Ferrater
(2986.C7) Cruchaga Tocornal
(2986.D5) Diez de Medina
(2991-2992) Ferrater (Table JX8)
(2994-2995) Ferrater, R. (Table JX8)

International law
Treatises (History and theory)
Modern
19th century
Spanish, Portuguese, and Latin-American publicists -- Continued

(2996) Ferrater to Gestoso
(3001-3002) Gestoso y Acosto (Table JX8)
(3003) Gestoso to Labra
(3007-3008) Labra y Cadrana (Table JX8)
(3015) Labra to López Sánchez
(3015.L5) López, José F.
(3017-3018) López Sánchez (Table JX8)
(3019) López to Madiedo
(3021-3022) Madiedo, Manuel M. (Table JX8)
(3027) Madiedo to Mozo
(3027.M5) Montúfar y Rivera Maestre
(3027.M6) Moreira de Almeida
(3028-3029) Mozo (Table JX8)
(3030) Mozo to Olivart
(3034-3035) Olivart (Table JX8)
(3036) Olivart to Pando
(3038-3039) Pando (Table JX8)
(3040) Pando to Pinheiro
(3040.P4) Pérez Gomar, Gregorio
(3041-3042) Pinheiro-Ferreira (Table JX8)
(3043) Pinheiro to Riquelme
(3045-3046) Riquelme (Table JX8)
(3047.R4) Rodríguez Saráchaga
(3048-3049) Seijas (Table JX8)
(3050) Seijas to Torres Campos
(3055-3056) Torres Campos (Table JX8)
(3058-3059) Tremosa y Nadal (Table JX8)
(3060) Tremosa to Z
(3085.A-Z) Other. By nationality, A-Z
(3085.H8) Hungarian

20th century
see KZ3092+

(3091) General works
(3096) Special topics

American publicists
(3110) A to Hershey
(3110.F6) Foulke, R.R.
(3110.H3) Hall, A.B.
(3131-3132) Hershey, Amos S. (Table JX8)
(3140) Hershey to Maxey
(3140.H8) Hyde, C.C.

International law
Treatises (History and theory)
Modern
20th century
American publicists -- Continued
(3151-3152) Maxey (Table JX8)
(3160) Maxey to Scott
(3160.R4) Root, Elihu
(3178-3179) Scott, J. Brown (Table JX8)
(3180) Scott to Taylor
(3180.S4) Singer, B.
(3180.S7) Stockton, C.H.
(3181-3182) Taylor, Hannis (Table JX8)
(3185) Taylor to Wilson
(3191-3192) Wilson, George C. (Table JX8)
(3195) Wilson to Z
English publicists
Including Canadian publicists
(3205) A to Baker
(3211-3212) Baker, Sir George S. (Table JX8)
(3215) Baker to Birkenhead
(3215.B3) Baty, Thomas
(3220-3221) Birkenhead, Frederick Edwin Smith, baron (Table JX8)
(3225) Birkenhead to Oppenehim
(3225.B8) Burns, C.D.
(3264-3265) Oppenheim, Lassa F.L. (Table JX8)
(3275) Oppenheim to Smith
(3275.P5) Plater, C.D.
(3281-3282) Smith, Frederick Edwin
see JX3220+
(3295) Smith to Z
French and Belgian publicists
(3310) A to Mérignhac
(3351-3352) Mérignhac (Table JX8)
(3375) Mérignhac to Z
German, Austrian, etc., publicists
(3425) A to Liszt
(3425.C9) Cybichowski
(3425.K7) Kohler
(3445-3446) Liszt, Franz von (Table JX8)
(3491) Liszt to Z
(3491.P6) Pohl, H.
(3491.S5) Schucking, W.M.A.
(3491.Z5) Zorn
(3545.A-Z) Italian publicists, A-Z
(3545.C3) Cavarreta

International law
Treatises (History and theory)
Modern
20th century
Italian publicists, A-Z -- Continued
(3545.D4) Diena, G.
(3545.L5) Lomonaco
(3545.M3) Marino
(3651.A-Z) Spanish publicists, A-Z
Including Portuguese and Latin American specialists
(3651.A6) Alvarez, A.
(3651.B3) Bevilagua, C.
(3651.C3) Cavalcanti
(3651.D4) Díaz de Medina
(3651.F3) Fernández Prida
(3651.F5) Flores y Flores
(3651.G2) García Alvarez
(3651.P7) Planos Suárez
(3651.R7) Romanos
(3651.S3) Sarmiento Laspiur
(3695.A-Z) Other. By nationality, A-Z
Dutch
(3695.D8L5) Jitta
(3695.D8L6) Louter
Norwegian
(3695.N6G5) Gjelsvik
Russian
(3695.R9K3) Kazanski
(3695.R9U4) Ulianitskii
Treatises on special topics
International persons
(4000) The individual as subject of international law
see KZ3920
The state as subject of international law
see KZ4002+
(4003) General special. The international community
Including fundamental rights of states from the standpoint of international law
see KZ3900+
Sovereign states
see KZ4034+
(4005) Unions of sovereign states. Alliances. Federation (from the standpoint of international law)
see KZ4053
(4008) Suzerain states
see KZ4060

International law
Treatises on special topics
International persons
The state as subject of international law -- Continued
Semisovereign, dependent, and vassal states
see KZ4059+
(4011) General works
see KZ4059
(4015) Mediatized states
see KZ4067
Protected states. Protectorates. Spheres of influence. Mandates. International trusteeships
(4021) General works
see KZ4061
(4023.A-Z) By region or country, A-Z
see the country
(4025) Vassal states
see KZ4060
(4027) Colonies (from viewpoint of international law)
see KZ4066
Servitudes
see KZ3679.5
Neutralized states. Neutralization
(4031) General works
see KZ4057
(4033.A-Z) Special states, A-Z
e. g.
see KZ4112+
(4033.B4) Belgium
see KZ4196
(4033.D4) Dominican Republic
see KZ4131
(4033.L9) Luxembourg
see KZ4198
(4033.S9) Switzerland
see KZ4236
(4035) Regions: Rivers, canals, etc. (General)
see KZ4110.A+
Sovereignty
see KZ4041+
(4041) General (from standpoint of international law)
see KZ4041
(4044) Recognition of sovereignty
see KZ4041+
Transfer of sovereignty. State succession
(4053) General works
see KZ4024+

International law
Treatises on special topics
International persons
The state as subject of international law
Sovereignty
Transfer of sovereignty. State succession -- Continued
(4054) International plebiscite
Special
(4055) State dismemberment. Civil war
see KZ4028
(4061) Dissolution of a state
see KZ4028
(4068.A-Z) Other, A-Z
(4068.C7) Condominiums
see KZ4051
(4068.E92) Exclaves
Free cities
see KZ3673
(4068.G6) Governments in exile
(4068.I6) Internationalized territories. "Free cities"
see KZ3673
(4068.S5) Servitudes
see KZ3679.5
(4068.S8) State bankruptcy
Means of protecting independence. Self-preservation. Noninterference
see KZ6360+ KZ6374+
(4071) General works
(4077) Exterritorial self-defense
(4079.A-Z) Other special, A-Z
e.g.
(4079.N4) Necessity, Doctrine
(4079.P7) Propaganda
(4081) International courtesy. Comitas. Court-oisie. Precedence
(4084) International status of particular states, regions, organizations, etc.
For regions, see KZ4110.A+
For countries, see KZ4112+
For gulfs and bays, see KZ3870+
For straits, see KZ3760+
For rivers, see KZ3700
For islands, see KZ3880+
(4084.A13) Aegean Islands (Greece and Turkey)
(4084.A15) Aland Islands
(4084.A34) Afghanistan

International law
Treatises on special topics
International persons
The state as subject of international law
International status of particular states, regions, organizations, etc. -- Continued

(4084.A43) Algeria
(4084.A45) Alsace
(4084.A5) Antarctica
see KZ4110.P65
Arabistan see JX4084.K45
(4084.A68) Arctic regions
see KZ4110.P65
(4084.A7) Armenia
(4084.A8) Austria
(4084.A86) Aves Island
(4084.B3) Bali (Island)
(4084.B314) Baltic Sea
(4084.B3146) Baltic States
(4084.B315) Baltic Straits
Including Skagerrak, Kattegat and The Sound
(4084.B32) Bangladesh
(4084.B35) Barents Sea
(4084.B38) Berlin
(4084.B4) Bessarabia
(4084.B55) Black Sea
(4084.B75) British West Indies
(4084.B8) Bukowina
(4084.C33) Cameroon
(4084.C34) Canary Islands
(4084.C5) China
(4084.C52) China (People's Republic of China, 1949-)
(4084.C6) Commonwealth of Nations
(4084.C63) Constance, Lake of
(4084.C86) Cyprus
(4084.C9) Czechoslovakia
(4084.D64) Dodecanese
(4084.D68) Dover, Strait of
(4084.E65) Epirus (Greece and Albania)
(4084.E9) Euphrates River
(4084.F34) Falkland Islands
Formosa see JX4084.T25
(4084.G3) Germany (General) and Federal Republic, 1949-
(4084.G4) Germany (Democratic Republic, 1949-)
(4084.G5) Gibraltar
(4084.G52) Gibraltar, Strait of
(4084.H34) Ḥalā'ib

International law
Treatises on special topics
International persons
The state as subject of international law
International status of particular states, regions, organizations, etc. -- Continued

(4084.H66) Hong Kong
(4084.I65) Imia Islands (Greece)
(4084.I7) Irian Barat, Indonesia
(4084.I8) Israel. Palestine
(4084.J3) Japan
(4084.J4) Jerusalem
(4084.J67) Jordan (Territory under Israeli occupation, 1967-)
Kangwane (South Africa) see JX4084.S62
(4084.K34) Kashmir
Kattegat (Denmark and Sweden) see JX4084.B315
(4084.K45) Khuzistan, Iran. Arabistan
(4084.K48) Kiel Canal (Germany)
(4084.K55) Knights of Malta
(4084.K67) Korea
(4084.K673) Korea (Democratic People's Republic)
(4084.K82) Kuril Islands
(4084.K83) Kwantung, Leased Territory, China
(4084.M24) Maddalena Island (Italy)
Including Maddalena Archipelago (Italy)
(4084.M28) Magellan, Strait of
(4084.M3) Malacca, Strait of
Malta, Knights of see JX4084.K55
(4084.M44) Memel (Klaipéda, Lith.)
(4084.M65) Montenegro (Yugoslavia)
Namibia see JX4084.S68
(4084.N4) Near East
(4084.N45) Netherlands Antilles
(4084.N65) North Sea
(4084.P27) Pacific Islands (Ter.)
Palestine see JX4084.I8
(4084.P28) Paracel Islands
Including Spratly Islands
(4084.P39) Persian Gulf
(4084.P4) Persian Gulf States
(4084.P65) Polar regions
(4084.P66) Pomerian Bay
(4084.P9) Puerto Rico
(4084.R5) Rhodesia, Southern
(4084.R65) Romania
(4084.R9) Ryukyu Islands
(4084.S3) Saarland

International law
Treatises on special topics
International persons
The state as subject of international law
International status of particular states, regions, organizations, etc. -- Continued

(4084.S32) Sabah
(4084.S36) San Andres y Providencia (Colombia)
(4084.S45) Senkaku Islands
(4084.S5) Silesia
Skagerrak (Denmark and Norway) see JX4084.B315
Sound, The (Denmark and Sweden) see JX4084.B315
(4084.S62) South Africa
(4084.S63) South China Sea islands
(4084.S65) South Moluccas
Southern Rhodesia see JX4084.R5
(4084.S68) Southwest Africa. Namibia
(4084.S7) Spanish Sahara
(4084.S75) Spitsbergen Island
Strait of Gibraltar see JX4084.G52
(4084.S88) Sudetenland
(4084.S94) Svalbard
(4084.T25) Taiwan
(4084.T27) Tajikstan
(4084.T45) Tibet (China)
(4084.T47) Timor Timur (Indonesia)
(4084.T5) Titicaca Lake
(4084.T62) Tok Island (Korea)
(4084.T67) Transkei
(4084.T7) Trentino-Alto Adige (Italy)
(4084.U4) Ukraine
(4084.V5) Vietnam
West Bank of the Jordan River see JX4084.J67
(4084.W45) White Russia

Right of domain and property
Territory
see KZ3670+
(4085) General works
Special
Acquisition of territory
see KZ3679
(4088) General works
(4093) By occupation and possession
(4095) By discovery
(4098) By cession. Annexation
(4099) Leased territories. Military bases

International law
Treatises on special topics
Right of domain and property
Territory
Special -- Continued
Boundaries
see JZ3684+ KZ3683.2+
(4111) General works (Collections, etc.)
Natural boundaries
(4115) General works
see KZ3685
(4118) Mountains
see KZ3685
(4122) Rivers
see KZ3685
(4125) Lakes
see KZ3685
Coast. Territorial waters
see KZA1500; KZA1540+
(4131) General works
(4135) Three-mile limit
see KZA1540+
(4137) Bays
see JZ3870+ KZ3870+
(4138) Gulfs and harbors
see JZ3870+ KZ3870+
(4141) Straits
see JZ3760+ KZ3760+
(4143) Continental shelf
see KZA1630+
(4144) Contiguous zones, Maritime
see KZA1540+
(4144.5) Economic zones, Maritime
see KZA1560+
(4145) Artificial boundaries
see KZ3685
(4147) Adjoining territory. Nuisances
see KZ3679.5
(4148) Islands
see KZ3880+
(4149) Archipelagoes
see KZ3880+
(4150) International rivers and waterways
see KZ3686+
(4155) Interoceanic canals
see KZ3710+

International law
Treatises on special topics -- Continued
Treaties and convention. Treaty making
see KZ1298+
For the effect of treaties on law of war see KZ6404
(4161) Early works to 1800
Treatises
(4165) English
(4166) French
(4167) German
(4169) Other
(4171.A-Z) Special topics. By subject, A-Z
see KZ1287+
(4171.A3) Accession
(4171.C6) Clausula rebus sic stantibus
(4171.D8) Duration
(4171.G8) Guaranty treaties
(4171.I6) Interpretation
(4171.L3) Language
(4171.O3) Obligation
(4171.O32) Obsolescence
(4171.P3) "Pacta sunt servanda"
(4171.P4) Peace treaties
(4171.P77) Provisional application
(4171.R3) Ratification
(4171.R37) Reciprocity
(4171.R4) Reservations
(4171.R45) Revision
(4171.S72) State succession
(4171.T5) Termination
(4171.T6) Third parties
(4171.U5) Unequal treaties
(4171.V5) Violation
(4171.W3) War
(4172) International legislation
see KZ1287+
Jurisdiction. Competence
(4173) General
see KZ4017; KZ6265 (Courts); KZ6283
(4175) Exterritoriality
(4185) Jurisdiction over property
(4190) Jurisdiction over shipping
(4195) Exterritorial crime
Nationality and alienage. Allegiance. Citizenship
see K3224+
History
(4203) General

International law
Treatises on special topics
Nationality and alienage. Allegiance. Citizenship
History -- Continued
Ancient
(4204) General
(4205.A-Z) By state or nation, A-Z
(4205.H4) Hebrews
(4206) Medieval (General)
(4207) Modern
Special countries see JX4265+
Laws. Legislation
(4209) Collections of the laws of different countries
(4209.52) Special countries
(4211) General works
Nationality
(4215) General works
(4216) Naturalization
see K3226
(4226) Expatriation
(4231.A-Z) Other special, A-Z
(4231.C5) Children
(4231.D5) Diplomatic and consular personnel
(4231.D7) Double allegiance
(4231.M3) Marriage and nationality
(4231.M5) Minorities
(4231.O7) Option of nationality
(4231.R5) Repatriation
(4231.S8) Statelessness
see K7128.S7
(4241) Domicile
Passports
see K3273
(4251) General works
(4253.A-Z) Special countries, A-Z
Aliens
see K3274+
(4255) General works
(4261) Expulsion. Deportation
Internationally protected persons
(4262) General works
(4262.5) Crimes against internationally protected persons
(4263.A-Z) Other special topics, A-Z
For taxation of aliens, see K4535
(4263.A8) Arrest and imprisonment
(4263.A9) Assistance to aliens
(4263.L2) Labor. Occupations. Professions

International law
Treatises on special topics
Nationality and alienage. Allegiance. Citizenship
Other special topics, A-Z -- Continued
(4263.M6) Military service
(4263.P6) Alien property
see K728+
Protection of nationals abroad by their home states
(4263.P7) General works
(4263.P8.A-Z) Special cases, A-Z
(4263.P8.W4) White affair
(4263.P82) Protection of stockholders abroad by their home state
(4263.T8) Travellers in foreign countries
For passports see K3273
Special countries
United States
(4265.A1-.A5) Collections. Documents
(4265.A7-Z) Monographs
(4270.A-Z) Other countries, A-Z
Subarrange each in the following order: (1) Collections (Documents, etc.); (2) Other works
Right of asylum. Extradition
see K3268.3; K5441+
(4275) Collections
Treatises
(4280) Early works (prior to 1800)
(4281) English
(4282) French and Belgian
(4283) German
(4284) Italian
(4285) Spanish, Portuguese, and Latin American
(4286) Scandinavian
(4288.A-Z) Other, A-Z
(4292.A-Z) Special topics. By subject, A-Z
(4292.L5) Legations
(4292.P6) Political offenses
(4292.P8) Provisional arrest
(4292.R4) Refugees
(4292.S5) Ships
By country
United States
(4301) Collections (Documents, etc.)
(4302) Separate documents. By date
(4305) Treatises and other general works
(4311) Addresses, essays, lectures
(4316.A-Z) Canada and other British American, A-Z
(4318.A-Z) West Indies other than British, A-Z

International law
Treatises on special topics
Right of asylum. Extradition
By country -- Continued

(4321) Mexico
(4326.A-Z) Central America, A-Z
(4335.A-Z) South America, A-Z
Europe
(4341) Great Britain
(4345.A-Z) Other European, A-Z
Asia
(4351) United States possessions (Philippines)
(4353.A-Z) British possessions, A-Z
(4357.A-Z) Other European possessions, A-Z
(4365.A-Z) Native states, A-Z
Africa
(4371.A-Z) British possessions, A-Z
(4377.A-Z) Other European possessions, A-Z
(4384.A-Z) Native states, A-Z
(4387.A-Z) Australia, A-Z
(4391) New Zealand
Oceania
(4394) United States possessions (Hawaii, etc.)
(4398.A-Z) Other, A-Z
(4399.A-Z) Cases. By name, A-Z

Jurisdiction over the high seas. Maritime law
see KZA1002+

(4408) Collections
Treatises
see KZA1145

(4410) Early works (prior to 1800)
(4411) English
(4412) French and Belgian
(4413) German
(4414) Italian
(4415) Spanish, Portuguese, and Latin American
(4416) Scandinavian
(4418.A-Z) Other, A-Z
(4419) Addresses, essays, lectures
(4421) Codes
(4422.A-Z) By region or country, A-Z
Special topics
The open and closed sea
see KZA1340

(4423) Early works to 1800
(4425) Recent

International law
Treatises on special topics
Jurisdiction over the high seas. Maritime law
Special topics -- Continued

(4426) Ocean bottom (Maritime law)
see subclass KZA

(4427) Offshore structures. Artificial islands
see K4202

(4431) Navigation laws (Treatises only)

(4434) Collisions at sea

(4436) Shipwreck, salvage
see K1188.A8

(4437) Marine insurance
see K1226+

Piracy
see K5277

(4444) General works. Treatises

(4446.A-Z) Cases, A-Z

(4447) Slavers, slave trade, etc.

Right of visit and search see KZ6578

(4449.A-Z) Other special, A-Z

(4449.A25) Access to the sea
see KZA1555

(4449.A5) Airports (Floating)

(4449.A6) Angary

(4449.D4) Death on the high seas

(4449.N3) Nationality of ships
see K4158

(4449.R3) Responsibility of shipments

(4449.S4) Seizure of vessels and cargoes
see KZ6580

(4449.S5) Shipmasters

(4449.W27) Warships
see KZ6574

International disputes and collisions
Measures short of war
see KZ6374+ JZ6374+

(4471) General works

(4472) Diplomatic protests

(4473) Diplomatic negotiations for pacific settlement
see JZ5597+ JZ6045

(4475) Mediation
see JZ6045

(4478) Arbitration
see KZ6115+

(4481) Intervention
see KZ6368+

International law
Treatises on special topics
International disputes and collisions
Measures short of war -- Continued
(4484) Retorsion
see KZ6362+
(4486) Reprisals
(4489) Boycott
(4491) Embargo
see KZ6365
(4494) Pacific blockade
see KZ6366
Law of war and humanitarian law
see KZ6378+
(4505) Collections
(4507) Codes
(4508) History
Treatises
(4510) Early works (prior to 1800)
(4511) English
(4512) French and Belgian
(4513) German
(4514) Italian
(4515) Spanish, Portuguese, and Latin American
(4516) Scandinavian
(4518.A-Z) Other, A-Z
(4521) Addresses, essays, lectures
Philosophy and ethics of law
see JZ6390+ U21+
(4525) Treaties, Effect of
see KZ6404
(4530) Region of war
see KZ6398.R45
Kinds of war
see KZ6397
(4541) Civil war
see KZ6397
Declaration and outbreak
see KZ6398.82+
(4552) General
(4556) Hostilities prior to declaration
(4561) Declaration
(4564) Necessity for declaration
Belligerency
see KZ6415+
(4571) General
(4574) Recognition of belligerency

International law
Treatises on special topics
International disputes and collisions
Law of war and humanitarian law
Belligerency
Special -- Continued
(4581) Alliance, succor, etc. (Specifically during state of war)
see KZ6417
(4591) Belligerents and noncombatants
(4595) Martial law
see K3345
Belligerent measures. Warfare
see KZ6429+
(5001) General
Special
Invasion. Belligerent occupation
(5003) General
see KZ6429+
(5003.5) Money. Occupation currency
(5005) Permissible violence
see KZ6436
(5011) Devastation
(5117) Bombardments and sieges
see KZ6437
(5121) Deceit, spies, etc.
(5123) Guerrilla warfare
(5124) Air warfare
see KZ6665+
Arms and instruments of war
(5127) General works
(5131) Prohibited instruments and methods
see KZ5598.2+
(5133.A-Z) Special. By subject, A-Z
(5133.A7) Atomic bomb
see KZ5647+
Biological warfare
see KZ5865.B56
(5133.C5) Chemical and biological warfare
see KZ5824+ KZ5865.B56
(5133.D55) Directed energy weapons
see KZ5840+
(5133.G3) Gases (Asphyxiating and poisonous)
see KZ5824+
(5133.I5) Incendiary weapons
see KZ5636.2+
(5135.A-Z) Special topics, A-Z

International law
Treatises on special topics
International disputes and collisions
Law of war and humanitarian law
Belligerency
Special
Belligerent measures. Warfare
Special
Special topics, A-Z -- Continued

(5135.C3) Cables
(5135.F7) Fortifications
(5135.M45) Mercenaries
(5135.M5) Military necessity
(5135.R3) Railroads
(5135.T5) Wireless telegraph

Treatment of the wounded. Geneva and Hague conventions. Humanitarian law
Including works on the Geneva and Hague conventions collectively
see KZ6440+

Official publications
Geneva, 1864
see KZ6464

(5136.A2) Preparatory conferences and committees. Preliminary drafts
(5136.A21) Preliminary correspondence
(5136.A22) Proceedings
(5136.A225) Resolutions. Final act
Text of convention
(5136.A23) English or French and English
(5136.A235.A-Z) Other languages, A-Z
(5136.A24A-.A24Z) Other documents. Declaration of accession, etc. By country, A-Z

Hague (III), 1899
see KZ6015+

(5136.A25) Preparatory conferences and committees. Preliminary drafts
(5136.A26) Preliminary correspondence
(5136.A27) Proceedings
(5136.A2725) Resolutions. Final act
Text of convention
(5136.A28) English or French and English
(5136.A2835A-.A2835Z) Other languages, A-Z
(5136.A29A-.A29Z) Other documents. Declaration of accession, etc. By country, A-Z

International law
Treatises on special topics
International disputes and collisions
Law of war and humanitarian law
Belligerency
Special
Treatment of the wounded. Geneva and Hague conventions
Official publications -- Continued
Geneva, 1906
see KZ6450+

(5136.A3) Preparatory conferences and committees. Preliminary drafts
(5136.A31) Preliminary correspondence
(5136.A32) Proceedings
(5136.A325) Resolutions. Final act
Text of convention
(5136.A33) English or French and English
(5136.A335A-.A335Z) Other languages, A-Z
(5136.A34A-.A34Z) Other documents. Declaration of accession, etc. By country, A-Z

Hague (X), 1907
see KZ6020+

(5136.A35) Preparatory conferences and committees. Preliminary drafts
(5136.A36) Preliminary correspondence
(5136.A37) Proceedings
(5136.A3725) Resolutions. Final act
Text of convention
(5136.A38) English or French and English
(5136.A3835A-.A3835Z) Other languages, A-Z
(5136.A39A-.A39Z) Other documents. Declaration of accession, etc. By country, A-Z

Geneva, 1929
see KZ6452+

(5136.A4) Preparatory conferences and committees. Preliminary drafts
(5136.A41) Preliminary correspondence
(5136.A42) Proceedings
(5136.A425) Resolutions. Final act
Text of convention
(5136.A43) English or French and English
(5136.A435A-.A435Z) Other languages, A-Z
(5136.A44A-.A44Z) Other documents. Declaration of accession, etc. By country, A-Z

International law
Treatises on special topics
International disputes and collisions
Law of war and humanitarian law
Belligerency
Special
Treatment of the wounded. Geneva and Hague conventions
Official publications -- Continued
Geneva, 1949
see KZ6454+
(5136.A45) Preparatory conferences and committees. Preliminary drafts
(5136.A46) Preliminary correspondence
(5136.A47) Proceedings
(5136.A4725) Resolutions. Final act
Text of convention
(5136.A48) English or French and English
(5136.A4835A-.A4835Z) Other languages, A-Z
(5136.A49A-.A49Z) Other documents. Declaration of accession, etc. By country, A-Z
Geneva, 1974-1977
(5136.A5) Preparatory conferences and committees. Preliminary drafts
(5136.A51) Preliminary correspondence
(5136.A52) Proceedings
(5136.A5225) Resolutions. Final act
Text of convention
(5136.A53) English or French and English
(5136.A5335A-.A5335Z) Other languages, A-Z
(5136.A54A-.A54Z) Other documents. Declaration of accession, etc. By country, A-Z
(5136.A9-Z) Other works
Prisoners of war
see KZ6486.52+
(5141.A1) Texts of international conventions. By date
(5141.A2-Z) Other works
(5143) Hostages
see KZ6517
Protection of civilians
see KZ6510+
(5144.A1) Text of international conventions
(5144.A2-Z) Other works
Intercourse of belligerents
(5145) General works

International law
Treatises on special topics
International disputes and collisions
Law of war and humanitarian law
Belligerency
Special
Intercourse of belligerents -- Continued
(5147) Protective signs
(5148) Flag of truce
(5151) Safe conduct
(5161) Deserters
Termination of belligerency
see KZ6730+
(5166) General works
(5169) Cartels
(5173) Truce and armistices
(5177) Capitulations
(5181) Treaties of peace
Conquest of territory see JX4093
Control of means of communication during war see JX5135.A+
(5187) Postliminium
Maritime war
see KZ6540+
Collections
(5203) Congresses. Conferences
e. g. Declaration of London
(5205) Other
History
(5207) General works
(5208) Declaration of London, 1909
see JX5203
Treatises
(5210) Early works (prior to 1800)
(5211) English
(5212) French and Belgian
(5213) German
(5214) Italian
(5215) Spanish, Portuguese, and Latin American
(5216) Scandinavian
(5218.A-Z) Other, A-Z
(5221) Addresses, essays, lectures
(5225) Blockade
(5228) Capture
Contraband
(5231) Theory
(5232.A-Z) Lists. By country, A-Z

International law
Treatises on special topics
International disputes and collisions
Law of war and humanitarian law
Maritime war -- Continued

(5234) Doctrine of continuous voyage
(5237) Innocent passage
(5239) War vessels in neutral ports
(5241) Privateers and letters of marque
Treatment of the wounded and shipwrecked. Hospitals ships
(5243.A1) Texts of international conventions. By date
(5243.A2-Z) Other works
(5244.A-Z) Other, A-Z
(5244.A7) Armed merchant ships
(5244.C6) Converted merchant ships
(5244.M6) Mines
(5244.S8) Submarines
Prize law
see KZ6590+
(5245) Collections
Treatises
(5250) Early works (prior to 1800)
(5251) English
(5252) French and Belgian
(5253) German
(5254) Italian
(5255) Spanish, Portuguese, and Latin American
(5256) Scandinavian
(5258.A-Z) Other, A-Z
(5261.A-Z) By region or country, A-Z
(5263) Prize courts
(5266) Procedure
(5268) Right of visit and search
Including Convoy
see KZ6578
Effect on commercial relations of belligerents
Including trading with the enemy
(5270) General works
see subclass JZ
(5271.A-Z) Special topics, A-Z
see KZ6404
(5271.C5) Contracts
(5271.L4) Licenses
(5271.M6) Moratorium
Enemy aliens
(5275) General works

International law
Treatises on special topics
International disputes and collisions
Law of war and humanitarian law
Enemy aliens -- Continued
(5276.A-Z) By region or country, A-Z
Property in war
(5278) Collections
Treatises
(5280) Early works (prior to 1800)
(5281) English
(5282) French and Belgian
(5283) German
(5284) Italian
(5285) Spanish, Portuguese, and Latin American
(5286) Scandinavian
(5288.A-Z) Other, A-Z
(5291) Addresses, essays, lectures
Enemy property
Including wartime control of alien property
see K730
(5295) General works
(5298) Public property
(5305) Private property
(5311) Scientific collections, art treasures, libraries, churches, etc.
(5313.A-Z) By region or country, A-Z
(5316) Neutral property and trade
(5321) Requisitions
(5326) Damages. Claims, indemnity, etc.
Right of visit and search see JX5268
Neutrality
see KZ6419+
(5355) Collections
Treatises
(5360) Early works (prior to 1800)
(5361) English
(5362) French and Belgian
(5363) German
(5364) Italian
(5365) Spanish, Portuguese, and Latin American
(5366) Scandinavian
(5368.A-Z) Other, A-Z
(5371) Addresses, essays, lectures
(5383) Armed neutrality
Class here theoretical discussions only
see KZ6423

International law
Treatises on special topics
International disputes and collisions
Law of war and humanitarian law
Neutrality -- Continued
(5388) Asylum. Internment
(5390) Exportation of munitions of war
Infractions of neutrality. Prohibited acts
see KZ6425.5
(5391) General works
(5393) Fitting out of war vessels for belligerents
(5395) Foreign enlistment. Hostile military expeditions. Filibustering
(5397.A-Z) Other, A-Z
(5397.A4) Aerial warfare
(5397.L6) Loans
(5397.N5) Neutral trade with belligerents
(5397.P3) Passage of troops and goods
(5397.P7) Press
(5397.R4) Refueling of war ships
Procedure in international disputes see JX1901+
International responsibility. International delinquencies
For responsibility or delinquency inherent in a particular subject listed elsewhere, see the subject, e. g. JX4263.P6, Alien property; JX4171.V5, Violations of treaties
(5401) General works
Responsibility of the state
Including responsibility for acts of organs and agents of the state
see K967
(5402) General works
Denial of justice to aliens
see K3274+
(5404) Nonpayment of contract debts and damages
(5405) Nuclear hazards and damages
(5407) Mass media
(5408) Acts of Unsuccessful insurgent governments
Acts of private persons
(5410) General works
(5410.2) Hostile acts against foreign states
Injuries and losses to aliens caused by mob violence, riots, etc.
(5410.3) General works
Riots against foreign missions see JX1683.P7
Responsibility of international agencies
see K967.5

International law
Treatises on special topics
International responsibility. International delinquencies
Responsibility of international agencies -- Continued
(5411) General works
League of Nations see JX1975+
United Nations see JX1976+
International unions, bureaus, etc. see JX1995
International offenses
Class here works on criminal law aspects of violations of international law
(5415) General works
(5417) Criminal responsibility of individuals
(5418) Crimes against humanity. Genocide
see K5302
(5419) Offenses against peace. Aggression
see K5240+
(5419.5) War crime trials
see KZ1168+
(5420) Terrorism
see K5256
Vandalism
Class here works on destruction of cultural or artistic works of racial, religious, or social collectivities
(5420.52) General works
see K5303
Piracy at sea see JX4444+
Piracy in the air, hijacking of aircraft see K5276
Slave trade see JX4447
International criminal jurisdiction and courts
(5425) General works
(5428) International criminal courts
Including proposed courts
Criminal trials in general
see subclass K
(5430) General works
War crime trials
see KZ1168+
(5433) General works
World War II
(5433.5) Collected trials
(5434) General works
Trials by international military tribunals
see KZ1168+
(5436) General works
(5437) Nuremberg Trial of Major German War Criminals, 1945-1946 (Table JX10)

International law
Treatises on special topics
International responsibility. International delinquencies
International offenses
Criminal trials
War crime trials
World War II
Trials by international military tribunals -- Continued
(5438) The Tokyo War Crimes Trial, 1946-1948 (Table JX10)
Trials by national courts other than those of the country of the defendant (sitting at home or abroad)
see the country
Collected trials
(5439) War crime trials, Nuremberg, 1946-1949 (subsequent proceedings) (Table JX10)
see KZ1175+
(5440) Other collected trials
(5441.A-Z) Particular trials. By first named defendant or best known (popular) name, A-Z
Subarrange each by Table JX11
e.g.
(5441.E3) Eichman trial
see KMK
(5441.J8) Justice case
see KZ1179.J89
(5441.M3) Manila war crime trial, 1946
see KZ1183+
Yamashita, Tomoyuki see KZ1184.Y36
Trials by the courts of defendant's own country
For trials by the courts of a particular country, see the country
For trials by the courts of countries in the same region, see the region
(5445) Other wars
Piracy cases see JX4446.A+
(5460.A-Z) Mock trials. By first named "defendant" or best known (popular) name, A-Z
Remedies
(5482) General works
(5482.5) Exhaustion of local remedies
Claims and reparation
Including restitution, recompensation, and satisfaction
For collections of cases and claims see KZ238+
(5483) General works

International law
Treatises on special topics
International responsibility. International delinquencies
Remedies
Claims and reparation -- Continued
(5485) Calvo doctrine and clause
Drago doctrine see JX1393.D8
(5486.A-Z) By region or country, A-Z
(5501-5531) Finance
see class H; K4430+
(5561-5681) Communication
see subclass HE; K4240+
Transportation
(5701) Railways
see K4061+
(5731) Maritime (commercial) law
see K1150+
(5751) Waterways and water transport
see K4150+
Aeronautics
see K4091+
(5760) Periodicals. Societies
(5762) Congresses. Conferences
(5763) International public agencies
(5768) Collections
Treaties
(5769.A2) Collections
(5769.A3-Z) Separate treaties
(5770) History
(5771) General works
(5775.A-Z) Special topics, A-Z
(5775.C7) Crimes aboard aircraft. Hijacking of aircraft
see K5276
(5775.L5) Licensing
(5775.S3) Salvage
see class K
(5775.T7) Traffic control
(5810) Space law
see KZD1002+
(6001-6650) Private international law. Conflict of laws
see K7051+

International relations

Class here works on (1) the science of international relations, i.e. the analysis of contemporary international politics and policy objectives, and of national trends in the foreign policy of states, as they affect relations in the international community, and (2) international associations of autonomous bodies (i.e. states or organizations) and on their interaction relating to the security of the international community

For the law and the rules of conduct binding upon states in the international community, and for the law establishing and governing intergovernmental organization, see subclass KZ or the pertinent regional class K subclasses, e. g. KJE for the regional organization of Europe

Bibliography

see class Z

<2> Bibliography of bibliography

<3> General bibliography

<4> Library catalogs. Union lists

Including sales catalogs

5 Indexes to periodical articles, collections, etc.

For indexes to a particular publication, see the publication

Bibliography of periodicals see JZ5.5

Periodicals

For periodicals consisting primarily of informative materials (newsletters, bulletins, etc.) relating to a particular subject, see the subject

For collected papers, proceedings, etc. of a particular congress, see the congress

For society publications, see the society

5.5 Bibliography of periodicals

For indexes to a particular periodical, see the periodical

For indexes to periodicals articles see JZ5

By language

European

6.5 English

e. g.

6.5.A53 (American) Foreign service journal

6.5.B74 British review of international studies

6.5.C6 Columbia journal of international studies

6.5.I53 International affairs

6.5.I64 International relations

6.5.J47 Jerusalem journal of international affairs

6.5.K66 Korean journal of international relations

6.5.L6 London quarterly of world affairs

6.5.M54 Millennium

7 Italian

e. g.

Periodicals
By language
European
Italian -- Continued
7.C67 Comunita internazionale
7.R63 Revista di studi politici internazionali
8 German
e. g.
8.B45 Beiträge zur Konfliktforschung
8.I68 Internationale Politik und Gesellschaft
9 Spanish. Portuguese
Including all Latin American journals
e. g.
9.N84 Nuevo Mundo
11 French
e. g.
11.M65 Le monde diplomatique
11.P6 Politique etrangere
11.2 Russian
Including works in original script or transliterated in Roman characters
11.3.A-Z Other European periodicals. By language, A-Z
Asian
Including works in original script or transliterated in Roman characters
12 Japanese
e. g.
12.K6 Kokusai seyi
13 Chinese
14 Indian
Including works in Sanskrit
14.2.A-Z Other Asian periodicals, A-Z
Korean journal of international relations see JZ6.5.K66
15.A-Z African/Middle Eastern periodicals, A-Z
Including Arabic, Hebrew, etc.
18.A-Z Other, A-Z
21 Annuals. Yearbooks
Class here annual surveys on international affairs and accounts of the trends in international politics
e. g.
21.A58 Annuaire politique
21.A64 Annuario di politica internazionale
21.I6 The Indian yearbook of international affairs
21.I63 The international yearbook of foreign policy analysis
21.J18 Jahrbuch der internationalen Politik und Wirtschaft
21.Y4 The yearbook of world affairs
22 Monographic series (numbered)

Societies, associations, academies, institutes, etc., for the study of international relations
Class here works on individual learned societies and their activities
Including reports, bylaws, proceedings, directories, etc. and works about a society
For a society limited to a particular subject, see the subject
For substantive periodicals authored by such societies see JZ6.5+

24.A-Z International, A-Z
International Peace Research Institute see JZ5518.I64
By region or country
The Americas
27.A-Z North America. United States and Canada, A-Z
e. g.
27.A54 American Enterprise Institute for Public Policy Research
27.C4 Center for Strategic and International Studies
27.C6 Council on Foreign Relations, Inc.
27.F67 Foreign Policy Institute
27.I68 International Studies Association
Central and South American regions or countries see JZ35.A+
European regions or countries
31.A-Z Great Britain, A-Z
e. g.
31.R627 Royal Institute of International Affairs
32.A-Z France, A-Z
33.A-Z Germany, A-Z
e. g.
33.D4 Deutsche Gesellschaft für Auswärtige Politik. Forschungsinstitut
34.A-Z Italy, A-Z
35.A-Z Spain and Portugal, A-Z
Including all Latin American countries
35.2.A-Z Russia, A-Z
35.3.A-Z Scandinavian, A-Z
35.4.A-Z Other European, A-Z
Asian regions or countries
36.A-Z India, A-Z
36.2.A-Z Japan, A-Z
36.3.A-Z Other Asian, A-Z
37.A-Z African and Middle Eastern, A-Z
38.A-Z Other, A-Z
43.A-Z Conferences. Symposia, A-Z
e. g.
43.C65 Coloquio Internacional de Primavera

JZ

Conferences. Symposia, A-Z -- Continued
43.C66 Conference on the United Nations of the Next Decade
43.F85 Fulbright Colloquium on Ethics and International relations
43.I55 Institut international d'études diplomatiques. Conference
43.I57 International Political Science Association World Conference (Congress; varies)
43.I58 International Slavic Conference
43.L77 London Conference on Cognitive Process Models of Foreign Policy (1973)
43.P85 Pugwash Conference on Science and World Affairs
43.T73 Transatlantic Colloquy on Cross-border Relations: European and North American perspectives (1987)
43.T75 Trilateral Commission. Plenary Meeting
<60> Intergovernmental congresses and conferences
see KZ60+
Sources
63 General (collective and selective)
Including reading, basic documents for the study of international relations, politics and diplomacy
For collections limited to a region or country see JZ221+
<64> General collections of treaties and other instruments of international law, and cases combined
see KZ64
95 Protocols of diplomatic congresses
<118-194> Treaties and conventions
see KZ118+
<199-220> Judicial decisions and awards. Law reports. Arbitration cases
see KZ199+
By region or country
The Americas and West Indies
221-230 General (Table JZ1)
<231-239> United States
see KZ231+
351-360 Canada (Table JZ1)
360.5 Greenland (Table JZ2)
361-370 Mexico (Table JZ1)
Central America
381-390 Belize (Table JZ1)
391-400 Costa Rica (Table JZ1)
401-410 Guatemala (Table JZ1)
411-420 Honduras (Table JZ1)
421-430 Nicaragua (Table JZ1)
431-440 Panama (Table JZ1)
441-450 El Salvador (Table JZ1)
West Indies. Caribbean Area
450.5 General (Table JZ2)
451-460 Cuba (Table JZ1)

Sources
By region or country
The Americas and West Indies
West Indies. Caribbean Area -- Continued
461-470 Haiti (Table JZ1)
471-480 Dominican Republic (Table JZ1)
483 Puerto Rico (Table JZ2)
484 Virgin Islands of the United States. Danish West Indies (Table JZ2)
485-488 British West Indies (Table JZ1a)
Including Guyana (British Guiana)
<491> Danish West Indies
see JZ484
493 Netherlands Antilles. Dutch West Indies (Table JZ2)
Including Curaçao
For Suriname (Dutch Guiana) see JZ574
495 French West Indies (Table JK2)
Including Guadeloupe and Martinique
For French Guiana see JZ577
South America
501-510 General (Table JZ1)
511-520 Argentina (Table JZ1)
521-530 Bolivia (Table JZ1)
531-540 Brazil (Table JZ1)
541-550 Chile (Table JZ1)
551-560 Colombia (Table JZ1)
561-570 Ecuador (Table JZ1)
Guiana
571 General (Table JZ2)
Guyana. British Guiana see JZ485+
574 Suriname. Dutch Guiana (Table JZ2)
577 French Guiana (Table JZ2)
581-590 Paraguay (Table JZ1)
591-600 Peru (Table JZ1)
601-610 Uruguay (Table JZ1)
611-620 Venezuela (Table JZ1)
620.5 Falkland Islands (Table JZ2)
Europe
621-630 General (Table JZ1)
Great Britain
631-640 General (Table JZ1)
Class here works on England and on England, Wales Scotland, and Northern Ireland combined
641 Wales (Table JZ2)
642 Scotland (Table JZ2)
643 Northern Ireland (Table JZ2)
645 Ireland. Eire (Table JZ2)

Sources
By region or country
Europe -- Continued
Gibraltar see JZ1046
Austria. Austro-Hungarian Monarchy
For Hungary see JZ661+
651-660 General (Table JZ1)
661-670 Hungary (Table JZ1)
675-678 Czechoslovakia (to 1993). Czech Republic (Table JZ1a)
680.5 Slovakia (1993-) (Table JZ2)
681-690 France (Table JZ1)
690.5 Monaco (Table JZ2)
Germany. Federal Republic of Germany, 1990-
Including West Germany (Federal Republic of Germany 1949-1990)
691-700 General (Table JZ1 modified)
700.A-Z Individual states, A-Z
700.B34 Baden
700.B36 Bavaria
East Germany (Democratic Republic of Germany, 1949-1990) see JZ700.G47
700.G47 Germany, East (Democratic Republic of Germany, 1949-1990)
700.P78 Prussia (Duchy)
700.W82 Württemberg
701-710 Greece (Table JZ1)
Italy
711-720 General (Table JZ1 modified)
720.A-Z Individual states, A-Z
720.T87 Tuscany (Grand Duchy)
720.V45 Venice (Republic)
722 Andorra (Table JZ2)
723 San Marino (Table JZ2)
724 Malta (Table JZ2)
The Benelux countries. Low countries
Holland see JZ741+
731-740 Belgium (Table JZ1)
The Netherlands. Holland
741-750 General (Table JZ1 modified)
750.A-Z Individual provinces, A-Z
Including historic (defunct) jurisdictions
750.5 Luxembourg (Table JZ2)
Russia. Soviet Union (to 1991)

Sources
By region or country
Europe
Russia. Soviet Union (to 1991) -- Continued
751-760 General (Table JZ1 modified)
Including works on, and proceedings of, the Commonwealth of Independent States; of former Soviet Republics (collectively); and of other historic (defunct) states, etc.
760.A-Z Individual states, republics, etc., A-Z
Byelorussian SSR see JZ760.4
Georgian SSR see JZ925
White Russia see JZ760.4
760.2 Russia (Federation) (Table JZ2)
Caucasus
Georgia (Republic) see JZ925
Armenia (Republic) see JZ923
Azerbaijan see JZ924
760.4 Belarus (Table JZ2)
760.5 Moldova (Table JZ2)
760.6 Ukraine (Table JZ2)
760.7 Poland (Table JZ2)
760.8 Finland (Table JZ2)
Baltic countries
760.9 Estonia (Table JZ2)
760.92 Latvia (Table JZ2)
760.93 Lithuania (Table JZ2)
Scandinavia
761-770 General (Table JZ1)
771-780 Denmark (Table JZ1)
For Greenland see JZ360.5
781-790 Iceland (Table JZ1)
791-800 Norway (Table JZ1)
801-810 Sweden (Table JZ1)
811-820 Spain (Table JZ1)
Gibraltar see JZ1046
821-830 Portugal (Table JZ1)
831-840 Switzerland (Table JZ1)
840.5 Liechtenstein (Table JZ2)
Southeastern Europe. Balkan States
Greece see JZ701+
841-850 Turkey (Table JZ1)
Including the Ottoman Empire
850.3 Cyprus (Table JZ2)
850.5 Albania (Table JZ2)
851-860 Bulgaria (Table JZ1)
861-870 Montenegro (Table JZ1)

JZ

Sources
By region or country
Europe
Southeastern Europe. Balkan States -- Continued
871-880 Romania (Table JZ1)
881-890 Yugoslavia (to 1992). Serbia (Table JZ1)
893 Croatia (Table JZ2)
894 Bosnia and Hercegovina (Table JZ2)
896 Slovenia (Table JZ2)
897 Macedonia (Republic) (Table JZ2)
Asia
Middle East. Southwest Asia
898 General (Table JZ2)
900 Armenia (to 1921) (Table JZ2)
901 Bahrain (Table JZ2)
Gaza see JZ906
904 Iran (Table JZ2)
905 Iraq (Table JZ2)
906 Israel. Palestine (Table JZ2)
907 Jerusalem (Table JZ2)
908 Jordan (Table JZ2)
West Bank (Territory under Israeli occupation, 1967-) see JZ906
910 Kuwait (Table JZ2)
911 Lebanon (Table JZ2)
912 Oman (Table JZ2)
913 Palestine (to 1948) (Table JZ2)
914 Qatar (Table JZ2)
915 Saudi Arabia (Table JZ2)
916 Syria (Table JZ2)
917 United Arab Emirates (Table JZ2)
918 Yemen (Table JZ2)
919 Yeman (People's Democratic Republic) (to 1990) (Table JZ2)
Caucasus
923 Armenia (Republic) (Table JZ2)
924 Azerbaijan (Table JZ2)
925 Georgia (Republic) (Table JZ2)
Turkey see JZ841+
Cyprus see JZ850.3
Central Asia
930 Kazakhstan (Table JZ2)
931 Kyrgyzstan (Table JZ2)
932 Tadjikistan (Table JZ2)
933 Turkmenistan (Table JZ2)
934 Uzbekistan (Table JZ2)
South Asia. Southeast Asia. East Asia

Sources
By region or country
Asia
South Asia. Southeast Asia. East Asia -- Continued
934.5 General (Table JZ2)
For works on both Asia and Pacific areas combined see JZ1105+
935 Afghanistan (Table JZ2)
936 Bangladesh (Table JZ2)
937 Bhutan (Table JZ2)
938 Brunei (Table JZ2)
939 Burma. Myanmar (Table JZ2)
940 Cambodia (Table JZ2)
China (to 1949)
941-950 General (Table JZ1 modified)
950.A-Z Provinces, A-Z
950.A63 An-tung sheng
950.C53 Ch'a-ha-erh sheng
950.H64 Ho-Chiang sheng
950.H75 Hsi-k'ang sheng
950.H76 Hsing-an sheng
950.J44 Je-ho sheng
950.L53 Liao-pei sheng
950.N46 Neng-Chiang sheng
950.N56 Ning-hsia sheng
950.P56 Pin-Chiang sheng
950.S85 Sui-yuan sheng
950.S87 Sung-Chiang sheng
950.T35 T'ai-wan sheng
951-960 China (Republic, 1949-). Taiwan (Table JZ1)
China (People's Republic, 1949-)
961-970 General (Table JZ1 modified)
970.A-Z Provinces, autonomous regions and municipalities, A-Z
970.H66 Hong Kong
970.M33 Macau
India
971-980 General (Table JZ1 modified)
980.A-Z States, Union Territories, etc., A-Z
980.A64 Andaman and Nicobar Islands
980.A65 Andrah Pradesh
980.A78 Arunchal Pradesh
980.A88 Assam
980.B55 Bihar
980.C35 Calcutta/Bengal Presidency
980.C53 Chandighar
980.D34 Dadra and Nagar Haveli

Sources
By region or country
Asia
South Asia. Southeast Asia. East Asia
India
States, Union Territories, etc., A-Z -- Continued

980.D45 Delhi
980.G63 Goa, Daman, and Diu
980.G85 Gujarat
980.H37 Haryana
980.H56 Himachal Pradesh
980.H84 Hyderabad
980.J35 Jaipur
980.J36 Jammu and Kashmir
980.K37 Karnataka
980.K47 Kerala
980.L35 Lakshadweep
980.M34 Madhya Pradesh
980.M35 Madras Presidency
980.M36 Maharashtra
980.M37 Manipur
980.M45 Meghalaya
980.M59 Mizoram
980.N36 Nagaland
980.O75 Orissa
980.P66 Pondicherry
980.P85 Punjab
980.R35 Rajasthan
980.S55 Sikkim
980.T35 Tamil Nadu
980.T75 Tripura
980.U77 Uttar Pradesh
980.W47 West Bengal
980.3 French Indochina (Table JZ2)
Hong Kong see JZ970.H66
980.6 Indonesia (Table JZ2)
981-990 Japan (Table JZ1)
991 Korea (South) (Table JZ2)
992 Democratic People's Republic of Korea. Korea (North) (Table JZ2)
992.3 Korea (to 1945) (Table JZ2)
993 Laos (Table JZ2)
Macau see JZ970.M33
Malaysia
995 General (Table JZ2)
Individual states
995.3 Straits Settlements (to 1942) (Table JZ2)

Sources
By region or country
Asia
South Asia. Southeast Asia. East Asia
Malaysia
Individual states -- Continued

995.5 Federated Malay States (1896-1942) (Table JZ2)
995.7 Malayan Union (1946-1947) (Table JZ2)
995.8 Malaya (1948-1962) (Table JZ2)
996.A-Z States of East and West Malaysia (1957-), A-Z
996.F44 Federal Territory (Kuala Lumpur)
996.J65 Johor
996.K44 Kedah
996.K46 Kelantan
996.L33 Labuan
996.M35 Malacca
996.N45 Negri Sembilan
996.P35 Pahang
996.P47 Perak
996.P48 Perlis
996.P56 Pinang
996.S33 Sabah
Previously North Borneo
996.S37 Sarawak
996.S45 Selangor
996.T47 Terengganu
997 Maldives (Table JZ2)
998 Mongolia (Table JZ2)
Myanmar see JZ939
999 Nepal (Table JZ2)
1000 Pakistan (Table JZ2)
1001-1010 Philippines (Table JZ1)
1011 Singapore (Table JZ2)
1012 Sri Lanka. Ceylon (Table JZ2)
1013 Thailand (Table JZ2)
1014 Vietnam (1976-) (Table JZ2)
Including the periods through 1945
1016 Vietnam (Republic). South Vietnam (1946-1975) (Table JZ2)
1017 Vietnam (Democratic Republic). North Vietnam (1946-1975) (Table JZ2)
Africa
1020 Algeria (Table JZ2)
1021 Angola (Table JZ2)
1022 Benin (Table JZ2)
1023 Botswana (Table JZ2)
1024 British Central Africa Protectorate (Table JZ2)

JZ

Sources
By region or country
Africa -- Continued
1025 British Indian Ocean Territory (Table JZ2)
1026 British Somaliland (Table JZ2)
1027 Burkina Faso (Table JZ2)
1028 Burundi (Table JZ2)
1029 Cameroon (Table JZ2)
1030 Cape Verde (Table JZ2)
1031 Central African Republic (Table JZ2)
1032 Chad (Table JZ2)
1033 Comoros (Table JZ2)
1034 Congo (Brazzaville) (Table JZ2)
Congo (Democratic Republic) see JZ1099
1035 Côte d'Ivoire. Ivory Coast (Table JZ2)
1036 Djibouti (Table JZ2)
1037 East Africa Protectorate (Table JZ2)
1038 Egypt (Table JZ2)
1038.5 Eritrea (Table JZ2)
1039 Ethiopia (Table JZ2)
1040 French Equatorial Africa (Table JZ2)
1041 French West Africa (Table JZ2)
1042 Gabon (Table JZ2)
1043 Gambia (Table JZ2)
1044 German East Africa (Table JZ2)
1045 Ghana (Table JZ2)
1046 Gibraltar (Table JZ2)
1047 Guinea (Table JZ2)
1048 Guinea-Bissau (Table JZ2)
1049 Equatorial Guinea (Table JZ2)
1050 Ifni (Table JZ2)
1051 Italian East Africa (Table JZ2)
1052 Italian Somaliland (Table JZ2)
1053 Kenya (Table JZ2)
1054 Lesotho (Table JZ2)
1055 Liberia (Table JZ2)
1056 Libya (Table JZ2)
1057 Madagascar (Table JZ2)
1058 Malawi (Table JZ2)
1059 Mali (Table JZ2)
1060 Mauritania (Table JZ2)
1061 Mauritius (Table JZ2)
1062 Mayotte (Table JZ2)
1063 Morocco (Table JZ2)
1064 Mozambique (Table JZ2)
1065 Namibia (Table JZ2)
1066 Niger (Table JZ2)

Sources
By region or country
Africa -- Continued
1067 Nigeria (Table JZ2)
1068 Réunion (Table JZ2)
1069 Rwanda (Table JZ2)
1070 Saint Helena (Table JZ2)
1071 Sao Tome and Principe (Table JZ2)
1072 Senegal (Table JZ2)
1073 Seychelles (Table JZ2)
1074 Sierra Leone (Table JZ2)
1075 Somalia (Table JZ2)
South Africa, Republic of
1081-1090 General (Table JZ1 modified)
1090.A-Z Provinces and self-governing territories, etc., A-Z
Including former independant homelands
1090.B66 Bophuthatswana
1090.C36 Cape of Good Hope. Kaapland (to 1994)
1090.C57 Ciskei
1090.E36 Eastern Cape
Eastern Transvaal see JZ1090.M68
1090.F74 Free State. Orange Free State
1090.G38 Gauteng
1090.K93 KwaZulu-Natal. Natal
Including former KwaZulu Homeland areas
1090.M68 Mpulamanga. Eastern Transvaal
Natal see JZ1090.K93
1090.N64 North West
1090.N66 Northern Cape
1090.N67 Northern Province. Northern Transvaal
Northern Transvaal see JZ1090.N67
Orange Free State. Oranje Vrystaat see JZ1090.F74
1090.T73 Transkei
1090.T74 Transvaal
1090.V46 Venda
1090.W47 Western Cape
1091 Spanish West Africa (to 1958) (Table JZ2)
1092 Spanish Sahara (to 1975) (Table JZ2)
1093 Sudan (Table JZ2)
1094 Swaziland (Table JZ2)
1095 Tanzania (Table JZ2)
1096 Togo (Table JZ2)
1097 Tunisia (Table JZ2)
1098 Uganda (Table JZ2)
1099 Zaire. Congo (Democratic Republic) (Table JZ2)
1100 Zambia (Table JZ2)
1101 Zanzibar (to 1964) (Table JZ2)

Sources
By region or country
Africa -- Continued
1103 Zimbabwe (Table JZ2)
Pacific Area
1105 General (Table JZ2)
Including works on both Pacific and Asian areas combined
Australia
1111-1120 General (Table JZ1 modified)
1120.A-Z States and territories, A-Z
Including external territories
1120.A88 Australian Capital Territory
Australian Antarctic Territory (External territory) see JZ1153
1120.N48 New South Wales
1120.N67 Norfolk Island (External territory)
1120.N673 Northern Territory
1120.Q84 Queensland
1120.S68 South Australia
1120.T38 Tasmania
1120.V53 Victoria
1120.W48 Western Australia
New Zealand
1121 General (Table JZ2)
1122.A-Z Regions and overseas territories, A-Z
Ross Dependency see JZ1153
Other Pacific Area jurisdictions
1125 American Samoa (Table JZ2)
1126 British New Guinea (Territory of Papua) (Table JZ2)
1127 Cook Islands (Table JZ2)
1128 Easter Island (Table JZ2)
1129 Fiji (Table JZ2)
1130 French Polynesia (Table JZ2)
1131 German New Guinea (to 1914) (Table JZ2)
1132 Guam (Table JZ2)
1133 Kiribati (Table JZ2)
1134 Marshall Islands (Table JZ2)
1135 Micronesia (Federated States) (Table JZ2)
1136 Midway Islands (Table JZ2)
1137 Nauru (Table JZ2)
1138 Netherlands New Guinea (to 1963) (Table JZ2)
1139 New Caledonia (Table JZ2)
1140 Niue (Table JZ2)
1141 Northern Mariana Islands (Table JZ2)
1142 Pacific Islands (Trust Territory) (Table JZ2)
1143 Palau (Table JZ2)
1144 Papua New Guinea (Table JZ2)

Sources
By region or country
Pacific Area
Other Pacific Area jurisdictions -- Continued
1145 Pitcairn Island (Table JZ2)
Samoa see JZ1152
1146 Solomon Islands (Table JZ2)
1147 Tonga (Table JZ2)
1148 Tuvalu (Table JZ2)
1149 Vanuatu (Table JZ2)
1150 Wake Islands (Table JZ2)
1151 Wallis and Futuna Islands (Table JZ2)
1152 Western Samoa. Samoa (Table JZ2)
1153 Antarctica (Table JZ2)
1160 Encyclopedias
1161 Dictionaries. Terms and phrases. Vocabularies
Directories
1163 General
1164 By specialization
<1168-1229> War crime trials
see KZ1168+
Research
Including methods of bibliographic research
1234 General works
1235 Electronic data processing
Study and teaching
1237 General works
1238.A-Z By region or country, A-Z
Societies, associations, academies, institutes, etc., for the study of international relations see JZ24+
Conferences. Symposia see JZ43.A+
1242 General works
1243.A-Z Manuals and other works for particular groups of users, A-Z
Relation to other disciplines and topics
1249 Relation to social (behavioral) sciences
<1250> Relation to international law
see KZ1250
1251 Sociology of international relations and politics
1252 International economic policies and theories
1253 Political and social psychology
1253.2 Gender theory and feminist theory in international relations
1253.5 Linguistics. Language
Cf. JZ1434 Diplomatic language
1254 Science and technology
<1256-1280> Theory and principles of the Law of Nations
see KZ1256+

Scope of international relations. Political theory. Diplomacy
Including history of international relations
1305 General works
Concepts and principles
1306 Political ethics. Political morality and moralism
Including ethics (morality) in international decisionmaking and diplomacy
1306.5 Political aesthetics. Aesthetics in international negotiations
1307 Political realism. Realist theory
International order. World order. Cosmopolitanism
1308 General works
Power and power politics. World politics
1310 General works
1312 Hegemony. Hegemonic power
1313 Balance of power. International equilibrium. Concert of nations
For Balkan question see JZ1648
For Far Eastern question see JZ1720
Cf. JZ1355 Congress of Vienna
1313.3 Non-alignment
1314 Alliance politics
Including alliance formation and management
For particular alliances see JZ1346+
1315 Revolution and world order
For the revolutionary state see JC491
The State system. The nation-state
For nature, concepts, and forms of the state see JC11+
1316 General works
National interest see JZ1320.3
1317 Concept of super-powers
1317.2 Warlordism
Cf. KZ4029 Failed state
Diplomacy. Diplomatic and consular service see JZ1400+
International cooperation. Global governance. Globalization
For economic aspects of globalization see HF1365
1317.5.A-Z Societies. Associations. Institutes. Academies, etc. By name, A-Z
1317.5.C655 Commission on Global Governance
Cf. JZ5518.S86 Stockholm Initiative on Global Security and Governance
1318 General works

Scope of international relations. Political theory. Diplomacy
Concepts and principles
International order. World order. Cosmopolitanism
International cooperation. Global governance. Globalization -- Continued
International regimes
Class here works on theory and analysis of regime formation and creation as a means of conflict resolution in the international community
For regimes governing particular areas of international law, see the subject in K or KZ, e. g. KZA, Regime of the Oceans; KWX, Antarctic legal regime
For international organization see JZ5566
For international security see JZ5586+

1319 General works
Interdependence and transnationalism. Domestic dimension (factors)
1320 General works
<1320.2> National self-determination
see KZ1269
1320.3 National self-interest
1320.4 World citizenship
1320.5 Principle of good neighbourliness. Global neighbourhood
1320.7 Interregionalism. Transregionalism
<1321-1323.5> Law and legal regimes governing the global commons
see KZ1321+
International cooperation and diplomacy defined by subject areas
1324 Environmental diplomacy. International politics of the environment
For environmental law and regimes see K3581+
By period
<1328> Ancient
see KZ1328
<1329> Early/Medieval
see KZ1329
Modern
1329.5 General works
1330 Peace of Westphalia to the Treaty of Utrecht (1648-1713)
Treaty of Utrecht to the French Revolution (1713-1789)
For peace treaties in general see KZ184+
1335 General works
Treaty of Paris, 1763
For the text of the treaty see KZ1336+
1336 General works

Scope of international relations. Political theory. Diplomacy
By period
Modern
Treaty of Utrecht to the French Revolution (1713-1789)
Treaty of Paris, 1763 -- Continued
1338.A-Z Special topics, A-Z
1338.L4 League of the Neutrals
French Revolution to the Congress of Vienna (1789-1815)
1345 General works
Particular congresses, alliances, etc.
1346 Congress of Rastatt
1347 Treaty of Ghent
Holy Alliance, 1815 see JZ1358
1351.A-Z Other, A-Z
Congress of Vienna to the American Civil War (1815-1861)
1352 General works
1355 Congress of Vienna, 1814-1815
Cf. JZ1313 Balance of power
1358 Holy Alliance, 1815
1361 Congress of Troppau, 1820
1363 Congress of Laibach, 1821
1365 Congress of Verona, 1822
1367 Congress of Panama, 1826
Cf. F1404 Pan American conferences
1369 Treaty of Paris, 1856
Class here publications of the English Maritime League
Including works on the Declaration of Paris
For the text of the treaty see KZ1369
American Civil War to the First Conference of the Hague (1861-1899)
1373 General works
Particular congresses and conferences
Class here general works
For final acts or treaties see KZ1373+
1377 Saint Petersburg Convention, 1868
1379 London Conference, 1871
1381 Brussels Conference, 1874
1383 Congress of Berlin, 1878
1385 Berlin West Africa Conference, 1884-1885
Cf. DT31+ Partition of Africa
Cf. DT652 Congo
Pan-American Congress, 1889-1890
1387 General works
1387.2 Pan-American Union, 1890

Scope of international relations. Political theory. Diplomacy
By period
Modern -- Continued
First Conference of the Hague to creation of the United Nations (1899-1945)

1391 General works
1391.2 Triple Entente, 1907
1392 World War I
1392.5 World War II
The Hague and Geneva Conferences and Conventions
1393 General (Collective)
Particular Conferences and Conventions
see the subject, e. g. KZ6464.2 Geneva Convention, July 6, 1906 (Relief of sick and wounded in war)
League of Nations see JZ4853+
United Nations see JZ4935+
Subsequent conferences or conflicts (1945-)
1394 General works
1395.A-Z Conferences or conflicts, A-Z
1395.I73 Italo-Ethiopian War, 1935-1936
1395.K67 Korean War, 1950-1953
1395.P47 Persian Gulf War, 1991
1395.R87 Russo-Japanese War, 1904-1905
1395.S56 Sino-Japanese War, 1937-1945
1395.S68 South African War, 1899-1902
1395.S73 Spanish Civil War, 1936-1939
1395.V54 Vietnam War, 1961-1975
Diplomatic and consular service
1400 Periodicals
Annuals. Yearbooks see JZ21
1402 Societies. Associations. Academies. Institutes, etc. By name, A-Z
Codes
see the appropriate country in class K subclasses
1403 Study and teaching. Schools
1405 General works
Organs and agencies conducting diplomatic and consular affairs. Diplomatic and consular officials
For the laws governing the diplomatic and consular service, including powers, diplomatic privileges and immunities, diplomatic gifts, etc., see the appropriate jurisdiction in class K subclasses
Biographies of diplomats, see classes D - F
1410 General works
1412 Heads of state

Scope of international relations. Political theory. Diplomacy
Diplomatic and consular service
Organs and agencies conducting diplomatic and consular affairs. Diplomatic and consular officials -- Continued
1416 Secretary of State. Minister of Foreign Affairs
Class here general works
For the Department of Foreign Affairs of an individual country, see the country
Ambassadors. Plenipotentiaries
1418 General works
1420 Appointment
1422 Credentials
1424 Diplomatic registers
Duties. Functions
1426 General works
To the home government
1427 Diplomatic protection of citizens abroad
1428 Protection of interests
1429 To the foreign government
1432 Extraterritoriality
1434 Diplomatic language, style, etc.
Cf. CD70+ Practice of special chancelleries
1436 Diplomatic etiquette. Ceremonials
Including precedence
1438 Dress
1440 Diplomatic couriers
1442 Diplomatic envoys
Consuls. The consular service
For consular laws (codes) governing the consular service, including privileges and immunities, consular jurisdiction, etc., see the appropriate jurisdiction in class K subclasses, e.g. KK5445+ Germany
For consular courts and procedure, see the appropriate jurisdiction in class K subclasses, e.g. KK3693 Courts of special jurisdiction
1444 General works
Including history
1446 Consular functions
Including administration of estates, functions in international (foreign) trade, certifications, etc.
1448 Police
Agents of foreign principals
1450 General works
1452 Attachés
1454 Trade missions
Scope of international relations with regard to countries, territories, regions, etc. By country, territory, or region

Scope of international relations. Political theory. Diplomacy
Scope of international relations with regard to countries, territories, regions, etc. By country, territory, or region -- Continued
The Americas and West Indies
1464 General (Collective)
1466 Pan-Americanism
Including the Pan-American conferences, e.g. American Congress (Panama, 1826); International American Conference (1889-1948); and Inter-American Conference (1954-)
Cf. F1404+ Pan American conferences
Cf. F1418 Relations between the United States and Latin America
United States
For documents see KZ231+
Cf. KF4650+ Foreign relations legislation (U.S.)
1467 Collections
History
Cf. E183.8.A+ History. Foreign and general relations (U.S.)
1469 General works
By period
1472 Colonial to 1776
1473 1776-1800/1815
1800/1815-1861
1474 General works
1474.2 Oregon question
Cf. F880 Oregon (United States local history)
1861-1880
1476 General works
Confederate States see E488
1478 1880-1900
For the Treaty of Paris, 1898, see subclass KZ
Cf. DS679 Annexation of Philippines (Spanish-American War, 1898)
Cf. DU627.3+ Annexation of Hawaiian Islands
Cf. F1975 Annexation of Puerto Rico (Spanish-American War, 1898)
1479 1900-1945
1480 General (Table JZ3)
Particular theories or questions
1482 Monroe Doctrine
Class here general and theoretical works
For application to particular events, see the period in class E and F

JZ

Scope of international relations. Political theory. Diplomacy
Scope of international relations with regard to countries, territories, regions, etc. By country, territory, or region
The Americas and West Indies
United States
Particular theories or questions -- Continued
1483 Boundary questions (older and general)
For boundary treaties see KZ176+
1484 Eastern policy
1485 Great Lakes
Panama Canal see JZ3715+
1515 Canada (Table JZ3)
1517 Greenland (Table JZ3)
1519 Latin America (General) (Table JZ3)
Including Mexico, Central and South America combined
Mexico
1520 General (Table JZ3)
1520.3 Cardenas doctrine
Central America
1522 General (Table JZ3)
1523 Belize (Table JZ3)
Including Belize questions
1524 Costa Rica (Table JZ3)
1526 Guatemala (Table JZ3)
1527 Honduras (Table JZ3)
Including British Honduras questions
1529 Nicaragua (Table JZ3)
1530 Panama (Table JZ3)
For Panama Canal see JZ3715+
1532 El Salvador (Table JZ3)
West Indies. Caribbean Area
Including Federation of the West Indies, 1958-1962
1534 General (Table JZ3)
1535 Cuba (Table JZ3)
1536 Haiti (Table JZ3)
1537 Dominican Republic (Table JZ3)
1538 Puerto Rico (Table JZ3)
1540 Virgin Islands of the United States. Danish West Indies (Table JZ3)
1541 British West Indies (Table JZ3)
1542 Netherlands Antilles. Dutch West Indies (Table JZ3)
Including Curaçao
For Suriname (Dutch Guiana) see JZ1555
1543 French West Indies (Table JZ3)
Including Guadeloupe and Martinique
For French Guiana see JZ1556
South America

Scope of international relations. Political theory. Diplomacy
Scope of international relations with regard to countries, territories, regions, etc. By country, territory, or region
The Americas and West Indies
South America -- Continued
1545 General (Table JZ3)
Argentina
1546 General (Table JZ3)
Drago doctrine
1547 Bolivia (Table JZ3)
1548 Brazil (Table JZ3)
1549 Chile (Table JZ3)
1550 Colombia (Table JZ3)
1552 Ecuador (Table JZ3)
Guianas
1553 General (Table JZ3)
Guyana. British Guiana see JZ1541
1555 Suriname. Dutch Guiana (Table JZ3)
1556 French Guiana (Table JZ3)
1557 Paraguay (Table JZ3)
1559 Peru (Table JZ3)
1560 Uruguay (Table JZ3)
1561 Venezuela (Table JZ3)
1562 Falkland Islands (Table JZ3)
Europe. European Community. European Union
1570 General (Table JZ3)
Great Britain
1572 General (Table JZ3)
Class here works on England and England, Wales, Scotland and Northern Ireland combined
1574 Wales (Table JZ3)
1575 Scotland (Table JZ3)
Gibraltar see JZ1811
1577 Northern Ireland (Table JZ3)
1578 Ireland. Eire (Table JZ3)
Austria. Austro-Hungarian Monarchy
1582 General (Table JZ3)
1583 Hungary (Table JZ3)
1584 Czechoslovakia (to 1993). Czech Republic (Table JZ3)
1585 Slovakia (1993-) (Table JZ3)
1587 France (Table JZ3)
1588 Monaco (Table JZ3)
Germany
Including the Federal Republic of Germany (to 1992)
1592 General (Table JZ3)
1592.2 International relations of German states to one another
1593 Danzig (Table JZ3)

Scope of international relations. Political theory. Diplomacy
Scope of international relations with regard to countries, territories, regions, etc. By country, territory, or region
Europe. European Community. European Union
Germany -- Continued

1593.5 Saar (to 1949) (Table JZ3)
1593.6 Rhine River and Valley (Table JZ3)
1595.A-Z Individual states, A-Z
1595.B3 Baden (Table JZ4)
1595.B36 Bavaria (Table JZ4)
1595.G4 Germany, Democratic Republic (1949-1992) (Table JZ4)
1595.P78 Prussia (Duchy) (Table JZ4)
1595.W82 Württemberg (Table JZ4)
1598 Greece (Table JZ3)
1600 Italy (Table JZ3)
1602 Vatican City. Stato Pontificio (Table JZ3)
Including Papal States, territories, regions, etc., and including periods before the Lateran treaty of 1929
1605 Andorra (Table JZ3)
1606 San Marino (Table JZ3)
1607 Malta (Table JZ3)
Benelux countries. Low countries
1608 General (Table JZ3)
Holland see JZ1611+
1609 Belgium (Table JZ3)
The Netherlands. Holland
1611 General (Table JZ3)
1612.A-Z Individual provinces, A-Z
1614 Luxembourg (Table JZ3)
Russia. Soviet Union (to 1991)
Including works on the Commonwealth of Independant States, and on the former Soviet republics treated collectively
1615 General (Table JZ3)
1616 Russia (Federation, 1992-) (Table JZ3)
1618.A-Z Individual states, republics, etc., A-Z
Byelorussian SSR see JZ1620
Estonia see JZ1629
Finland see JZ1627
Latvia see JZ1630
Lithuania see JZ1631
Poland see JZ1625
1620 Belarus (Table JZ3)
1622 Moldova (Table JZ3)
1624 Ukraine (Table JZ3)
1625 Poland (Table JZ3)

Scope of international relations. Political theory. Diplomacy
Scope of international relations with regard to countries, territories, regions, etc. By country, territory, or region
Europe. European Community. European Union -- Continued

1627 Finland (Table JZ3)
Baltic States
1628 General works
1629 Estonia (Table JZ3)
1630 Latvia (Table JZ3)
1631 Lithuania (Table JZ3)
Scandinavia
1633 General works
1635 Denmark (Table JZ3)
For Greenland see JZ1517
1636 Iceland (Table JZ3)
1637 Norway (Table JZ3)
1639 Sweden (Table JZ3)
Spain
1641 General (Table JZ3)
1642.A-Z Individual states, provinces, regions, etc., A-Z
e.g.
1642.C3 Catalonia (Table JZ4)
Gibraltar see JZ1811
1644 Portugal (Table JZ3)
1646 Switzerland (Table JZ3)
1647 Liechtenstein (Table JZ3)
Southeastern Europe. The Balkan States
1648 General (Table JZ3)
Greece see JZ1598
1649 Turkey (Table JZ3)
1650 Cyprus (Table JZ3)
1652 Albania (Table JZ3)
1654 Bulgaria (Table JZ3)
1656 Montenegro (Table JZ3)
Romania
1658 General (Table JZ3)
1659.A-Z Individual provinces , etc., A-Z
Including historic provinces, etc.
e.g.
1659.W32 Wallachia (Table JZ4)
1661 Yugoslavia (to 1992). Serbia (Table JZ3)
1662 Croatia (Table JZ3)
1664 Bosnia and Hercegovina (Table JZ3)
1666 Slovenia (Table JZ3)
1668 Macedonia (Republic) (Table JZ3)
Asia

Scope of international relations. Political theory. Diplomacy
Scope of international relations with regard to countries, territories, regions, etc. By country, territory, or region
Asia -- Continued
Middle East. Southwest Asia
1670 General (Table JZ3)
1672 Armenia (to 1921) (Table JZ3)
1674 Bahrain (Table JZ3)
1676 Gaza (Table JZ3)
1680 Iran (Table JZ3)
1682 Iraq (Table JZ3)
1684 Israel. Palestine (Table JZ3)
1685 Jerusalem (Table JZ3)
1687 Jordan (Table JZ3)
West Bank (Territory under Israeli occupation, 1967-) see JZ1684
1689 Kuwait (Table JZ3)
1691 Lebanon (Table JZ3)
1693 Oman (Table JZ3)
Palestine (to 1948) see JZ1684
1700 Qatar (Table JZ3)
1702 Saudi Arabia (Table JZ3)
1703 Syria (Table JZ3)
1704 United Arab Emirates (Table JZ3)
1705 Yemen (Table JZ3)
1706 Yemen (People's Democratic Republic) (to 1990) (Table JZ3)
Caucasus
1708 Armenia (Republic) (Table JZ3)
1709 Azerbaijan (Table JZ3)
1710 Georgia (Republic) (Table JZ3)
Turkey see JZ1649
Cyprus see JZ1650
Central Asia
1711.5 General (Table JZ3)
1712 Kazakhstan (Table JZ3)
1714 Kyrgyzstan (Table JZ3)
1715 Tajikistan (Table JZ3)
1717 Turkmenistan (Table JZ3)
1718 Uzbekistan (Table JZ3)
South Asia. Southeast Asia. East Asia
1720 General (Table JZ3)
For works on both Asia and Pacific areas combined see JZ1980
1722 Afghanistan (Table JZ3)
1724 Bangladesh (Table JZ3)
1725 Bhutan (Table JZ3)

Scope of international relations. Political theory. Diplomacy
Scope of international relations with regard to countries, territories, regions, etc. By country, territory, or region
Asia
South Asia. Southeast Asia. East Asia -- Continued

1726 Brunei (Table JZ3)
1727 Burma. Myanmar (Table JZ3)
1729 Cambodia (Table JZ3)
China (to 1949)
1730 General (Table JZ3)
1731.A-Z Provinces, A-Z
1731.A63 An-tung sheng (Table JZ4)
1731.C53 Ch'a-ha-erh sheng (Table JZ4)
Fukien Province. Fuijan Sheng see JZ1733
1731.H64 Ho-Chiang Sheng (Table JZ4)
1731.H75 Hsi-k'ang sheng (Table JZ4)
1731.H76 Hsing-an sheng (Table JZ4)
1731.J44 Je-ho sheng (Table JZ4)
Kwangsi Province. Kuang-hsi see JZ1733
Kwangtung Province. Guangdong Sheng see JZ1733
1731.L53 Liao-pei sheng (Table JZ4)
1731.N46 Neng-Chiang sheng (Table JZ4)
1731.N56 Ning-hsia sheng (Table JZ4)
1731.P56 Pin-Chiang sheng (Table JZ4)
Sikang Province see JZ1733
1731.S85 Sui-yuan sheng (Table JZ4)
1731.S86 Sung-Chiang sheng (Table JZ4)
1731.T35 T'ai-wan sheng (Table JZ4)
1733 China (Republic, 1949-). Taiwan (Table JZ3)
China (People's Republic, 1949-)
1734 General (Table JZ3)
1735.A-Z Provinces, autonomous regions and municipalities, A-Z
1735.H66 Hong Kong
1735.M33 Macau
India
1737 General (Table JZ3)
1738.A-Z States, Union Territories, etc., A-Z
Including historic (defunct) jurisdictions (e. g. princely states, presidencies, etc.)
1738.A64 Andaman and Nicobar Islands (Table JZ4)
1738.A65 Andrah Pradesh (Table JZ4)
1738.A78 Arunchal Pradesh (Table JZ4)
1738.A88 Assam (Table JZ4)
1738.B55 Bihar (Table JZ4)
1738.C35 Calcutta/Bengal Presidency (Table JZ4)

Scope of international relations. Political theory. Diplomacy
Scope of international relations with regard to countries, territories, regions, etc. By country, territory, or region
Asia
South Asia. Southeast Asia. East Asia
India
States, Union Territories, etc., A-Z -- Continued

1738.C53 Chandighar (Table JZ4)
1738.D34 Dadra and Nagar Haveli (Table JZ4)
1738.D45 Delhi (Table JZ4)
1738.G63 Goa, Daman, and Diu (Table JZ4)
1738.G85 Gujarat (Table JZ4)
1738.H37 Haryana (Table JZ4)
1738.H56 Himachal Pradesh (Table JZ4)
1738.H84 Hyderabad (Table JZ4)
1738.J35 Jaipur (Table JZ4)
1738.J36 Jammu and Kashmir (Table JZ4)
1738.K37 Karnataka (Table JZ4)
1738.K47 Kerala (Table JZ4)
1738.L35 Lakshadweep (Table JZ4)
1738.M34 Madhya Pradesh (Table JZ4)
1738.M35 Madras Presidency (Table JZ4)
1738.M36 Maharashtra (Table JZ4)
1738.M37 Manipur (Table JZ4)
1738.M45 Meghalaya (Table JZ4)
1738.M59 Mizoram (Table JZ4)
1738.N35 Nagaland (Table JZ4)
1738.O75 Orissa (Table JZ4)
1738.P66 Pondicherry (Table JZ4)
1738.P85 Punjab (Table JZ4)
1738.R35 Rajasthan (Table JZ4)
1738.S55 Sikkim (Table JZ4)
1738.T36 Tamil Nadu (Table JZ4)
1738.T75 Tripura (Table JZ4)
1738.U77 Uttar Pradesh (Table JZ4)
1738.W47 West Bengal (Table JZ4)
1741 French Indochina (Table JZ3)
Hong Kong see JZ1735.H66
1743 Indonesia (Table JZ3)
1745 Japan (Table JZ3)
1747 Korea (South) (Table JZ3)
1748 Democratic People's Republic of Korea. Korea (North) (Table JZ3)
1750 Korea (to 1945) (Table JZ3)
1752 Laos (Table JZ3)
Macau see JZ1735.M33
Malaysia

Scope of international relations. Political theory. Diplomacy
Scope of international relations with regard to countries, territories, regions, etc. By country, territory, or region
Asia
South Asia. Southeast Asia. East Asia
Malaysia -- Continued
1755 General (Table JZ3)
1756.A-Z Individual states, A-Z
1756.F44 Federated Malay States (1896-1942) (Table JZ4)
1756.M34 Malaya (1948-1962) (Table JZ4)
1756.M35 Malayan Union (1946-1947) (Table JZ4)
1756.S87 Straits Settlements (to 1942) (Table JZ4)
1756.5.A-Z States of East and West Malaysia (1957-), A-Z
Brunei see JZ1726
1756.5.F44 Federal Territory (Kuala Lumpur) (Table JZ4)
1756.5.J65 Johor (Table JZ4)
1756.5.K44 Kedah (Table JZ4)
1756.5.K46 Kelantan (Table JZ4)
1756.5.L33 Labuan (Table JZ4)
1756.5.M35 Malacca (Table JZ4)
1756.5.N45 Negri Sembilan (Table JZ4)
1756.5.P35 Pahang (Table JZ4)
1756.5.P46 Perak (Table JZ4)
1756.5.P48 Perlis (Table JZ4)
1756.5.P56 Pinang (Table JZ4)
1756.5.S33 Sabah (Table JZ4)
Previously North Borneo
1756.5.S37 Sarawak (Table JZ4)
1756.5.S45 Selangor (Table JZ4)
1756.5.T47 Terengganu (Table JZ4)
1757 Maldives (Table JZ3)
1758 Mongolia (Table JZ3)
Myanmar see JZ1727
1760 Nepal (Table JZ3)
1761 Pakistan (Table JZ3)
1763 Philippines (Table JZ3)
1765 Singapore (Table JZ3)
1766 Sri Lanka. Ceylon (Table JZ3)
1767 Thailand. Siam (Table JZ3)
1769 Vietnam (1976-) (Table JZ3)
Including the periods up through 1945
1770 Vietnam (Republic). South Vietnam (1946-1975) (Table JZ3)
1771 Vietnam (Democratic Republic). North Vietnam (1946-1975) (Table JZ3)
Africa
1773 General (Table JZ3)

Scope of international relations. Political theory. Diplomacy
Scope of international relations with regard to countries, territories, regions, etc. By country, territory, or region
Africa -- Continued

1774 Algeria (Table JZ3)
1775 Angola. Portuguese West Africa (Table JZ3)
1777 Benin. Dahomey (Table JZ3)
1779 Botswana (Table JZ3)
1780 British Central Africa Protectorate (Table JZ3)
1782 British Indian Ocean Territory (Table JZ3)
1783 British Somaliland (Table JZ3)
1784 Burkina Faso. Upper Volta (Table JZ3)
1786 Burundi. Ruanda-Urundi (Table JZ3)
1787 Cameroon (Table JZ3)
1788 Cape Verde (Table JZ3)
1789 Central African Republic. Central African Empire. Ubangi Shari (Table JZ3)
1790 Chad (Table JZ3)
1791 Comoros (Table JZ3)
1792 Congo (Brazzaville). Moyen-Congo (Table JZ3)
Congo (Democratic Republic) see JZ1940
1793 Côte d'Ivoire. Ivory Coast (Table JZ3)
1795 Djibouti. French Somaliland. Afars and Issas (Table JZ3)
1796 East Africa Protectorate (Table JZ3)
1797 Egypt. United Arab Republic (Table JZ3)
1798 Eritrea (Table JZ3)
1799 Ethiopia. Abyssinia (Table JZ3)
1800 French Equatorial Africa (Table JZ3)
1803 French West Africa (Table JZ3)
1805 Gabon (Table JZ3)
1807 Gambia (Table JZ3)
1808 German East Africa (Table JZ3)
1810 Ghana (Table JZ3)
1811 Gibraltar (Table JZ3)
1812 Guinea. French Guinea (Table JZ3)
1814 Guinea-Bissau. Portuguese Guinea (Table JZ3)
1816 Equatorial Guinea. Spanish Guinea (Table JZ3)
1817 Ifni (Table JZ3)
1818 Italian East Africa (Table JZ3)
1820 Italian Somaliland (Table JZ3)
1822 Kenya (Table JZ3)
1824 Lesotho. Basutoland (Table JZ3)
1826 Liberia (Table JZ3)
1828 Libya (Table JZ3)
1830 Madagascar. Malagasy Republic (Table JZ3)
1835 Malawi. Nyasaland (Table JZ3)
1838 Mali. French Sudan (Table JZ3)

Scope of international relations. Political theory. Diplomacy
Scope of international relations with regard to countries, territories, regions, etc. By country, territory, or region
Africa -- Continued

1841 Mauritania (Table JZ3)
1843 Mauritius (Table JZ3)
1846 Mayotte (Table JZ3)
1849 Morocco (Table JZ3)
1852 Mozambique. Portuguese East Africa (Table JZ3)
1855 Namibia. German South Africa. Southwest Africa (Table JZ3)
1859 Niger (Table JZ3)
1862 Nigeria. Colony and Protectorate of Nigeria (Table JZ3)
1870 Réunion (Table JZ3)
1876 Rwanda. Ruanda-Urundi (Table JZ3)
1882 Saint Helena (Table JZ3)
1885 Sao Tome and Principe (Table JZ3)
1890 Senegal (Table JZ3)
1894 Seychelles (Table JZ3)
1897 Sierra Leone (Table JZ3)
1900 Somalia. Somali Republic (Table JZ3)
South Africa, Republic of
1905 General (Table JZ3)
1908.A-Z Provinces and self-governing territories, etc., A-Z
Including former independant homelands
1908.B66 Bophuthatswana (Table JZ4)
1908.C36 Cape of Good Hope (Kaapland) (to 1994) (Table JZ4)
1908.C57 Ciskei (Table JZ4)
1908.E36 Eastern Cape (Table JZ4)
Eastern Transvaal see JZ1908.M68
1908.F74 Free State. Orange Free State (Table JZ4)
1908.G38 Gauteng (Table JZ4)
1908.K83 KwaZulu-Natal. Natal (Table JZ4)
Including former KwaZulu Homeland areas
1908.M68 Mpulamanga. Eastern Transvaal (Table JZ4)
Natal see JZ1908.K83
1908.N64 North West (Table JZ4)
1908.N66 Northern Cape (Table JZ4)
1908.N67 Northern Province (Table JZ4)
Northern Transvaal see JZ1908.N67
Orange Free State (Oranje Vrystaat) see JZ1908.F74
1908.T73 Transkei (Table JZ4)
1908.T74 Transvaal (Table JZ4)
1908.V46 Venda (Table JZ4)
1908.W47 Western Cape (Table JZ4)
1917 Spanish West Africa (to 1958) (Table JZ3)
1918 Spanish Sahara (to 1975) (Table JZ3)

Scope of international relations. Political theory. Diplomacy
Scope of international relations with regard to countries, territories, regions, etc. By country, territory, or region
Africa -- Continued
1920 Sudan (Table JZ3)
1923 Swaziland (Table JZ3)
1927 Tanzania. Tanganyika (Table JZ3)
1930 Togo. Togoland (Table JZ3)
1933 Tunisia (Table JZ3)
1936 Uganda (Table JZ3)
1940 Zaire. Congo (Democratic Republic) (Table JZ3)
1944 Zambia. Northern Rhodesia (Table JZ3)
1947 Zanzibar (to 1964) (Table JZ3)
1950 Zimbabwe. Southern Rhodesia (Table JZ3)
Pacific Area
1980 General works
Including works on both Pacific and Asian areas combined
Australia
1990 General (Table JZ3)
1995.A-Z States and territories, A-Z
Australian Antarctic Territory see JZ2060
1995.A88 Australian Capital Territory
1995.N48 New South Wales
1995.N67 Norfolk Island
1995.N673 Northern Territory
1995.Q84 Queensland
1995.S68 South Australia
1995.T38 Tasmania
1995.V63 Victoria
1995.W48 Western Australia
2015 New Zealand (Table JZ3)
Ross Dependency see JZ2060
Other Pacific Area jurisdictions
2020 American Samoa (Table JZ3)
2021 British New Guinea (Territory of Papua) (Table JZ3)
2022 Cook Islands (Table JZ3)
2024 Easter Island (Table JZ3)
2026 Fiji (Table JZ3)
2028 French Polynesia (Table JZ3)
2030 German New Guinea (to 1914) (Table JZ3)
2032 Guam (Table JZ3)
2037 Kiribati (Table JZ3)
2038 Marshall Islands (Table JZ3)
2040 Micronesia (Federated States) (Table JZ3)
2042 Midway Islands (Table JZ3)
2043 Nauru (Table JZ3)
2044 Netherlands New Guinea (to 1963) (Table JZ3)

Scope of international relations. Political theory. Diplomacy
Scope of international relations with regard to countries, territories, regions, etc. By country, territory, or region
Pacific Area
Other Pacific Area jurisdictions -- Continued
2046 New Caledonia (Table JZ3)
2047 Niue (Table JZ3)
2048 Northern Mariana Islands (Table JZ3)
2049 Pacific Islands (Trust Territory) (Table JZ3)
2050 Palau (Table JZ3)
2051 Papua New Guinea (Table JZ3)
2052 Pitcairn Island (Table JZ3)
Samoa see JZ2059
2053 Solomon Islands (Table JZ3)
2054 Tonga (Table JZ3)
2055 Tuvalu (Table JZ3)
2056 Vanuatu (Table JZ3)
2057 Wake Islands (Table JZ3)
2058 Wallis and Futuna Islands (Table JZ3)
2059 Western Samoa. Samoa (Table JZ3)
2060 Antarctica (Table JZ3)
<2064-3669> Publicists. Writers on public international law (jus naturae et gentium)
see KZ2064+
State territory and its parts
3674 Periodicals
3675 General works
Boundaries
For non-legal works on boundary disputes see classes D - F
For boundary treaties see KZ176+
<3684> General
see JC323, Political geography; KZ3684, Law of nations
3685 Natural boundaries
Including mountains, rivers, lakes, etc.
For particular rivers, mountains, etc., see the region
For maritime boundaries see KZA1430+
International waters
3686 General works
The oceans
Including high seas areas and zones
For use of the ocean, see the subject, e. g. K4150+ Navigation; K3891+ High seas fisheries and fishery zones
For law of the sea, see subclass KZA
3690 General works
3691.A-Z Particular high seas areas and zones, A-Z
Including territorial waters

State territory and its parts
International waters
The oceans
Particular high seas areas and zones, A-Z -- Continued
3691.I64 Indian Ocean Region
3691.M44 Mediterranean Region
3691.N67 North Atlantic Region
3691.P33 Pacific Ocean Region
3691.S68 South Atlantic Region
Rivers, lakes and landlocked seas
For their function as international waterways, i.e., highways of transportation, see subclass HE
3700 General works
3705.A-Z Particular rivers, lakes, and landlocked seas, A-Z
Interoceanic canals
Cf. HE528+ Transportation
3710 General works
Panama Canal
3715 General works
Traffic and tolls see HE537+
Construction and maintenance see TC774+
3720 Nicaragua Canal
3730 Suez Canal
3740 Donau Canal
3750.A-Z Other interoceanic canals, A-Z
Straits
Class here works on the linkages between oceans and seas
3760 General works
Particular straits
3780 Black Sea Straits. Bosphorus and Dardanelles
3810 Baltic Straits
Including Skagerrak, Kattegat, and the Sound
3825 Strait of Dover
3835 Epirus (Geeece and Albania)
3845 Strait of Gibraltar
3855 Magellan Straits
3865 Malacca Straits
Gulfs and bays
3870 General works
3875.A-Z Particular gulfs and bays, A-Z
3875.A68 Aqaba, Gulf of
3875.P48 Persian Gulf
3875.S53 Sidra, Gulf of
3876 Antarctica
Cf. KWX1+ Law
3877 Outer space, the moon and other celestial bodies
Cf. KZD1002+ Space law

	The international community and its members
	Cf. KZ3900+ The state in international law
3900	General works
4034	Sovereign states
	Alliances see JZ1314
4059	Semi-sovereign, dependent, and vassal states. Subnational governments
	International organizations and associations
4835.A-Z	Periodicals
	e.g.
4835.I58	International association statutes series
4835.I583	International organization
4836.A-Z	Annuals. Yearbooks
	e.g.
4836.I58	International Geneva Yearbook
4836.Y43	Yearbook of international organizations
4837	Handbooks
4838	Directories
4839	General works
	Including compends, form books, popular works, essays, festschriften, etc.
4840.A-Z	Manuals and other works for particular groups of users. By user, A-Z
	Political non-governmental organizations. NGOs
	Including international freedom and liberation organizations
	For political organizations limited in their jurisdiction by subject, see the subject
4841	General works
4842.A-Z	Universal organizations. By name, A-Z
	e.g.
4842.A66	Amnesty International
4842.I68	Inter-Parliamentary Union. IPU
4842.S63	Socialist International
	War Resisters International see JZ5576
4842.W67	World Association of World Federalists
4842.W673	World Federation Movement
4842.W675	World Future Council
	Regional organizations
4843.A-Z	Organizations in the Americas. By name, A-Z
4844.A-Z	Organizations in Europe. By name, A-Z
	e.g.
4844.P36	Pan-European Union
4844.U65	Union of European Federalists
4845.A-Z	Organizations in Asia. By name, A-Z
4846.A-Z	Organizations in the Middle East. By name, A-Z
	e.g.
4846.H37	Harakat al-muqawamah al-Islamiyah

International organizations and associations

Political non-governmental organizations. NGOs

Regional organizations

Organizations in the Middle East. By name, A-Z -- Continued

4846.L4 League of Arab States

Cf. KME51+ Regional comparative and uniform law

Palestinian Liberation Organization (PLO) see DS119.7+

4847.A-Z Organizations in Africa. By name, A-Z

African National Congress see JQ1900+

4848.A-Z Organizations in Pacific Area. By name, A-Z

e.g.

4848.P3 Pacific Economic Cooperation Council

Cf. KVE401+ Regional comparative and uniform law

Intergovernmental organizations. IGOs

4850 General works

Universal

4852 General works

League of Nations

4853 Bibliography

4860 Periodicals

4860.3 Annuals. Yearbooks

<4860.5> Official journal

see KZ4860.5

League of Nations documents see JZ4895+

4861 Intergovernmental congresses and conferences. League of Nations conferences. By name of the congress or conference

Non-governmental congresses and conferences see JZ4871

<4862-4867> Official acts. Official reports

see KZ4862+

4868 Dictionaries. Thesauri

4869 Handbooks. Manuals. Reference aids

Including all organs of the League, international unions, bureaus, etc. under direction of the League

Form books. Graphic materials see JZ4871

Directories

4870 General

4870.2 List of delegates

4870.5.A-Z Societies. Associations. Academies. Institutes, etc., A-Z

4870.7 Conferences. Symposia

4871 General works

Including collections, compends, essays, festschriften, form books, etc.

International organizations and associations
Intergovernmental organizations. IGOs
Universal
League of Nations -- Continued
League internal (intra-organizational) and external (foreign) relations
Including member nations, and relations with its specialized agencies

4871.3	General works
4871.5.A-Z	Membership and League relations with member nations, A-Z
4871.7.A-Z	Relation with non-member nations, A-Z
4871.8.A-Z	Relation with other international organizations, A-Z
	The Covenant of the League of Nations
4872	General works
	Organs and international unions, bureaus, etc. under direction of the League
	Class here general works on organs and institutions of the League collectively
<4873-4884>	Organization law
	see KZ4873+
4887	General works
4887.5.A-4887.Z	By organ, union, bureau, etc., A-Z
4887.5.A77	Assembly
	For list of delegates see JZ4870.2
4887.5.B87	Bureau International d'assistance
4887.5.C68	Council
4887.5.I55	International Commission for Air Navigation
4887.5.I65	International Institute for Unification of Private Law
4887.5.I67	International Institute of Intellectual Cooperation
4887.5.I68	International Relief Union
4887.5.N35	Nansen International Office for Refugees
4887.5.P74	Preparatory Commission for the Disarmament Conference
4887.5.S43	Secretariat
	League of Nations documents
	Official records
4895	Assembly (Conference of the Members of the League)
4910	Council
	International unions, bureaus, organizations, etc. under the direction of the League
4920	International Institute for Unification of Private Law
4923	International Institute of Intellectual Cooperation
4926	International Commission for Air Navigation

International organizations and associations
Intergovernmental organizations. IGOs
Universal
League of Nations
The Covenant of the League of Nations
League of Nations documents
Official records
International unions, bureaus, organizations, etc. under the direction of the League -- Continued
4929 Bureau International d'assistance
4932 International Relief Union
4934 Nansen International Office for Refugees
United Nations
Including works on the specialized agencies agencies of the United Nations treated collectively
Bibliography
General bibliography
Including indexes, registers and other finding aids
Class here bibliographies that cover all United Nations bodies
4935 Serials
4935.C87 Current bibliographic information (1971-1993)
4935.D35 Daily List of Documents Issued at Headquarters
4935.M66 Monthly bibliography (1978-)
Including predecessor Monthly List of Books Catalogued at the Library of the United Nations
4935.R43 READEX Electronic Index to United Nations Document and Publications (CD-ROM) (1990-)
4935.U53 UNBIS Plus (CD-ROM) (1995-)
4935.U54 UNDOC: Current Index (1979-)
Including predecessor United Nations Documents Index: United Nations and Specialized Agencies Documents and Publications, 1950-1963, and UNDEX
4935.U65 United Nations Publications Catalogue (1985-)
Including predecessors United Nations Sales Publications and United Nations Publications

International organizations and associations
Intergovernmental organizations. IGOs
Universal
United Nations
Bibliography
General bibliography -- Continued

4936 Monographs. By date

e. g. Bibliography of United Nations thesauri, classifications, nomenclatures; Books in Print of the United Nations System (1992), Directory of United Nations Documents and Archival sources (1991), Directory of United Nations Serial Publications (1988), The complete Reference Guide to United Nations Sales Publications, 1946-1978 (1982), A Guide to the Use of United Nations Documents (1962), United Nations Document Series Symbols, 1978-1984 (1986), United Nations Documentation: A Brief Guide (1994)

By United Nations organs, bodies and programs
Collective see JZ5005
Individual see JZ5006+
International Court of Justice. Indexes, registers and digests to decisions and pleadings see KZ199+
Administrative Tribunal
see KZ5274
By United Nations mandate see JZ4971+

4945 Periodicals

Class here periodicals and series available through standing orders or subscriptions

e. g.

4945.A66 Annual Review of United Nations Affairs
4945.D56 The Diplomatic World Bulletin and Delegates World Bulletin
4945.J68 Journal of the United Nations
4945.U63 UN Chronicle
Yearbook of the United Nations see JZ4947
4947 Yearbook of the United Nations
<4949> United Nations Juridical Yearbook
see KZ4949
UN International Commission Yearbook see KZ21
4952 Monographic series (numbered)
e. g.
4952.U65 The United Nations Blue Book Series
United Nations documents and publications see JZ5010+

International organizations and associations
Intergovernmental organizations. IGOs
Universal
United Nations -- Continued
Inter-governmental congresses and conferences
4954 General works
UN conferences see JZ5090
<4968> Encyclopedias
see KZ4968
4969 Dictionaries
e.g.
4969.D74 Dreisprachenliste: Vereinte Nationen
4970 Handbooks. Reference aids
Class here works on facts and functions of the UN
For UN lawmaking and development of international law see KZ4992.7+
United Nations activities by mandate. United Nations and particular disciplines and topics
4971 International security, disarmament, and conflict resolution
e. g. The Blue Helmets; Palestine question: a select bibliography (1976-1993); The United Nations and Cambodia; The United Nations and El Salvador
4972 Economic and financial questions, trade and development
4972.3 Education
4972.5 Environmental affairs
4973 Social issues. Health
4973.5 Humanitarian aid. Refugee assistance. Disaster relief
4974 Human rights
Including women's rights, children's rights, and indigenous people's rights
e. g. United Nations Activities in the Field of Human Rights; The United Nations and Human Rights
4975 Trusteeship Issues and Decolonization
e. g. The United Nations and Namibia
4976 Administrative, personnel, and budgetary questions
4978 Form books. Graphic materials
Directories
4979 General
e. g. Directory for the United Nations System; A Guide to Information at the United Nations (1995); Who is Who in the United Nations and Related Agencies (1992)
4980 Lists of member-nations, delegations, observers, etc.
4981 Lists of missions, observer missions, etc.
4981.P47 Permanent Missions to the United Nations

International organizations and associations
Intergovernmental organizations. IGOs
Universal
United Nations
Directories -- Continued

4982 Lists of United Nations depository libraries, United Nations information centers, etc.

4983.A-Z Societies. Associations. Academies. Institutes, etc. By name, A-Z
e. g.

4983.A33 Academic Council on the United Nations Systems. ACUNS

4983.U65 United Nations Association for the United States

4984 Conferences. Symposia

4984.5 General works

4984.6 Popular works, juvenile literature, etc.

Genesis of the United Nations

4986 General works

4988 Intergovernmental preliminary congresses and conferences related to the establishment of the UN
Including Dumbarton Oaks Conversations (1944) and San Francisco Conference (1945)

The United Nations system. Organization law.
Constitution of the United Nations
see KZ4985+

United Nations internal (intra-organizational) and external (foreign) relations
Including member nations, observers, and relations to its specialized agencies

4995 General works

4997.5.A-Z Membership and relations with member nations, A-Z

5002.A-Z Relations with non-member nations, A-Z

5003.A-Z Relation with intergovernmental organizations and other international organizations, A-Z
For observer questions see KZ4998.7

United Nations organs, bodies and programs
Class here works on structure, organs, programs and bodies of the United Nations
Including bibliography

5005 General (Collective)

Individual
General Assembly

5006.A66 Annotated Preliminary List of Items to be included in the Provisional Agenda of the [] Session of the General Assembly (1964?-)

JZ

International organizations and associations
Intergovernmental organizations. IGOs
Universal
United Nations
United Nations organs, bodies and programs
Individual
General Assembly -- Continued
5006.I64 Index to proceedings of the General Assembly (1950/51-)
5006.I65 Index to Resolutions of the General Assembly, 1946-1970 (1972)
5006.2 General works
Security Council
5006.5.I64 Index to Proceedings of the Security Council (1964-)
5006.5.I65 Index to Resolutions of the Security Council, 1946-1991 (1992)
5006.5.R46 Repertoire of the Practice of the Security Council
5006.7 General works
Economic and Social Council
5007.I64 Index to Proceedings of the Economic and Social Council (1952-)
5007.3 General works
Trusteeship Council
5007.5.I64 Index to Proceedings of the Trusteeship Council (1952-)
5007.7 General works
5008 Secretariat
5008.5 Office of the United Nations High Commissioner for Human Rights
5009 Office of the United Nations High Commissioner for Refugees
5009.5.A-Z Other United Nations organs, bodies and programs, A-Z
5009.5.A44 Alliance of Civilizations. UNAOC
5009.5.I68 International Trade Centre. UNCTAD/GATT
5009.5.T73 Trade and Development Board. TDBOR
5009.5.U54 UNICEF. United Nations International Children's Emergency
5009.5.U545 United Nations Conference on Trade and Development. UNCTAD
5009.5.U55 United Nations Development Programme. UNDP
5009.5.U553 United Nations Educational, Scientific, and Cultural Organization. Unesco
For official records of Unesco see JZ5220
5009.5.U555 United Nations Environment Programme. UNEP

International organizations and associations
Intergovernmental organizations. IGOs
Universal
United Nations
United Nations organs, bodies and programs
Individual
Other United Nations organs, bodies and programs -- Continued

5009.5.U558 United Nations Human Settlements Programme. UN-HABITAT
5009.5.U56 United Nations International Drug Control Programme. UNDCP
5009.5.U563 United Nations Office for Project Services. UNOPS
5009.5.U565 United Nations Population Fund. UNFPA
5009.5.U57 United Nations Research Institute for Social Development. UNRISD
5009.5.U575 United Nations University. UNU
5009.5.W67 World Food Council. WFC
5009.5.W675 World Food Programme. WFP
5009.5.W69 World Meteorological Organization

United Nations documents and publications
Official records
General Assembly Official Records. GAOR. By session, e. g. regular, special, and emergency session

5010.2 Regular session

Within each session, subarrange by plenary meetings, annexes, committee meeting records and supplements

Plenary meetings. Verbatim records of meetings

Document series symbol since 5th Session A/PV.-

Beginning with 31st Session, document series symbol includes session number, e. g. A/31/PV.-, etc.

Annexes. By agenda item numbers

Committee meeting records

General Committee

Document series symbol A/BUR/session/SR.-

Special Political Committee

Document series symbol A/SPC/session/SR.-

Beginning with 48th Session, merged with the Decolonization Committee to constitute the Fourth Committee

International organizations and associations
Intergovernmental organizations. IGOs
Universal
United Nations
United Nations documents and publications
Official records
General Assembly Official Records. GAOR. By session, e. g. regular, special, and emergency session
Regular session
Committee meeting records -- Continued
First Committee (Disarmament and International Security)
Document series symbol A/C.1/session/PV.-
Second Committee (Economic and Financial)
Document series symbol A/C.2/session/PV.-
Third Committee (Social, Humanitarian and Cultural)
Document series symbol A/C.3/session/SR.-
Fourth Committee (Special Political and Decolonization. Previously Trusteeship)
Document series symbol A/C.4/session/SR.-
Fifth Committee (Administrative and Budgetary)
Document series symbol A/C.5/session /SR.-
Sixth Committee (Legal)
Document series symbol A/C.6/session/SR.-
Supplements
Here are entered supplements in numerical order; the listing begins with the 36th Session (1981/82) and includes later changes and new supplements issued for subsequent sessions
Supplement No. 1: Report of the Secretary-General on the Work of the Organization
Supplement No. 2: Report of the Security Council (2nd- Session)
Supplement No. 3: Report of the Economic & Social Council (2nd- Session)
Supplement No. 4: Report of the International Court of Justice (33rd- Session)
Supplement No. 5: Financial Report and Audited Financial Statements for the Biennium (37th- Session)
Supplement No. 5A: United Nations Development Programme: financial report and audited financial statements

International organizations and associations
Intergovernmental organizations. IGOs
Universal
United Nations
United Nations documents and publications
Official records
General Assembly Official Records. GAOR. By session, e. g. regular, special, and emergency session
Regular session
Supplements -- Continued
Supplement No. 5B: United Nations Children's Fund: financial report and audited financial statements
Supplement No. 5C: United Nations Relief and Works Agency for Palestine Refugees in the Near East: financial report and audited financial statements
Supplement No. 5D: United Nations Institute for Training and Research: financial report and audited financial statements
Supplement No. 5E: Voluntary funds administered by the United Nations High Commissioner for Refugees: audited financial statements
Supplement No. 5F: Fund of the United Nations Environment Programme: financial report and audited financial statements (37th- session)
Supplement No. 5G: United Nations Population Fund (formerly United Nations Fund for Population Activities): financial report and audited financial statements
Supplement No. 5H: United Nations Habitat and Human Settlements Foundations: financial report and audited financial statements (37th- session)
Supplement No. 6: Programme Budget for the Biennium (alternate title: Medium-Term Plan for the Period ...) (30th- Session)
Supplement No. 7: Advisory Committee on Administrative and Budgetary Questions. Report on the Proposed Programme Budget for the Biennium (33rd- Session)
Supplement No. 8: Report of the Commission on Human Settlements

International organizations and associations
Intergovernmental organizations. IGOs
Universal
United Nations
United Nations documents and publications
Official records
General Assembly Official Records. GAOR. By session, e. g. regular, special, and emergency session
Regular session
Supplements -- Continued
Supplement No. 9: Report of the United Nations Joint Staff Pension Board
Supplement No. 10: Report of the International Law Commission
Supplement No. 11: Report of the Committee on Contributions
Supplement No. 12: Report of the United Nations High Commissioner for Refugees
Supplement No. 13: Report of the Commissioner-General of the United Nations Relief and Works Agency for Palestine Refugees in the Near East
Supplement No. 14: Report of the Executive Director of the United Nations Institute for Training and Research
Supplement No. 15: Report of the Trade and Development Board
Supplement No. 16: Report of the Industrial Development Board (22nd to 40th Session)
Supplement No. 17: Report of the United Nations Commission on International Trade Law
Supplement No. 18: Report of the Committee on the Elimination of Racial Discrimination
Supplement No. 19: Report of the World Food Council
Supplement No. 20: Report of the Committee on the Peaceful Uses of Outer Space
Supplement No. 21: Report of the Committee on Information
Supplement No. 22: Report of the Special Committee Against Apartheid (26th Session - 48th Session)

International organizations and associations
Intergovernmental organizations. IGOs
Universal
United Nations
United Nations documents and publications
Official records
General Assembly Official Records. GAOR. By session, e. g. regular, special, and emergency session
Regular session
Supplements -- Continued
Supplement No. 22: Report of the Ad Hoc Committee on the Elaboration of an International Convention Dealing with the Safety and Security of United Nations and Associated Personnel (49th Session)
Supplement No. 22: Report of the Ad Hoc Committee on the Establishment of an International Criminal Court (50th- Session)
Supplement No. 23: Report of the Special Committee on the Situation with Regard to the Implementation of the Declaration of the Granting of Independence to Colonial Countries and Peoples (24th- Session)
Supplement No. 24: Report of the United Nations Council for Namibia (24th - 44th Session)
Supplement No. 24: Report of the Preparatory Committee for the World Conference on Human Rights (46th - 47th Session)
Supplement No. 24: Report of the Preparatory Committee for the World Summit for Social Development (48th - 49th Session)
Supplement No. 25: Report of the Governing Council. United Nations Environment Programme (28th- Session)
Supplement No. 26: Report of the Committee on Relations with the Host Country (27th- Session)
Supplement No. 27: Report of the Committee on Disarmament (34th - 38th Session)
Supplement No. 28: Report of the Ad Hoc Committee on the World Disarmament Conference (29th - 41st Session)

International organizations and associations
Intergovernmental organizations. IGOs
Universal
United Nations
United Nations documents and publications
Official records
General Assembly Official Records. GAOR. By session, e. g. regular, special, and emergency session
Regular session
Supplements -- Continued
Supplement No. 29: Report of the Ad Hoc Committee on the Indian Ocean (28th- Session)
Supplement No. 30: Report of the International Civil Service Commission (30th- Session)
Supplement No. 31: Report of the Council of the United Nations University (30th - 47th Session)
Supplement No. 32: Report of the Committee on Conferences (33rd- Session)
Supplement No. 33: Report of the Special Committee on the Charter of the United Nations and on the Strengthening of the Role of the organization (31st- Session)
Supplement No. 34: Report of the Joint Inspection Unit (35th- Session)
Supplement No. 35: Report of the Committee on the Exercise of the Inalienable Rights of the Palentinian People (31st- Session)
Supplement No. 36: Report of the Ad Hoc Committee on the Drafting of an International Convention Against Apartheid in Sports (32nd - 40th Session)
Supplement No. 36: Report of the Committee on the Development and Utilization of New and Renewable Sources of Energy (43d - 45th Session)
Supplement No. 36: Report of the Preparatory Committee for the Global Conference on the Sustainable Development of Small Island Developing States (48th Session)
Supplement No. 36: Report of the United Nations High Commissioner for Human Rights (49th- Session)

International organizations and associations
Intergovernmental organizations. IGOs
Universal
United Nations
United Nations documents and publications
Official records
General Assembly Official Records. GAOR. By session, e. g. regular, special, and emergency session
Regular session
Supplements -- Continued
Supplement No. 37: Report of the Intergovernmental Committee on Science and Technology for Development (35th - 46th Session)
Supplement No. 37: Report of the Preparatory Committee for the United Nations Conference on Human Settlements (HABITAT II) (49th- Session)
Supplement No. 38: Report of the Committee for Programme and Coordination (31st - 41st Session)
Supplement No. 38: Report of the Committee on the Elimination of Discrimination against Women (42nd- Session)
Supplement No. 39: Report of the High-level Meeting on the Review of Technical Co-operation among Developing Countries (35th- Session)
Supplement No. 40: Report of the Human Rights Committee
Supplement No. 41: Report of the Special Committee on Enhancing the Effectiveness of the Principle on Non-Use of Force in International Relations (33rd - 42nd Session)
Supplement No. 41: Report of the Ad Hoc Committee of the Whole for the Preparation of the International Development Strategy for the Fourth United Nations Development Decade (44th - 45th Session)

International organizations and associations
Intergovernmental organizations. IGOs
Universal
United Nations
United Nations documents and publications
Official records
General Assembly Official Records. GAOR. By session, e. g. regular, special, and emergency session
Regular session
Supplements -- Continued
Supplement No. 41: Report of the Ad Hoc Committee of the Whole for the Final Review and Appraisal of the United Nations Programme of Action for African Economic Recovery and Development, 1986-1990(46th Session)
Supplement No. 41: Report of the Committee on the Rights of the Child (47th- Session)
Supplement No. 42: Report of the Disarmament Commission (33rd- Session)
Supplement No. 43: Report of the Preparatory Committee for the United Nations Conference on New and Renewable Sources of Energy (35th Session)
Supplement No. 43: Report of the Ad Hoc Comnmittee on the Drafting of an International Convention against the Recruitment, Use, Financing and Training of Mercenaries (36th - 44th Session)
Supplement No. 43: Report of the Intergovernmental Group to Monitor the Supply and Shipping of Oil and Petroleum Products to South Africa (45th - 48th Session)
Supplement No. 43: Report of the High-level Open-ended Working Group on the Financial Situation of the United Nations (49th- Session)
Supplement No. 44: Report of the Committee of Governmental Experts to Evaluate the Present Structure of the Secretariat in the Administrative, Finance and Personnel Areas (37th Session)

International organizations and associations
Intergovernmental organizations. IGOs
Universal
United Nations
United Nations documents and publications
Official records
General Assembly Official Records. GAOR. By session, e. g. regular, special, and emergency session
Regular session
Supplements -- Continued
Supplement No. 44: Report of the Committee on the Development and Utilization of New and Renewable Sources of Energy (38th - 41st Session)
Supplement No. 44: Report of the Intergovernmental Group to Monitor the Supply and Shipping of Oil and Petroleum Products to South Africa (43rd - 44th Session)
Supplement No. 44: Report of the Committee against Torture (45th Session)
Supplement No. 44: Report of the Intergovernmental Group to Monitor the Supply and Shipping of Oil and Petroleum Products to South Africa (46th Session)
Supplement No. 44: Report of the Committee on Torture (47th- Session)
Supplement No. 45: Report of the Preparatory Committee for the United Nations Conference on the Least Developed Countries (35th - 36th Session)
Supplement No. 45: Report of the United Nations Scientific Committee on the Effects of Atomic Radiaiton (37th Session)
Supplement No. 45: Report of the Committee on the Elimination of Discrimination against Women (38th - 41st Session)
Supplement No. 45: Report of the Intergovernmental Group to Monitor the Supply and Shipping of Oil and Petroleum Products to South Africa (42nd Session)
Supplement No. 45: Report of the United Nations Scientific Committee on the Effects of Atomic Radiation (43rd Session)

International organizations and associations
Intergovernmental organizations. IGOs
Universal
United Nations
United Nations documents and publications
Official records
General Assembly Official Records. GAOR. By session, e. g. regular, special, and emergency session
Regular session
Supplements -- Continued
Supplement No. 45: Report of the Preparatory Committee of the Whole for the Special Session of the General Assembly Devoted to International Economic Co-operation, in Particular to the Revitalization of Economic Growth and Development of the Developing Countries (44th Session)
Supplement No. 45: Report of the Commission against Apartheid in Sports (45th - 47th Session)
Supplement No. 46: Report of the Preparatory Committee for the Second United Nations Conference on the Exploration and Peaceful Uses of Outer Space (37th Session)
Supplement No. 46: Report of the Preparatory Committee for the Internationsl Conference on the Question of Palestine (38th Session)
Supplement No. 46: Report of the Preparatory Committee for the Third Special Session of the General Assembly Devoted to Disarmament (42nd Session)
Supplement No. 46: Report of the Committee against Torture (43rd - 44th Session)
Supplement No. 46: Report of the Preparatory Committee for the United Nations Conference on Environment and Development (45th Session)
Supplement No. 46: Report of the Committee against Torture (46th Session)
Supplement No. 46: Report of the United Nations Scientific Committee on the Effects of Atomic Radiation (46th - Session)

International organizations and associations
Intergovernmental organizations. IGOs
Universal
United Nations
United Nations documents and publications
Official records
General Assembly Official Records. GAOR. By session, e. g. regular, special, and emergency session
Regular session
Supplements -- Continued
Supplement No. 47: Report of the Ad Hoc Committee on Subsidiary Organs (35th Session)
Supplement No. 47: Report of the Preparatory Committee for the United Nations Conference on New and Renewable Sources of Energy (36th Session)
Supplement No. 47: Report of the Interim Committee on New and Renewable Sources of Energy (37th Session)
Supplement No. 47: Resolutions and Decisions Adopted by the General Assembly (38th Session)
Supplement No. 47: Report of the Preparatory Committee for the United Nations Conference for the Promotion of International Cooperation in the Peaceful Uses of Nuclear Energy (39th - 41st Session)
Supplement No. 47: Report of the Commission against Apartheid in Sports (44th Session)
Supplement No. 47: Report of the Open-ended Working Group on the Question of Equitable Representation on and Increase in the Membership of the Security Council (48th- Session)
Supplement No. 48: Resolutions and Decisions Adopted by the General Assembly (35th Session)
Supplement No. 48: REport of the Preparatory Committee for the United Nations Conference for the Promotion of International Cooperation in the Peaceful Uses of Nuclear Energy (36th - 37th Session)

International organizations and associations
Intergovernmental organizations. IGOs
Universal
United Nations
United Nations documents and publications
Official records
General Assembly Official Records. GAOR. By session, e. g. regular, special, and emergency session
Regular session
Supplements -- Continued
Supplement No. 48: Report of the Committee on the Review and Appraisal of the Implementation of the International Devleopment Strategy for the Third United Nations Development Decade (46th Session)
Supplement No. 48: Report of the Preparatory Committee for the United Nations Conference on Environment and Development (46th Session)
Supplement No. 48: Report of the Preparatory Committee for the Fiftieth Anniversary of the United Nations (47th- Session)
Supplement No. 49: Report of the Preparatory Committee for the Second Special Session of the General Assembly Devoted to Disarmament (36th Session)
Supplement No. 49: Report of the Preparatory Committee for the International Conference on the Question of Palestine (37th Session)
Supplement No. 49: Report of the Preparatory Committee for the 40th Anniversary of the United Nations (39th Session)
Supplement No. 49: Report of the Group of High-level Intergovernmental Experts to Review the Efficiency of the Administrative and Financial Functioning of the United Nations (41st Session)
Supplement No. 49: Resolutions and Decisions Adopted by the General Assembly (43rd- Session)
Supplement No. 51: Resolutions and Decisions Adopted by the General Assembly (36th - 37th, and 39th Session)

International organizations and associations
Intergovernmental organizations. IGOs
Universal
United Nations
United Nations documents and publications
Official records
General Assembly Official Records. GAOR. By session, e. g. regular, special, and emergency session
Regular session
Supplements -- Continued
Supplement No. 51: Report of the Preparatory Committee for the Internationsl Conference on the Relationship between Disarmament and Development (40th - 41st Session)
Supplement No. 52: Report of the Ad Hoc Committee to Review the Implementation of the Charter of Economic Rights and Duties of States (40th Session)
Supplement No. 53: Resolutions and Decisions Adopted by the General Assembly (40th Session)

5010.3 Special sessions
Subarrange by plenary meetings, annexes, committee meeting records and supplements
1st Special Session (28 April - 15 May 1947)
On constituting and instructing a special committee to prepare for the consideration of question of Palestine at the 2nd regular session
Plenary Meetings, 68th-79th, and Annexes (Vol. I)
General Committee: verbatim record of meetings, 28th-34th (Vol. II)
Main Committees: verbatim records of meetings (Vol. III)

International organizations and associations
Intergovernmental organizations. IGOs
Universal
United Nations
United Nations documents and publications
Official records
General Assembly Official Records. GAOR. By session, e. g. regular, special, and emergency session
Special sessions -- Continued
2nd Special Session (16 April - 14 May 1948)
On the question of the future government of Palestine
Plenary Meetings: summary records of meetings, 129th-135th (Vol. I)
Main Committees: summary records of meetings (Vol. II)
Annex to Volumes I and II
Supplement No. 1: United Nations Palestine Commission: Report, A/532
Supplement No. 2: Resolutions (A/555)
3rd Special Session (21-25 August, 1961)
On the grave situation in Tunisia obtaining since 19 July 1961
Plenary Meetings (A/PV.996-1006) & annexes
Supplement No. 1: Resolutions (A/4860)
4th Special Session (14 May - 27 June 1963)
On the financial situation of the Organization
Plenary Meetings (A/PV.1203-1205)
Annexes
Fifth Committee: Summary Records of Meetings (A/C.5/SR.984-1005)
Supplement No. 1: Resolutions (A/5441)
5th Special Session (21 April - 13 June 1967)
On question of South West Africa; comprehensive review of the whole question of peace-keeping operations in all their aspects
Plenary Meetings (A/PV.1502-1524)
Annexes
Summary Reocrd of the 1680th Meeting of the Fourth Committee (a/C.4/SR.1680)
Supplement No. 1: Resolutions (A/6657)

International organizations and associations
Intergovernmental organizations. IGOs
Universal
United Nations
United Nations documents and publications
Official records
General Assembly Official Records. GAOR. By session, e. g. regular, special, and emergency session
Special sessions -- Continued
6th Special Session (9 April - 2 May 1974)
To study the problems of raw materials and development
Plenary Meetings (A/PV.2207-2231)
Annexes
Summary Records of Meetings: General Committee and Ad Hoc Committee of the 6th Special Session (A/BUR/SR.217 and A/ AC.166/SR.1-21)
Supplement No. 1: Resolutions (A/9559)
7th Special Session (1-16 September 1975)
On development and international economic cooperation
Plenary Meetings (A/PV.2326-2349), Summary records of the 1st to the 3rd meetings: Ad Hoc Committee of the 7th special session (A/ AC.176SR.1-3) and Annexes
List of Delegations
Supplement No. 1: Resolutions (A/10301)
8th Special Session (20-21 April 1978)
On financing of the United Nations Interim Force in Lebanon
Plenary Meetings (A/S-8/PV.1-2), Sessional Fascicle: Fifth Committee and Annexes
Summary Records of the 1st-3rd Meeting: Fifth Committee (A/C.5/S-8/SR.1-3)
Supplement No. 1: Resolutions and Decisions (A/S-8/10)
9th Special Session (24 april - 3 May 1978)
On question of Namibia
Plenary Meetings (A/S09/PV.1-15) and Ad Hoc Committee of the 9th Special Session: Sessional Fascicle and Annexes
Supplement No. 1: Report of the United Nations Council for Namibia (A/S-9/4)

International organizations and associations
Intergovernmental organizations. IGOs
Universal
United Nations
United Nations documents and publications
Official records
General Assembly Official Records. GAOR. By session, e. g. regular, special, and emergency session
Special sessions -- Continued
10th Special Session (23 May - 30 June 1978)
i.e. 1st special session of the General Assembly on disarmament
Plenary Meetings (A/S-10/PV.1-27), Ad Hoc Committee of the 10th Special Session: Session Fascicle and Annexes
Verbatim Records of the Ad Hoc Committee of the 10th Special Session (A/S-10/AC.1/PV.1-16)
Supplement No. 1: Report of the Preparatory Committee for the Special Session of the General Assembly Devoted to Disarmament (A/S-10/1, Vols. I-VII)
Supplement No. 2: Special Report of the Conference of the Committee on Disarmament (A/S-10/2, Vols. I-II & Addendum)
Supplement No. 3: Special Report of the Ad Hoc Committee on the World Disarmament Conference (A/S-10/3, Vols. I-II)
Supplement No. 4: Resolutions and Decisions (A/S-10/4)

International organizations and associations
Intergovernmental organizations. IGOs
Universal
United Nations
United Nations documents and publications
Official records
General Assembly Official Records. GAOR. By session, e. g. regular, special, and emergency session
Special sessions -- Continued
11th Special Session (25 August - 15 September 1980)
On assessment of the progress made in the establishment of the new international economic order and appropriate action for the promotion of the development of developing countries and international economic cooperation
Plenary Meetings (A/S-11/PV.1-21), Ad Hoc Committee of the 11th Special Session: Sessional Fascicle and Annexes
Summary Reocrd of the 1st-5th Meeting (A/S-11/AC.1/SR.1-5)
Supplement No. 1: Report of the Committee of the Whole Established Under General Assembly Resolution 32/174 (A/S-11/1)
Supplement No. 2: Report of the Preparatory Committee for the New International Devleopment Strategy (A/S-11/2)
Supplement No. 3: Resolutions and Decisions (A/S-11/3)

International organizations and associations
Intergovernmental organizations. IGOs
Universal
United Nations
United Nations documents and publications
Official records
General Assembly Official Records. GAOR. By session, e. g. regular, special, and emergency session
Special sessions -- Continued
12th Special Session (7 June - 10 July 1982)
i.e. 2nd special session of the General Assembly devoted to disarmament: review of the implementation of the recommendations and decisions adopted by the General Assembly at its 10th Special Session; consideration and adoption of the Comprehensive Programme of Disarmament
Plenary Meetings (A/S-12/PV.1-20) and Annexes
Supplement No. 1: Report of the Preparatory Committee for the 2nd Special Session Devoted to Disarmament (A/S-12/1)
Supplement No. 2: Special Report of the Committee on Disarmament (A/S-12/2)
Supplement No. 3: Report of the Disarmament Commission (A/S-12/3)
Supplement No. 4: Report of the Ad Hoc Committee on the World Disarmament Conference (A/S-12/4)
Supplement No. 5: Report of the Ad Hoc Committee on the Indian Ocean (A/S-12/5)
Supplement No. 6: Resolutions and Decisions (A/S-12/6)
13th Special Session (17 May - 1 June 1986)
On the critical economic situation in Africa
Plenary Meetings (A/S-13/PV.1-8) and Annexes
Supplement No. 1: Report of the Preparatory Committee of the Whole for the Special Session of the General Assembly on the Critical Economic Situation in Africa (A/S-13/4)
Supplement No. 2: Resolutions and Decisions (A/S-13/16)

International organizations and associations
Intergovernmental organizations. IGOs
Universal
United Nations
United Nations documents and publications
Official records
General Assembly Official Records. GAOR. By session, e. g. regular, special, and emergency session
Special sessions -- Continued
14th Special Session (17-20 September 1986)
On question of Namibia
Plenary Meetings (A/S-14/PV.1-7) and Annexes
Supplement No. 1: Resolutions and Decisions (A/S-14/10)
15th Special Session (31 May - 25 June 1988)
i.e. 3rd Special session of the General Assembly devoted to disarmament: consideration and adoption of the Comprehensive Programme of Disarmament; role of the United Nations in the field of disarmament; World Disarmament Campaign; relationship between disarmament and development
Plenary Meetings (A/S-15/PV.1-22) and Annexes
Supplement No. 1: Report of the Preparatory Committee for the 3rd Special Session of the General Assembly Devoted to Disarmament (A/S-15/1)
Supplement No. 2: Report of the Conference on Disarmament to the 3rd Special Session of the General Assembly of the United Nations Devoted to Disarmament (A/S-15/2)
Supplement No. 3: Report of the Disarmament Commission (A/S-15/3)
Supplement No. 4: Report of the Ad Hoc Committee on the World Disarmament Conference (A/S-15/4)
Supplement No. 5: Report of the Ad Hoc Committee on the Indian Ocean (A/S-15/5)
Supplement No. 6: Resolutions and Decisions (A/S-15/6)

International organizations and associations
Intergovernmental organizations. IGOs
Universal
United Nations
United Nations documents and publications
Official records
General Assembly Official Records. GAOR. By session, e. g. regular, special, and emergency session
Special sessions -- Continued
16th Special Session (12-14 December 1989)
On Apartheid and its destructive consequences in southern Africa
Plenary Meetings (A/S-16/PV.1-6)
Ad Hoc Committee of the Whole of the 16th Special Session: summary records of the 1st-5th meetings (A/S-16/AC.1/SR.1-5)
Supplement No. 1: Report of the Ad Hoc Committee of the Whole of the 16th Special Session (A/S-16/4)
Supplement No. 2: (mistakenly issued as Supplement No. 5): Resolutions and Decisions (A/S-16/5)
17th Special Session (20-23 February 1990)
On question of international co-operation against illicit production, supply, demand, trafficking and distribution of narcotic drugs
Plenary Meetings, etc. to be issued
18th Special Session (23 April - 1 May 1990)
On international economic co-operation, in particular to the revitalization of economic growth and development of the developing countries
Plenary Meetings (A/S-18/PV.1-11 to be issued)
Supplement No. 1: Report of the Preparatory Committee of the Whole for the 18th Special Session of the General Assembly (A/S-18/7), to be issued
Supplement No. 2: Resolutions and Decisions (A/S-18/15)

5010.5 Emergency sessions

International organizations and associations
Intergovernmental organizations. IGOs
Universal
United Nations
United Nations documents and publications
Official records
General Assembly Official Records (GAOR). Documents Officiels de l'Assemblee. By session, e. g. regular, special, and emergency session
Emergency sessions
1st Emergency Special Session (1-10 November 1956)
On question considered by the Security Council at its 749th and 750th meetings: military operations in Egyptian territory - the Suez Canal Crisis
Plenary Meetings (A/PV.561-563, 565-567, 572) and Annexes
Supplement No. 1: Resolutions (1/3354)
2nd Emergency Special Session (4-10 November 1956)
On situation in Hungary
Plenary Meetings (A/PV.564, 568-571, 573) and Annex
Supplement No. 1: Resolutions (A/3355)
3rd Emergency Special Session (8-21 August 1958)
On questions considered by the Security Council at its 838th meeting: situation in Lebanon and Jordan
Plenary Meetings (A/PV.732-746) and Annexes
Supplement No. 1: Resolutions (A/3905)
4th Emergency Special Session (17-19 September 1960)
On question considered by the Security Council at its 906th meeting: the Congo situation
Plenary Meetings (A/PV.858963) and Annexes
Supplement No. 1: Resolutions (A/4510)
5th Emergency Special Session (17 June - 18 September 1967)
1967 Israeli Arab Conflict
Plenary Meetings (A/PV.1525-1559)
Supplement No. 1: Resolutions (A/6798)

International organizations and associations
Intergovernmental organizations. IGOs
Universal
United Nations
United Nations documents and publications
Official records
General Assembly Official Records (GAOR). Documents Officiels de l'Assemblee. By session, e. g. regular, special, and emergency session
Emergency sessions -- Continued
6th Emergency Special Session (10-14 January 1980)
On question by the Security Council at its 2185th to 2190th meetings: the situation in Afghanistan
Plenary Meetings (A/ES-6/PV.1-7) and Annexes
Supplement No. 1: Resolutions and Decisions (A/ES-6/7)
7th Emergency Special Session (12-29 July 1980)
On qustion of Palestine
Plenary Meetings and Annexes: to be issued
Supplement No. 1: Resolutions and Decisions (A/ES-7/14)
8th Emergency Special Session (3-14 September 1981)
On question of Namibia
Plenary Meetings (A/ES-8/PV.1-12) and Annexes
Supplement No. 1: Resolutions and Decisions (A/ES-8/13)
9th Emergency Special Session (19 January - 5 February 1982)
On situation in the occupied Arab territories
Plenary Meetings (A/ES-9/PV.1-12) and Annexes
Supplement No. 1: Resolutions and Decisions (A/ES-9/7)
General Assembly subsidiary bodies. Official records

International organizations and associations
Intergovernmental organizations. IGOs
Universal
United Nations
United Nations documents and publications
Official records
General Assembly subsidiary bodies. Official records -- Continued

5020.1 Disarmament Commission. Official records, 1994-
i.e. successor body to the Disarmament Commission established in 1952 under the Security Council
Meetings (Verbatim records), 184th- (18 April 1994-); Document series symbol A/CN.10/PV.-
For the Report of the Disarmament Commission to the General Assembly, see JZ5010.3, Supplement No. 42
For earlier meeting records, not issued as Official Records (A/CN.10/PV.1-193) see JZ5160

5020.2 Committee on the Peaceful Uses of Outer Space. Official records
Meetings (Verbatim records): issued as official records beginning with the 406th Meeting; Document series symbol A/AC.105/PV.-
For the Report of the Committee to the General Assembly, see JZ5010.2, Supplement No. 20

5020.3 Special Committee on the Situation with Regard to the Implementation of the Declaration on the granting of Independence to Colonial Countries and Peoples. Official records, 1994-
Meetings (Verbatim records); Document series symbol A/AC.109/PV.-
For the Report of the Committee to the General Assembly, see JZ5010.2, Supplement No. 23
For earlier meeting records, not issued as Official Records (A/AC.109/PV.1-1430) see JZ5160

International organizations and associations
Intergovernmental organizations. IGOs
Universal
United Nations
United Nations documents and publications
Official records
General Assembly subsidiary bodies. Official records -- Continued

5020.4 Committee on the Exercise of the Inalienable Rights of the Palestinian People. Official records, 1994-

Meetings (Verbatim records), 210th- (29 November 1994-); UN document series symbol: A/AC,183/PV.-

For the Report of the Committee to the General Assembly, see JZ5010.2, Supplement 35

For earlier meeting records not issued as Official Records and later meetings issued as summary records (e. g. A/AC.183/SR.211) see JZ5160

5030 Security Council Official Records. SCOR. By year

Subarrange by meetings, supplements, special supplements, resolutions and decisions

For the Report of the Security Council to the General Assembly, see JZ5010.2, Supplement No. 2

Meetings (1946-)

Document series symbol since the 5th year S/PV.-

Supplements

Issued quarterly since the 7th year (1952)

Special supplements

Class here special supplements beginning with the 36th year, 1981

Special Supplement No. 1: Report of the Trusteeship Council to the Security Council on the Trust Territory of the Pacific Island

Special Supplement No. 2: Report of the Security Council Commission of Enquiry established under resolution 496 (1981) (to 37th year)

Special Supplement No. 3: Supplementary Report of the Security Council Commission of Enquiry established under resolution 496 (1981) (to 37th year)

International organizations and associations
Intergovernmental organizations. IGOs
Universal
United Nations
United Nations documents and publications
Official records -- Continued

5040 Atomic Energy Commission Official Records, 1946-1951. By year (1st-6th)
Including records of meetings, supplements, special supplements, and including Index to Documents, 1 January 1946-30 April 1951 (AEC/C.1/81/Rev.1)
Superseded in 1951 by the International Atomic Energy Agency (IAEA)

5045 Disarmament Commission Official Records. DCOR, 1952-1959
Including records of meetings for the Commission and its 2 committees, supplements and Special Supplement No. 1 (1952)
Meetings (1952-1959), DC/PV.1-65
Committee 1: Meetings (1952), DC/C.1/PV.1-7
Committee 2: Meetings (1952), DC/C.2/PV.1-5
For the successor body see JZ5020.1

5050 Economic and Social Council Official Records. ESCOR. By year (beginning 1978)
Subarrange by plenary meetings, annexes (to 55th Session, 1973), supplements
Previously (to the 63rd Session, 1977) arranged by session
For the Report of the Conomic and Social Council to the General Assembly, see JZ5010.2, Supplement No. 3

Plenary Meetings (1946-)
Document series symbol since 1978 E/year/SR.- (e. g. E/1978/SR.1)
Previously (from the 11th Session, 1950 to 63rd Session, 1977) E/SR.-

Supplements
Including resolutions and decisions since 8th session (1949) in Supplement No. 1. Other supplements include sessional or annual reports of ECOSOC's functional commissions, standing committees, expert bodies and other related bodies (with supplement numbers varying from session to session)

Commission for Social Development

JZ

International organizations and associations
Intergovernmental organizations. IGOs
Universal
United Nations
United Nations documents and publications
Official records
Economic and Social Council Official Records. ESCOR. By year (beginning 1978)
Supplements -- Continued
Commission on Crime Prevention and Criminal Justice
Commission on Human Rights
Commission on Human Settlements
Commission on Narcotic Drugs
Commission on Population and Development
Commission on Science and Technology for Development
Commission on Sustainable Development
Commission on the Status of Women
Commission on Transnational Corporations
Committee for Development Planning
Committee on Economic, Social and Cultural Rights
Committee on Natural Resources
Committee on New and Renewable Sources of Energy and on Energy for Devlopment
Economic and Social Commission for Asia and the Pacific
Economic and Social Commission for Western Asia
Economic Commission for Africa
Economic Commission for Europe
Economic Commission for Latin America and the Caribbean
Population Commission
Statistical Commission
United Nations Children's Fund
United Nations Development Programme. Governing Council (to 1995)
United Nations Development Programme/ United Nations Population Fund. Executive Board (1995-)
Successor of the Governing Council of the UNDP

International organizations and associations
Intergovernmental organizations. IGOs
Universal
United Nations
United Nations documents and publications
Official records -- Continued

5060 Trusteeship Council Official Records. TCOR. 1947-

Issued separately for regular and special sessions up to 1978. Since 14th special and 46th (regular) session in 1979, regular and special session are included in combined fascicles and supplements

For the Report of the Trusteeship Council to the Security Council, see JZ5030, Special Supplement No. 1

Regular Sessions (1st-45th, 1947-1978). Regular Sessions and Special Sessions combined (46th-regular Session/17th-Special Session, 1979-)

Subarrange by meetings, sessional fascicles, annexes, supplements, special supplements, differing slightly during the first 3 sessions

Meetings: 1st-35th Session (1947-1965)

1st-2nd sessions verbatim; since 3rd session, summarized: since 7th session, meeting records bear the series symbol T/SR., followed by the meeting number. Since 36th session, meeting records are issued as masthead documents in series T/PV

Sessional Fascicles. 37th- Session (1970-)

Including agenda list of delegations, officers of the Council, check list of documents, annexes. May cover both, regular and special sessions combined

Annexes. 1st-37th Session (1947-1970)

Beginning with the 37th session, included in sessional fascicles. For the 5th-35th sessions, arranged by agenda items.

International organizations and associations
Intergovernmental organizations. IGOs
Universal
United Nations
United Nations documents and publications
Official records
Trusteeship Council Official Records. TCOR. 1947-
Regular Sessions (1st-45th, 1947-1978). Regular Sessions and Special Sessions combined (46th-regular Session/17th-Special Session, 1979-) -- Continued
Supplements
Resolutions and decisions are included in Supplement No. 1 of the 4th-46th, 48th-50th and 52nd session. Resolutions adopted at the 47th, 51st and 53rd sessions are included in Supplement No. 3. Resolutions and decisions adopted at the 54th session are included in Supplement No. 4
Other supplements include reports on visiting missions to the folowing trust territories: Cameroons (West Africa) under British Administration, see 13th, 17th, 23rd sessions; Cameroons (West Africa) under French Administration, see 13th, 17th, 23rd sessions; Mariana Islands District (Trust Territory of the Pacific Islands), see 43rd session; Marshall Islands (Trust Territory of the Pacific Islands), see 46th session; Micronesia, Federated States of (Trust Territory of the Pacific Islands), see 51st session; Nauru (Trust Territory in the Pacific), see 8th, 12th, 18th, 24th, 29th, 32nd sessions; New Guinea, see 8th, 12th, 18th, 24th, 29th, 32nd, 35th, 38th sessions; Pacific Islands, see 8th, 12th, 19th, 24th, 27th, 31st, 37th, 40th, 43rd, 46th, 47th, 50th, 53rd sessions; Palau (Trust Territory of the Pacific Islands), see 47th, 50th, 53rd-54th, 56th-57th, 59th-60th sessions; Papua New Guinea, see 39th session; Rwanda-Urundi (East Africa), see 4th, 11th, 15th, 21st, 26th sessions; Somaliland (East Africa) under Italian Administration, see 11th, 16th, 22nd sessions; Tanganyika (East Africa), see 4th, 8th 15th, 21st, 26th sessions; Togoland under French Administration, see 13th, 17th

International organizations and associations
Intergovernmental organizations. IGOs
Universal
United Nations
United Nations documents and publications
Official records
Trusteeship Council Official Records. TCOR. 1947-
Regular Sessions (1st-45th, 1947-1978). Regular Sessions and Special Sessions combined (46th-regular Session/17th-Special Session, 1979-) -- Continued

sessions; Togoland under British Administration, see 13th, 17th sessions; West Africa (Trust territories in), see 7th session; West Africa: Ewe and Togoland unification Problem, see 11th session, Second Part; Western Samoa, see 8th, 12th, 18th 24th sessions

Special Supplements

Issued infrequently, including questionnaires. Usually not numbered. Listed by session

11th Session: Questionnaire as approved by the Trusteeship Council at its 414th Meeting, 11th session, on 6 June 1952 (T/1010)

22nd Session: Special Questionnaire for the Trust Territory of New Guinea approved by the Trusteeship Council at its 22nd Session (t/1010/Add.1)

26th Session: Special Questionnaire for the Trust Territory of Nauru approved by the Trusteeship Council at its 26th Session, Special Supplement No. 1 (T/1010/Add.2)

27th Session: Questionnaire as approved by the Trusteeship Council at its 414th Meeting, 11th Session, on 6 June 1952, with amendments approved at its 1166th Meeting, 27th Session, on 7 July 1968 (T/1010/Rev.1)

Special Sessions

Since 14th special session in 1979, TCORs issued as one document, including regular sessions and special sessions

International organizations and associations
Intergovernmental organizations. IGOs
Universal
United Nations
United Nations documents and publications
Official records
Trusteeship Council Official Records. TCOR. 1947-
Special Sessions -- Continued
1st Special Session (27 September 1949)
On appointment of a member to the United Nations Visiting Mission to Trust Territories in West Africa
Meeting and Annexes
2nd Special Session (8 December 1949)
On responsibilities of the Trusteeship Council on the question of the disposal of the former Italian colonies and on the question of an international regime for the Jerusalem area and the protection of the Holy Places
Meetings and Annex
Supplement No. 1: Resolutions (T/433)
3rd Special Session (23 November 1950)
On question of the place of the sessions of the Trusteeship Council in 1951
Meeting (T/SR.314) and Annexes
4th Special Session (18 December 1951)
On date of the 10th session of the Trusteeship Council
Meeting
5th Special Session (24 October - 14 December 1955)
On the Togoland unification problem and the future of the Trust Territory of Togoland under British administration; arrangements for a periodic visiting mission to Trust Territories in the Pacific in 1956
Summary Records (T/SR.648-652) and Annex
Supplement No. 1: Resolutions (T/1217)
Supplement No. 2: Special Report on the Togoland unification problem and the future of the Trust Territory of Togoland under British administration (T/1218)
6th Special Session (19 December 1956 - 31 January 1957)
On the future of the Trust Territory of Togoland under French administration
Meetings (T/SR.746-751) and Annex

International organizations and associations
Intergovernmental organizations. IGOs
Universal
United Nations
United Nations documents and publications
Official records
Trusteeship Council Official Records. TCOR. 1947-
Special Sessions -- Continued
7th Special Session (12 - 20 September 1957)
On the future of Togoland under French administration: report of the United Nations Commission on Togoland under French administration
Summary Records (T/SR.841-847) and Annex
Supplement No. 1: Resolutions (T/1341)
Supplement No. 2: Report of the United Nations Commission on Togoland under French Administration (T/1343)
8th Special Session (13-17 October 1959)
On the future of Togoland under French administration, etc.
Summary Records (T/Sr.937-939) and Annexes
Supplement No. 1: Resolutions (T/1420)
9th Special Session (6-7 November 1958)
On terms of reference of the United Nations Visiting Mission to Trust Territories in West Africa, 1958
Meetings (T/SR.940-941) and Annex
Supplement No. 1: Resolutions (T/1421)
10th Special Session (2-14 December 1959)
On the future of the Trust Territory of the Cameroons under United Kingdom administration: report of the United Nations Plebiscite Commissioner on the plebiscite in the northern part of the Territory
Summary Reocrds (T/SR.1042-1043) and Annexes
Supplement No. 1: Resolutions (T/1498)

International organizations and associations
Intergovernmental organizations. IGOs
Universal
United Nations
United Nations documents and publications
Official records
Trusteeship Council Official Records. TCOR. 1947-
Special Sessions -- Continued
11th Special Session (10 April 1961)
On the future of the Trust Territory of the Cameroons under United Kingdom administration: report of the United Nations Plebiscite Commissioner for the Cameroons under United Kingdom Administration on the plebiscites in the southern and northern parts of the Territory
Meeting (T/SR.1135)
Supplement No. 1: Resolutions (T/1580)
12th Special Session (2 March 1965)
On arrangements for the dispatch of a periodic visiting mission to the Trust Territories of Nauru and New Guinea in 1965
Meeting (T/SR.1244)
13th Special Session (22-23 November 1967)
On the future of the Trust Territory of Nauru; terms of reference of the United Nations Visiting Mission to the Trust Territories of Nauru and New Guinea, 1968
Meetings: T/SR.1323-1324
Supplement No. 1: Resolutions (T/1678)
14th Special Session (12 and 15 February 1979)
On Marshall Islands: constitutional referendum on 1 March 1979; terms of reference of the United Nations Visiting Mission to the Trust Territory of the Pacific Islands, 1979
Sessional Fascicle
Supplement No. 1: Resolutions (T/1812)
Fascicle and supplement include 46th (regular) and the 14th special sessions

International organizations and associations
Intergovernmental organizations. IGOs
Universal
United Nations
United Nations documents and publications
Official records
Trusteeship Council Official Records. TCOR. 1947-
Special Sessions -- Continued
15th Special Session (16-20 December 1982)
On missions to observe plebiscites in Palau, the Marshall Islands and the Federated States of Micronesia and related petitions
Sessional Fascicle
Supplement No. 1: Resolutions (T/1859)
Fascicle and supplement include the 50th (regular) and the 15th special sessions
16th Special Session (4-6 February 1986)
On February 1986 plebiscite in Palau on the Compact of Free Associations and related petitions
Sessional Fascicle
Supplement No. 1: Resolutions and Decisions (T/1901)
Fascicle and supplement include the 16th special and 53rd (regular) sessions
17th Special Session (20-26 November 1986)
On December 1986 plebiscite in Palau on the Compact of Free Association and related petitions
Sessional Fascicle
Supplement No. 4: Resolutions and Decisions (T/1921)
Fascicle and supplement include 17th special, 54th (regular) and 18th special sessions
18th Special Session (13 August 1987)
Plebiscite in Palau on the Compact of Free Association
Sessional Fascicle
Supplement No. 4: Resolutions and Decisions (T/1921)
Fascicle and supplement combined coverage of 17th special, 54th (regular) and 18th special sessions

International organizations and associations
Intergovernmental organizations. IGOs
Universal
United Nations
United Nations documents and publications
Official records -- Continued
Trade and Development Board Official Records.
TDBOR. 1965- . By session
From the 1st-29th session, TDBORs consisted of records of meetings, annexes to those records, and supplement. Beginning with the 30th session (1965), the Board dispensed with summary records for its plenary meetings
For the Report of the Trade and Development Board (to the General Assembly), see JZ5010.2, Supplement No. 15

5070.2 Regular sessions, 1st- (April 1965-)
Beginning with the 9th session (1969), held in one, two or three parts
Meetings (1968-1984)
Issued for the 1st-29th session (TD/B/SR.1-653)
For a report on the work of each session, see Supplement No. 1A
Annexes. By agenda item
First published for the 2nd session (1965)

International organizations and associations
Intergovernmental organizations. IGOs
Universal
United Nations
United Nations documents and publications
Official records
Trade and Development Board Official Records. TDBOR. 1965- . By session
Regular sessions, 1st- (April 1965-) -- Continued
Supplements

Resolutions and decisions (occasionally "agreed conclusions") regularly included in Supplement No. 1

Since 26th session (1983), Supplement No. 1A regularly includes full version of the session report by the Trade and Development Board

Other supplements include reports of the following subsidiary bodies (with supplement numbers varying from session to session): Committee on Commodities, see 2nd- session (1965-) of the Trade and Development Board; Committee on Economic Co-operation Among Developing Countries, see 17th- session (1977/78-) of the Trade and Development Board; Committee on Invisibles and Financing Related to Trade, see 3rd- session (1966-) of the Trade and Development Board; Committee on Manufactures, see 2nd- Session (1965-) of the Trade and Development Board; Committee on Shipping, see 3rd- session (1966-) of the Trade and Development Board; Committee on Transfer of Technology, see 7th- special session (1976-) and later (regular) sessions of the Trade and Development Board; Intergovernmental Group on Supplementary Financing, see 9th session (1970) of the Trade and Development Board; Permanent Group on Synthetics and Substitutes, see 5th-11th session (1967-1971) of the Trade and Development Board; Special Committee on Preferences, see 8th- session (1969-) of the Trade and Development Board; Working Party on the Medium-Term Plan and the Programme Budget, see 20th- session (1979-) of the Trade and Development

International organizations and associations
Intergovernmental organizations. IGOs
Universal
United Nations
United Nations documents and publications
Official records
Trade and Development Board Official Records. TDBOR. 1965- . By session
Regular sessions, 1st- (April 1965-) -- Continued
Board

5070.3 Special sessions
1st Special Session (28-29 October 1965)
Recommendation on the location of the secretariat of UNCTAD pursuant to resolution 17 (II) of the Trade and Development Board
Meeting (TD/B/SR.56)
Annex
Supplement No. 1: Resolution (TD/B/72)
2nd Special Session (21 December 1966)
On review of the calendar of meetings of UNCTAD for 1967
Meeting (TD/B/SR.119)
Annex
Supplement No. 1: Decision (TD/B/117)
3rd Special Session (16 November 1967)
On the possibility of concerted action to deal with problems arising in international trade in rubber
Meeting (TD/B/SR.153)
Annex
Supplement No. 1: Resolution (TD/B/170; originally (mistakenly) symbolled TD/B/162)
4th Special Session (12-13 October 1970)
On report of the Special Committee on Preferences on the second part of its 4th session
Meetings (TD/B/SR. 266-267)
Supplement No. 1: Decision (TD/B/332)

International organizations and associations
Intergovernmental organizations. IGOs
Universal
United Nations
United Nations documents and publications
Official records
Trade and Development Board Official Records. TDBOR. 1965- . By session
Special sessions -- Continued
5th Special Session (24 April - 9 May 1973)
Review of the implementation of the policy measures within UNCTAD's competence as agreed upon within the context of the International Development Strategy; dissemination of information on mobilization of public opinion relative to problems of trade and development
Meetings (TD/B/SR.343-SR.352; SR.357
Supplement No. 1: Resolution and Decision (TD/B/445)
6th Special Session (10-22 March 1975)
On implementation of the International Development Strategy; implementation of the Declaration and Program of Action on the Establishment of a New International Economic Order
Meetings (TD/B/SR.413-525)
7th Special Session (8-20 March 1976)
On consideration of proposals for action by the UN Conference on Trade and Development at its 4th session
Meetings (TD/B/SR.444-447)
Annexes
Supplements Nos. 2-6; no Supplement No. 1
8th Special Session (25 April - 4 May 1977)
On review and appraisal of the implementation of the International Development Strategy, the Declaration and Programme of Action on the Establishment of a New International Economic Order, the Charter of Economic Rights and Duties of states, etc.
Meetings (TD/B/SR.457-461; 463-464)
Supplement No. 1: Agreed Conclusion and Decision (TD/B/669)

International organizations and associations
Intergovernmental organizations. IGOs
Universal
United Nations
United Nations documents and publications
Official records
Trade and Development Board Official Records. TDBOR. 1965- . By session
Special sessions -- Continued
9th Special Session (First part 5-10 September 1977; Second part 23-27 January 1978; Third part 6-11 March 1978
On UN Conference on Trade and Development resolutions 90 (IV) and 94 (IV), etc.
Meetings (TD/B/SR.478-494)
Annexes
Supplement No. 1: Resolution and Decisions (TD/B/701)
10th Special Session (19-17 March 1979)
On consideration of proposals for action by the UN Conference on Trade and Development at its 5th session, etc.
Meetings (TD/B/SR.511-517)
Annexes
Supplement No. 1: Decision (TD/B/745)
Supplements Nos. 2-4
11th Special Session (14 and 30 March 1980)
On contribution of UNCTAD to the preparation of the new International Development Strategy for the Third United Nations Development Decade, etc.
Meetings (TD/B/SR.527 and SR.532)
Annexes
No supplements
12th Special Session (25-30 April and 6 May 1983)
On consideration of proposals to be submitted to the UN Conference on Trade and Development at its 6th session, etc.
Meetings (TD/B/SR.610-614, SR.616 and SR.617)
Supplement No. 1: Decisions (TD/B/958, Vol. I)
Supplement No. 1A: Report on the session (TD/B/958, Vol. II)

International organizations and associations
Intergovernmental organizations. IGOs
Universal
United Nations
United Nations documents and publications
Official records
Trade and Development Board Official Records. TDBOR. 1965- . By session
Special sessions -- Continued
13th Special Session (2-6 April 1984)
On contribution of the UN Conference on Trade and Development to the review and appraisal by the General Assembly of the implementation of the International Development Strategy for the Third UN Development Decade
Meetings (TD/B/SR.637 and SR.640)
Annexes
Supplement No. 1: Decision (TD/B/996, Vol. I)
Supplement No. 1A: Report on the session (TD/B/996, Vol. II)
14th Special Session (10-15 and 27 June 1985)
On compensatory financing of export earnings shortfalls; report of the Expert Group convened pursuant to UN Conference on Trade and Development resolution 157 (VI)
Supplement No. 1: Decision (TD/B/1062, Vol.I)
Supplement No. 1A: Report on the session (TD/B/1062, Vol. II)
15th Special Session (18-20 May 1987)
On consideration of proposals to be submitted to the UN Conference on Trade and Development at its 7th session, etc.
Supplement No. 1: Decision (TD/B/1140, Vol. I)
Supplement No. 1A: Report on the session (TD/B/1140, Vol. II)
16th Special Session (8-9 and 16 March 1990)
On compensatory financing of export earnings shortfalls: report of the Intergovernmental Group of Experts
Supplement No. 1: Decision (TD/B/1256, Vol. I)
Supplement No. 1A: Report on the session (TD/B/1256, Vol. II)

International organizations and associations
Intergovernmental organizations. IGOs
Universal
United Nations
United Nations documents and publications
Official records
Trade and Development Board Official Records. TDBOR. 1965- . By session
Special sessions -- Continued
17th Special Session (2-13 December 1991 and 15-24 January 1992)
On preparations for the 8th session of the UN Conference on Trade and Development
Supplement No. 1 (Part I): Report on the 1st part of the session (TD/B/1319)
Supplement No. 1, Part II to be issued

5080 Meeting of States Parties. Official Records
On UN human rights treaties consisting solely of decisions adopted at the meetings

5080.2 International Convention on the Elimination of All Forms of Racial Discrimination. Meeting of States Parties. Official Records, 1969-1992
Decisions adopted at the 1st-14th Meeting, 1969-1992, (CERP/SP/-)

5080.4 International Covenant on Civil and Political Rights. Meeting of States Parties. Official Records, 1976
Decisions adopted at the 1st Meeting, 1976 (CCPR/SP/7)

Sales publications
Class here United Nations publications identified by a UN sales number, e. g. E.94.V.13

5090 United Nations Conferences
Subarrange by UN Document Numbers/Symbols
Including Final Acts, Reports, Proceedings, Official Records, etc.
.A/CONF.1/9 United Nations Conference on Declaration of Death of Missing Persons (1950)
.A/CONF.2/108 United Nations Conference of Plenipotentiaries on the Status of Refugees and Stateless Persons (1951)
.A/CONF.6/1 First United Nations Congress on the Prevention of Crimes and the Treatment of Offenders (1955)
.A/CONF.8/1 International Conference on the Peaceful Uses of Atomic Energy (1955)

International organizations and associations
Intergovernmental organizations. IGOs
Universal
United Nations
United Nations documents and publications
Sales publications
United Nations Conferences -- Continued
.A/CONF.13/38 United Nations Conference on the Law of the Sea (1958)
.A/CONF.19/8-9 Second United Nations Conference on the Law of the Sea (1960)
.A/CONF.62 Third United Nations Conference on the Law of the Sea (Official Records, issued in 17 vols.; 1973-1982)
.A/CONF.39/11 United Nations Conference on the Law of Treaties (1st Session, 1968)
Addendum 1: 2nd Session, 1969
.E/CONF.2/78 United Nations Conference on Trade and Employment (1948)
.E/CONF.7/7 United Nations Scientific Conference on the Conservation and Utilization of Resources (1949)
.E/CONF.12/12 United Nations Tin Conference (1950 and 1953)
.E/CONF.13/413 World Population Conference (1954)
.E/CONF.15/15 United Nations Sugar Conference (1953)
.E/CONF.16/23 United Nations Conference on Customs Formalities for the Temporary Importation of Private Road Motor Vehicles and for Tourism (1954)
.E/CONF.17/5/Rev United Nations Conference on the Status of Stateless Persons (1954)
Other sales publications. By UN sales number categories
Within each category, subarrange by UN sales number
5100 Category 0: UN materials printed in Geneva
Including publications of the Advisory Committee for the Co-ordination of Information Systems (ACCIS), United Nations Institute for Disarmament Research (UNIDIR) and miscellaneous publications
5101 Category I: General information and reference
Class here publications issued in this category beginning with the year 1994

International organizations and associations
Intergovernmental organizations. IGOs
Universal
United Nations
United Nations documents and publications
Sales publications
Other sales publications. By Un sales number categories
Category I: General information and reference
Yearbook of the United Nations (Vol. 48) see JZ4947
.94.I.3 Jerusalem: Visions of Reconciliation: An Israeli-Palestinian Dialogue
.94.I.4 United Nations Regional Cartographic Conference for the Americas
5102.01 Category II.A: Business, economics, science and technology
5102.02 Category II.B: Economic development
5102.03 Category II.C: World economy
5102.04 Category II.D: Trade, finance and commerce
5102.05 Category II.E: Economic Commission for Europe (ECE) publications
Serials
.E Economic Bulletin for Europe
.E Economic Survey of Europe
.T Transport Information
Monographs
94.II.E.3 Programme of Current Housing and Building Statistics for countries in the UN/ ECE Region
94.II.E.4 Trade Data Elements Directory (UNITED 1993)
5102.06 Category II.F: Economic and Social Commission for Asia and the Pacific (ESCAP) publications
5102.07 Category II.G: Economic Commission for Latin America and the Caribbean (ECLAC/CEPAL) publications
5102.08 Category II.H: Public Administration
5102.10 Category II.K: Economic Commission for Africa (ECA) publications
5102.11 Category II.L: Economic and Social Commission for Western Asia (ESCWA) publications
5103.01 Category III.A: United Nations University (UNU) publications
5103.02 Category III.B: United Nations Development Programme (UNDP) pulbications

International organizations and associations
Intergovernmental organizations. IGOs
Universal
United Nations
United Nations documents and publications
Sales publications
Other sales publications. By UN sales number categories -- Continued

5103.03 Category III.C: International Research and Training Institute for the Advancement of Women (INSTRAW) publications
5103.04 Category III.D: United Nations Environment Programme (UNEP) publications
5103.05 Category III.E: United Nations Industrial Development Organization (UNIDO) publications
5103.08 Category III.H: United Nations Fund for Population Activities (UNFPA) publications
5103.10 Category III.K: United Nations Institute for Training and Research (UNITAR) publications
5103.13 Category III.N: UNSDRI publications
5104 Category IV: Social questions
5105 Category V: International law
5107 Category VII: Security Council and peace-keeping operations
5108 Category VIII: Transport and communications
5109 Category IX: Disarmament and atomic energy
5110 Category X: International administration
5111 Category XI: Narcotic drugs
5113 Category XIII: Demography
5114 Category XIV: Human rights
5116 Category XVI: Public finance and fiscal questions
5117 Category XVII: International statistics
5120 Category XX: United Nations Children's Fund (UNICEF) publications
5125 Category XXV: United Nations Postal Administration
5160 Masthead documents. Working documents. Mimeographed documents

Arrange here UN bodies by their series symbols as represented by the UNDOC: Current Index. Arrange series symbols alphabetically

.A/AC.86/- General Assembly. Committee on Applications for Review of Administrative Tribunal Judg(e)ments

International organizations and associations
Intergovernmental organizations. IGOs
Universal
United Nations
United Nations documents and publications
Masthead documents. Working documents.
Mimeographed documents -- Continued

.A/AC.96/- General Assembly. Executive Committee of the High Commissioner's Programme
Cf. JZ5010, General Assembly Official Records. Supplement No. 12

.A/AC.105/- General Assembly. Committee on the Peaceful Uses of Outer Space
Cf. JZ5010, General Assembly Official Records. Supplement No. 20

.A/AC.105/C.2/- General Assembly. Committee on the Peaceful Uses of Outer Space. Legal Subcommittee

.A/AC.109/- Special Committee on the Situation with Regard to the Implementation of the Declaration on the Granting of Independence to Colonial Countries and Peoples
Cf. JZ5010, General Assembly Official Records. Supplement No. 23

.A/AC.115/- General Assembly. Special Committee against Apartheid
Cf. JZ5010, General Assembly Official Records. Supplement No. 22

.A/AC.159/- General Assembly. Ad Hoc Committee on the Indian Ocean
Cf. JZ5010, General Assembly Official Records. Supplement No. 29

.A/AC.172/- General Assembly. Committee on Conferences
Cf. JZ5010, General Assembly Official Records. Supplement No. 32

.A/AC.182/- General Assembly. Special Committee on the Charter of the UN and on the Strengthening of the Role of the Organization
Cf. JZ5010, General Assembly Official Records. Supplement No. 33

.A/AC.237/- General Assembly. Intergovernmental Negotiating Committee for a Framework Convention on Climate Change

International organizations and associations
Intergovernmental organizations. IGOs
Universal
United Nations
United Nations documents and publications
Masthead documents. Working documents.
Mimeographed documents -- Continued

.A/AC.240/- General Assembly. Preparatory Committee for the Fiftieth Anniversary of the UN
Cf. JZ5010, General Assembly Official Records. Supplement No. 48

.A/AC.241/- General Assembly. Intergovernmental Negotiating Committee for the Elaboration of an International Convention to Combat Desertification in those Countries Experiencing Serious Drought and/or Desertification, particularly in Africa

.A/AC.242/- General Assembly. Ad Hoc Committee on the Elaboration of an International Convention Dealing with the Safety and Security of UN and Associated Personnel
Cf. JZ5010, General Assembly Official Records. Supplement No. 22

.A/AC.243/- General Assembly. Ad Hoc Intergovernmental Working Group of Experts Established persuant to General Assembly Resolution 48/218

.A/BUR/- General Assembly. General Committee
Cf. JZ5010, General Assembly Official Records. Committee Meeting Records

.A/C.1/- General Assembly. First Committee (Disarmament and International Security)
Cf. JZ5010, General Assembly Official Records. Committee Meeting Records

.A/C.2/- General Assembly. Second Committee (Economic and Financial)
Cf. JZ5010, General Assembly Official Records. Committee Meeting Records

.A/C.3/- General Assembly. Third Committee (Social, Humanitarian and Cultural)
Cf. JZ5010, General Assembly Official Records. Committee Meeting Records

.A/C.4/- General Assembly. Forth Committee (Special Political and Decolonization. Previously Trusteeship)
Cf. JZ5010, General Assembly Official Records. Committee Meeting Records

International organizations and associations
Intergovernmental organizations. IGOs
Universal
United Nations
United Nations documents and publications
Masthead documents. Working documents.
Mimeographed documents -- Continued

.A/C.5/- General Assembly. Fifth Committee (Administrative and Budgetary)
Cf. JZ5010, General Assembly Official Records. Committee Meeting Records

.A/C.6/- General Assembly. Sixth Committee (Legal)
Cf. JZ5010, General Assembly Official Records. Committee Meeting Records

.A/CN.4/- General Assembly. International Law Commission
Cf. JZ5010, General Assembly Official Records. Supplement No. 10

.A/CN.9/- General Assembly. UN Commisstion on International Trade Law
Cf. JZ5010, General Assembly Official Records. Supplement No. 17

.A/CN.10/- General Assembly. Disarmament Commission
Cf. JZ5010, General Assembly Official Records. Supplement No. 42

.A/CN.9/WG.II/- General Assembly. UN Commission on International Trade Law. Working Group on International Contract Practices

.A/CONF.151/- General Assembly. UN Conference on Environment and Development

.A/CONF.157/- General Assembly. World Conference on Human Rights

.A/CONF.162/- Conference of Plenipotentiaries on a Draft Convention on Maritime Liens and Mortgages

.A/CONF.164/- General Assembly. UN Conference on Straddling Fish Stocks and Highly Migratory Fish Stocks

.A/CONF.165/- General Assembly. UN Conference on Human Settlements (Habitat II)

.A/CONF.166/- General Assembly. World Summit for Social Development

International organizations and associations
Intergovernmental organizations. IGOs
Universal
United Nations
United Nations documents and publications
Masthead documents. Working documents.
Mimeographed documents -- Continued

.A/CONF.167/- General Assembly. Global Conference on the Sustainable Development of Small Island Developing States

.A/CONF.169/- General Assembly. UN Congress on the Prevention of Crime and the Treatment of Offenders (9th)

.A/CONF.171/- General Assembly. International Conference on Population and Development

.A/CONF.172/- General Assembly. World Conference on Natural Disaster Reduction

.A/SPC/- General Assembly. Special Political Committee

Cf. JZ5010, General Assembly Official Records. Committee Meeting Records

.ACC/- Administrative Committee on Coordination

.ACC/ACCIS/- Administrative Committee on Coordination. Advisory Committee for Coordination of Information Systems

.ACC/SCN/- Administrative Committee on Coordination. Subcommittee on Nutrition

.ACC/DEC/- UN Administrative Tribunal. Judgements of the UN Administrative Tribunal (distribution limited; not for deposit)

.BWC/CONF.III/- Review Conference of the Parties to the Convention on the Prohibition of the Development, Production and Stockpiling of Bacteriological (Biological) and Toxin Weapons and on Their Destruction (3rd)

.CAT/C/- Convention against Torture and Other Cruel, Inhuman or Degrading Treatment of Punishment. Committee Against Torture

Cf. JZ5010, General Assembly Official Records. Supplement No. 44 and No. 46

.CCPR/C/- International Covenant on Civil and Political Rights. Human Rights Committee

.CCPR/SP/- International Covenant on Civil and Political Rights. Meeting of the States Parties

Cf. JZ5010, General Assembly Official Records. Supplement No. 40

International organizations and associations
Intergovernmental organizations. IGOs
Universal
United Nations
United Nations documents and publications
Masthead documents. Working documents.
Mimeographed documents -- Continued
.CD/- Conference on Disarmament
Cf. JZ5010, General Assembly Official Records. Supplement No. 27
.CD/NTB/- Conference on Disarmament. Ad Hoc Committee on a Nuclear Test Ban
.CD/OS/- Conference on Disarmament. Ad Hoc Committee on Prevention of an Arms Race in Outer Space
Conference on Disarmament. Ad Hoc Committee on Effective International Arrangements to Assure Non-Nuclear Weapon States against the Use or Threat of Use of Nuclear Weapons
.CD/TIA/- Conference on Disarmament. Ad Hoc Committee on Transparency in Armaments
.CEDAW/C/- Convention on the Elimination of All Forms of Discrimination against Women. Committee on the Elimination of Discrimination against Women
Cf. JZ5010, General Assembly Official Records. Supplement No. 38 and No. 45
.CERD/C/- International Convention on the Elimination of All Forms of Racial Discrimination
Cf. JZ5010, General Assembly Official Records. Supplement No. 18
.CRC/C/- Convention on the Rights of the Child. Committee on the Rights of the Child
Cf. JZ5010, General Assembly Official Records. Supplement No. 41
.DP/- UN Devlopment Programme. Governing Council
.DP/CP/- UN Development Programme. Governing Council. Country and Intercountry Programs and Projects
.DP/ID/SER.A/- UN Development Programme/UN Industrial Development Organization. Technical Report
.DP/ID/SER.B/- UN Development Programme/UN Industrial Development Organization. Terminal Report

International organizations and associations
Intergovernmental organizations. IGOs
Universal
United Nations
United Nations documents and publications
Masthead documents. Working documents.
Mimeographed documents -- Continued
.DP/ID/SER.C/- UN Development Programme/UN Industrial Development Organization. Report of the Evaluation Mission
Other intergovernmental organizations. Official records
5180 Food and Agriculture Organization. FAO
5185 General Agreement on Tariffs and Trade. GATT
From January 1, 1995, World Trade Organization. WTO
5190 International Atomic Energy Agency. IAEA
5195 International Civil Aviation Organization. ICAO
5200 International Labour Organisation. ILO
5220 United Nations Educational, Scientific and Cultural Organization. Unesco
For works about Unesco see JZ5009.5.U553
5225 United Nations Industrial Development Organization. UNIDO
5230 World Health Organization. WHO
Regional organizations. Regionalism
5330 General works (Collective)
By region or country
Americas
5331 General works
5331.5.A-Z By name of organization, A-Z
Europe
5332 General works
5332.5.A-Z By name of organization, A-Z
Asia
5333 General works
5333.5.A-Z By name of organization, A-Z
Africa
5334 General works
5334.5.A-Z By name of organization, A-Z
Arab countries
5335 General works
5335.5.A-Z By name of organization, A-Z
Pacific Area
5336 General works
5336.5.A-Z By name of organization, A-Z
Official records
The Americas
Including North, Central and Latin America

International organizations and associations
Intergovernmental organizations. IGOs
Regional organizations. Regionalism
Official records
The Americas -- Continued
5340 Organization of American States (OAS)
5360 Commission of the Cartagena Agreement. Andean Group
5370 Latin American Integration Association
5375 Caribbean Community
5380 Central American Common Market
5390 Inter-American Research and Documentation Center on Vocational Training (CINTERFOR)
Europe
5400 Council of Europe
5420 Organization for Security and Cooperation in Europe
5425 European Community (EC). European Union (EU)
5448 Western European Union (WEU)
Asia
Association of South East Asian States see JZ5490
5450 Southeast Asian Ministers of Education Organization
Africa
5454 African Economic Community
5455 Central African Customs and Economic Union
5456 East African Community
5458 Economic Community of Central African States
5459 Economic Community of West African States
5460 African Union
5464 Southern African Customs Union
5466 West African Customs Union
Arab organizations
5468 Arab Common Market
5470 Arab League Educational, Cultural and Scientific Organization
5473 Arab Maghreb Union
5475 Council for Arab Economic Unity
5480 League of Arab States
Pacific Area organizations
5485 South Pacific Commission
5490 Association of South East Asian Nations (ASEAN)
Other international organizations limited in jurisdiction by subject
see the subject, e. g. Organization for Economic Development (OECD), see K3824
Promotion of peace. Peaceful change
Bibliography see Z6464.Z9
Periodicals

Promotion of peace. Peaceful change
Periodicals -- Continued
Bibliography of periodicals see JZ5.5
By language
European
5511.2 English
5511.3 French
5511.4 German
5511.5 Italian
5511.6 Spanish. Portuguese
Including all Latin American journals
5511.7 Other European (not A-Z)
Asian
Including works in original script or transliterated inb Roman characters
5512 Japanese
5512.7 African/Middle Eastern
Including Arabic, Hebrew, etc.
Societies, associations, academies, institutes, etc., for peace promotion, research and education
For substantive publications authored by such societies, see the subject
For publications relating to conferences of such societies, see the conference
5514 Directories (General)
5518.A-Z International associations. By name, A-Z
e. g.
5518.A77 Association for International Conciliation
5518.C46 Central Organization for a Durable Peace
5518.C47 Chemin des enfants (Organization)
5518.C66 Commonwealth of World Citizens
5518.I58 International Institute for Peace
5518.I62 International Peace Bureau
5518.I64 International Peace Research Institute
5518.I66 International Society for Research on Aggression
5518.N48 New Commonwealth Society
5518.S86 Stockholm Initiative on Global Security and Governance
War Resisters International see JZ5576
5518.W65 World Council of Peace
5518.W66 World Federation Society
5518.W67 World Future Studies Federation
National associations
American (North and South America)
5520 Carnegie Endowment for International Peace
5520.5.A-Z Individual chapters or divisions, A-Z
e. g.

Promotion of peace. Peaceful change
Societies, associations, academies, institutes, etc. for peace promotion, research and education
National associations
American (North and South America)
Carnegie Endowment for International Peace
Individual chapters or divisions, A-Z -- Continued
<5520.5.D585> Division of international law
see KZ5520.5.D585
5521 Nuclear Age Peace Foundation
5524.A-Z Other societies and associations. By name, A-Z
5526.A-Z Other nations. By name or association, A-Z
e. g.
5526.G47 German Peace Research Association. Arbeitsgemeinschaft für Friedens- und Konfliktforschung
Congresses and conferences
International congresses and conferences
5527 General works
5527.5 International Peace Research Association. Conference
<5528> Intergovernmental congresses and conferences
see KZ5528
5530.A-Z Congresses with permanent organization. By name, A-Z
e.g.
Inter-Parliamentary Union. IPU see JZ4842.I68
5530.U65 Union des associations internationales (Brussels)
5530.U67 Universal peace congress
National congresses
5531.A-Z United States. By name of congress, A-Z
e. g.
5531.N3 National Security Affairs Conference
5532.A-Z Other countries. By name of congress, A-Z
5533 Encyclopedias. Dictionaries
5534 Peace research. Education for peace. Study and teaching
Cf. LC1090+ International education
5535 Illustrative materials
Including fiction (e. g. imaginary wars, including picture books)
5536 Museums and exhibitions devoted to the subject
5537 Celebrations. Festivals. "Peace day", etc.
5538 General works
Biography
5540 Collective
5540.2.A-Z Individual, A-Z
5542.A-Z Manuals and other works for particular groups of users, A-Z
History and theory of pacificism. By period
5544 Ancient
Modern

Promotion of peace. Peaceful change
History and theory of pacificism. By period
Modern -- Continued
5548 General works
5550 17th century
5552 18th century
19th century
World peace
5554 General works
International arbitration see KZ6115+
5556 International organization (General)
20th century
5560 General works
5562 Renunciation of war as an instrument of national politics
5566 International organization (General)
For IGOs see JZ4850+
5566.4 21st century
Militarism and pacifism
For the just war theory, see KZ6396
5567 General works
By region or country see JZ5584.A+
Peace movements. Antiwar movements. Nonviolence
Including antinuclear movements
5574 General works
Peaceful resistance
5575 General works
5576 War Resisters International
Societies, associations see JZ5518.A+
5577 Conscientious objectors
5577.5 Role of mass media
Role of women
5578 General works
5578.2.A-Z By region or country, A-Z
5579 Role of youth
By region or country see JZ5584.A+
5581 Peace ethics
Including popular ethical peace literature
For ethics of war see JZ6392
Peace research. Education for peace. Study and teaching see JZ5534
Societies. Associations. Academies. Institutes, etc. for peace promotion, research and education see JZ5514+
5584.A-Z By region or country, A-Z
International security. Disarmament. Global survival
Cf. BL65.S375 International security and religion

Promotion of peace. Peaceful change
International security. Disarmament. Global survival -- Continued
<5586> Bibliography
see KZ5586
5587 Annuals. Yearbooks
e. g. Yearbook of World Armaments and Disarmaments
5588 General works
International tension and conflict. Cold wars
5595 General works
5595.5 Sociology of international tensions
5596 Responsibility of statesmanship. Moral choice
Peace politics. Reduction of tension. International reconciliation
5597 General works
5599 World peace promotion through detente. Detente diplomacy
5600 Detente management. Policy aims
5601 Collaboration of nations. International cooperation
Including concepts of military cooperation
5603 International organization
Non-diplomatic (voluntary) methods of dispute resolution see KZ6009+
Arbitration and adjudication. The courts see KZ6115+
International politics in arms control, limitation and prohibition of armament. Disengagement
Cf. UA12.5 Disarmament inspection
5615.A-Z Intergovernmental congresses and conferences, A-Z
5625 General works
5630 Intelligence activities (General)
Conventional arms control
Class here works on land mines, booby traps, incendiary weapons (napalm, flame throwers, etc.), and fragments not detectible in the human body
<5640.2> Treaties and other international agreements
see KZ5637+
5645 General works
Nuclear weapons and weapon systems
Including manufacture, testing, and possession
For anti-nuclear movements (Peace movements) see JZ5574+
<5650.2> Treaties and other international agreements
see KZ5650+
5665 General works
Nonproliferation. Abolition
<5670.2> Nuclear nonproliferation treaties
see KZ5670+

Promotion of peace. Peaceful change
International security. Disarmament. Global survival
International tension and conflict. Cold wars
International politics in arms control, limitation and prohibition of armament. Disengagement
Nuclear weapons and weapon systems
Nonproliferation. Abolition -- Continued

5675 General works

Cessation of nuclear weapons tests

<5680.2> Treaties and other international agreements
see KZ5680+

5681 General works

Particular nuclear weapons and weapon systems

5685 Anti-ballistic missile systems

5686 Neutron weapons

Arms control and arms limitation with regard to international commons

5687 General works

Outer space. International security dimensions in the space age

Treaties and other international agreements see KZD1118+

5695 General works

5700 Satellites in outer space

5710 Space militarization. Arms race in outer space
Including particular weapons and weapon systems

The Oceans
Including sea-bed, ocean floor and subsoil

<5715.2> Treaties and other international agreements. Conventions
see KZ5715.2

5720 General works

Nuclear-weapon-free zones. Zones of peace

5725 General works

By region

Latin America

<5730.2> Treaties and other international agreements. Conventions
see KZ5730.2

5735 General works

Europe

<5740.2> Treaties and other international agreements. Conventions
see KZ5740.2

5745 General works

5760 Scandinavia

Middle East

Promotion of peace. Peaceful change
International security. Disarmament. Global survival
International tension and conflict. Cold wars
International politics in arms control, limitation and prohibition of armament. Disengagement
Nuclear weapons and weapon systems
Nuclear-weapon-free zones. Zones of peace
By region
Middle East -- Continued
<5765.2> Treaties and other international agreements. Conventions
see KZ5765.2
5770 General works
Africa
<5780.2> Treaties and other international agreements. Conventions
see KZ5780.2
5785 General works
5786 South Asia
5787 South Pacific
5788 Indian Ocean Zone of Peace
Chemical arms control
Including chemical and biological (bacterial) weapons, and including binary weapons and gases
Cf. UG447+ Military science
<5825.2> Treaties and other international agreements. Conventions
see KZ5825+
5830 General works
5832 Chemical-weapon-free zones
Gas (Asphyxiating and poisonous). Nerve gas
Treaties and other international agreements. Conventions
see KZ5825+
General works see JZ5830
Directed-energy weapons
<5840.2> Treaties and other international agreements. Conventions
see KZ5840.2
5855 General works
Incendiary weapons see JZ5640.2+
5865.A-Z Other types of weapon systems, A-Z
5865.B56 Biological weapons
5865.R35 Radiological weapons
Military pact systems
5900 General works
Supra-regional and regional defense organizations

Promotion of peace. Peaceful change
International security. Disarmament. Global survival
International tension and conflict. Cold wars
Military pact systems
Supra-regional and regional defense organizations -- Continued
North Atlantic Treaty Organization (NATO), 1949-
Including the North Atlantic Council and Military Commission
Cf. D845.2 Twentieth century history
<5925.2> Treaties and other international agreements. Conventions
see KZ5925+
5930 General works
European Defense Community (Proposed)
<5955.2> Draft treaty
see KZ5955
5957 General works
Warsaw Treaty Organization, 1955
<5965.2> Warsaw Treaty, 1955
see KZ5965
5967 General works
5980 Central Treaty Organization. Baghdad Pact
International peacekeeping forces see KZ6374+
6005 Post-Cold War security
6009.A-Z By region or country, A-Z
Pacific settlement of international disputes
6010 General works
6045 General diplomatic negotiations and consultations. Mediation and good offices
Preliminary processes other than arbitration
6060 Fact finding and inquiry
Cf. KZ6060+ Law of nations
<6144-6184> Arbitration tribunals and Permanent Court of Arbitration
see KZ6144+
<6250-6299> Judicial settlement of international disputes
see KZ6250+
6300 Nation-building
For works on nation-building activities in specific regions or countries see classes D-F
Non-military coercion
6360 General works
6362 Reprisals. Retorsion. Retaliation
6365 Embargo
6366 Blockade

JZ

Non-military coercion -- Continued
Intervention. Preventive diplomacy and other preventive measures
Including intervention by states or intergovernmental organization in civil wars
6368 General works
6369 Humanitarian intervention
6373 Sanctions
Including economic sanctions
Threat of force. Enforced peacekeeping measures short of war
Including use of international military forces
6374 General works
6377.A-Z By country providing peacekeeping forces, A-Z
Specific wars
see classes D, E, F
The armed conflict. War and order
<6378> Law of war
see KZ6378+
6385 General works
History
6387 General works
History of particular wars
see classes D - F
Peace treaties see KZ184+
Theoretical/political interpretation of a particular international conflict see JZ1329.5+
6388 Capitulations
For particular wars, see the war in classes D - F
Sociology and philosophy of war
6390 General works
6392 Ethics of war
Including religious-ethical aspects of force
Just war theory
see KZ6396
6400 Diplomacy. Effects of outbreak of war on diplomacy
Economic aspects. Economic exploitation
6401 General works
6402 Occupation of enemy territory
Arms and instruments of war (General)
see class U
6405.A-Z Works on diverse concepts and aspects of the subject, A-Z
6405.L33 Labor and war
6405.M37 Mass media
6405.M68 Moving pictures
The press see JZ6405.M37
Psychological warfare. Propaganda see UB275+

The armed conflict. War and order
Works on diverse concepts and aspects of the subject, A-Z -- Continued
Radio broadcasting see JZ6405.M37
6405.W66 Women and war
Neutrality. Non-participation in wars. Norms of neutrality
Class here social-scientific studies on norm theory, policy and standards of neutrality
6422 General works
6422.5.A-Z By region or country, A-Z
<6440-6530> Law of war and humanitarian law
see KZ6440+
6530 Humanitarian aspects of war

Governors' messages and other executive papers
For messages on a specific subject, see the subject
.xA15 Collections covering more than one administration
.xA17 Collections covering one administration
Veto messages
.xA18 Collections covering more than one administration
.xA19 Collections covering one administration
.xA2 Individual messages. By date (year) of message
.xA25 Lieutenant Governors' messages
Administrative papers
.xA3 Collections. Documents of several departments or agencies combined
.xA4 Secretary of State
(.xA5) Other departments or agencies limited to a particular subject
see the subject

	Governors' messages and other executive papers
	For messages on a specific subject, see the subject
.A15	Collections covering more than one administration
.A17	Collections covering one administration
	Veto messages
.A18	Collections covering more than one administration
.A19	Collections covering one administration
.A2	Individual messages. By date of message
.A25	Lieutenant Governors' messages
	Administrative papers
.A3	Collections. Documents of several departments or agencies combined
.A4	Secretary of State
(.A5)	Other departments or agencies limited to a particular subject
	see the subject

TABLES

.C2 General works

Legislative papers

For official gazettes, see class K

.G3 Joint sessions

.H Papers of a unicameral legislative body. Combined papers of a bicameral legislature

.H2 Debates. Proceedings. Sessional papers. Journals

Including calendars

.H5 Bills

.H7 Committee hearings, proceedings, reports

For committee papers on a special topic, see the topic

.J Upper House

.J2 Debates. Proceedings. Sessional papers. Journals

Including calendars

.J5 Bills

.J7 Committee hearings, proceedings, reports

For committee papers on a special topic, see the topic

.K Lower House

.K2 Debates. Proceedings. Sessional papers. Journals

Including calendars

.K5 Bills

.K7 Committee hearings, proceedings, reports

For committee papers on a special topic, see the topic

.M5 Indexes

.N Messages of heads of state (or heads of government) and other executive papers

Class here official messages and documents only

For the collected works of individual heads of state, see D-F

For messages on a specific subject, see the subject

.N15 Collections

.N3 Individual messages. By date of message

(.N5) Executive orders

see class K

.R Administrative papers

Collections. Documents of several departments or agencies combined

.R1 Collected

(.R3) Department of the Interior

see JL-JQ

(.R7) Other departments or agencies

see the subject

(.T3) State, provincial documents

see JL-JS

.xC2 General works
Legislative papers
For official gazettes, see class K
.xG3 Joint sessions
.xH Papers of a unicameral legislative body. Combined papers of a bicameral legislature
.xH2 Debates. Proceedings. Sessional papers. Journals
Including calendars
.xH5 Bills
.xH7 Committee hearings, proceedings, reports
For committee papers on a special topic, see the topic
.xJ Upper House
.xJ2 Debates. Proceedings. Sessional papers. Journals
Including calendars
.xJ5 Bills
.xJ7 Committee hearings, proceedings, reports
For committee papers on a special topic, see the topic
.xK Lower House
.xK2 Debates. Proceedings. Sessional papers. Journals
Including calendars
.xK5 Bills
.xK7 Committee hearings, proceedings, reports
For committee papers on a special topic, see the topic
.xM5 Indexes
.xN Messages of heads of state and other executive papers
Class here official messages and documents only
For the collected works of individual heads of state, see D-F
For messages on a specific subject, see the subject
.xN15 Collections
.xN3 Individual messages. By date of message
(.xN5) Executive orders
see class K
.xR Administrative papers
Collections. Documents of several departments or agencies combined
.xR1 Collected
(.xR3) Department of the Interior
see JL-JQ
(.xR7) Other departments or agencies
see the subject
(.xT3) State, provincial documents
see JL-JS

TABLES

1	Periodicals. Serials
2	Handbooks, manuals, etc.
3	Conventions. Congresses. By date
4	Associations and clubs (National)
6	General works. History
	Local
	Including political clubs
8.A-.W	By state
9.A-Z	By city

2 General works. History

Including periodicals, serials, handbooks, manuals, conventions, congresses, and national associations and clubs

Local

Including political clubs

4.A-.W By state

5.A-Z By city

.A6A-.A6Z General works. History

Including periodicals, serials, handbooks, manuals, conventions, congresses, and national associations and clubs

Local

Including political clubs

.A8A-.A8W By state

.A9A-.A9Z By city

.xA5-.xZ General works. History

Including periodicals, serials, handbooks, manuals, conventions, congresses, and national associations and clubs

Local

Including political clubs

.x2A-.x2W By state

.x3A-.x3Z By city

1	Periodicals. Serials
2	Societies
2.5	Museums. Exhibitions
(3)	Colonial period
	see JK99.A+
(5-6)	Constitution
	see KFC-KFZ
16	General works
	For Colonial period, see JK99
	Public administration
	Directories. Registers
30	Serials
31	Monographs
35	History
41	General works
45	Political corruption
49.A-Z	Other topics, A-Z
49.A8	Automatic data processing. Electronic data processing
	Including use of the Internet for the delivery of government services
	Benchmarking see J7 49.T67
49.C65	Communication systems
49.C7	Consultants. Executive advisory bodies
49.E84	Ethics. Political ethics
49.O4	Ombudsman
49.P36	Paperwork
	Political ethics see J7 49.E84
49.P64	Political planning. Public policy
	Public policy see J7 49.P64
49.P8	Publicity. Public relations
49.R4	Records. Public records management
49.S43	Secret and confidential information. Government information
49.T67	Total quality management. Benchmarking
49.W45	Whistle blowing
	Executive branch
50	General works
	Governor
51	General works
53.A-Z	Special. By subject, A-Z
53.L5	Lieutenant governor
53.S8	Staff
53.V4	Veto
	Civil service
55	General works
	Lists of officials. Registers see J7 30+

Public administration
Executive branch
Civil service -- Continued

57 Salaries. Fringe benefits
Class here works dealing with service under the state in all branches; not limited to civil service proper
Cf. J7 60.P4 Pensions

58 Appointments and removals

60.A-Z Special. By subject, A-Z
60.A3 Accidents
60.A33 Affirmative action programs
60.A35 Alcoholism
60.C53 Charitable contributions by employees
60.D5 Discipline
60.E57 Employee assistance programs
60.F54 Flexitime. Hours of labor
60.G7 Grievance procedures
60.H4 Health insurance
60.H68 Housing
60.I5 In-service training
60.I53 Interns
60.J63 Job sharing
60.L3 Labor productivity
60.L43 Leave
60.L5 Life insurance
60.P4 Pensions. Retirement
60.P44 Personnel management
60.P6 Political activity
60.P65 Positions
60.P7 Promotions
60.R3 Rating of employees
60.R4 Resignations
60.S5 Sick leave
60.S8 Suggestion awards. Incentive awards
60.T45 Temporary employment
60.T7 Travel
60.W6 Workers' compensation
Cf. KFA-KFZ, Law

60.5.A-Z Special classes of officials and employees, A-Z
60.5.A34 African Americans. Blacks
60.5.A43 Aged. Older employees. Age and employment
60.5.E9 Executives
60.5.H3 Handicapped. People with disabilities
60.5.H35 Mental disabilities, People with
60.5.M5 Minorities
Older employees see J7 60.5.A43
People with disabilities see J7 60.5.H3

TABLES

Public administration
Executive branch
Civil service
Special classes of officials and employees, A-Z -- Continued
60.5.V47 Veterans
60.5.V64 Volunteer workers
60.5.W6 Women
60.6.A-Z Special departments or agencies, A-Z
For departments or agencies limited to a particular subject, see the subject
60.6.C65 Community Affairs
60.6.E94 Executive Department
60.6.S43 Secretary of State
Legislative branch
Directories. Registers see J7 30+
66 History
For Colonial period, see JK83
68 Representation. Election districts
(69) Powers
see KFA-KFZ
71 Organization. Administration
74 Legislative reference bureaus
74.4 Legislative internships
74.5 Lobbying. Pressure groups
74.7 Ethics
(74.8) Investigations
see KFA-KFZ
75 Term of office. Term limits
76 Upper House
78 Lower House
(79-80) Contested elections
see KFA-KFZ
(81-85) Judiciary
see KFA-KFZ
87 Capital. Seat of government. Site of the capital
Public buildings
see JK1651.A2+
Supplies. Government property. Government purchasing
88.A1 General
88.A2-Z Special articles, A-Z
88.A4 Aircraft
88.C64 Computers
88.M7 Motor vehicles
88.P36 Paper
89 Political participation. Citizenship
Elections. Voting. Suffrage. Right to vote

Elections. Voting. Suffrage. Right to vote -- Continued
90 General works
91 Registered voters. Voter registration
Election returns. Statistics. Voting behavior
92 General works
93 By date of election
Subarrange by main entry
Campaign funds. Election finance. Political action committees. Campaign contributions
see JK1991.5.A+
Political parties
see JK2295.A+

	History see J8 31
1	Periodicals. Societies. Serials
2	Directories. Registers
5	Dictionaries
(9-17)	Constitutional history. Constitutional law. Constitutions see class K
	Treatises see J8 31
19	Separation of powers
20.A-Z	Special topics, A-Z
20.C58	Civil-military relations
	Federal and state relations see J8 20.S8
	Language question see P119.32
20.M5	Minorities
20.R43	Regionalism
20.S43	Secularism
20.S8	State rights. Federal-state relations. Central-local government relations
	Government. Public administration
	Directories. Registers see J8 2
	History see J8 31
29.A-Z	Special topics, A-Z
29.A33	Accountability
29.A8	Automatic data processing. Electronic data processing Including use of the Internet for the delivery of government services
	Benchmarking see J8 29.T67
	Business and politics. Pressure groups see J8 69.P7
29.C54	Communication systems
	Confidential information see J8 29.S4
29.C55	Consultants
29.C57	Correspondence
29.C6	Corruption. Political corruption
29.C75	Crisis management
29.D42	Decentralization
29.D45	Decision making
	Electronic data processing see J8 29.A8
29.E8	Ethics. Political ethics
29.I6	Intelligence service. Espionage
29.I63	Investigations
29.M37	Marketing
29.O35	Office practice
29.O4	Ombudsman
29.O73	Organizational change
29.P37	Paperwork
29.P64	Political planning. Public policy

	Government. Public administration
	Special topics, A-Z -- Continued
29.P75	Productivity
29.P85	Purchasing. Government purchasing
29.R4	Records. Public records
29.R46	Report writing. Government report writing
29.S4	Secret and confidential information. Government information
29.T4	Telecommunication systems
29.T67	Total quality management. Benchmarking
29.T7	Transportation
29.W55	Whistle blowing
(30)	Administrative law
	see class K
31	General works
	Executive branch
40	General works
(41)	The chief executive
	see J8 40
	Departments. Ministries
42	General works
	Civil service
(45)	Documents
	see J8 47
(46)	Treatises
	see J8 47
47	General works
49.A-.Z1	Special topics, A-Z
49.A25	Accidents
49.A4	Alcoholism
49.A6	Appointments and removals
49.C53	Charitable contributions
49.C55	Classification
49.D4	Details. Transfers
49.D5	Discipline
49.D77	Drug abuse. Drug testing
49.E48	Employee assistance programs. Problem employees
49.E87	Examinations
49.E9	Executives. Government executives
49.F55	Financial disclosure
49.H35	Handicapped. People with disabilities
49.H39	Health and hygiene. Medical care
49.H4	Health insurance
49.H6	Homosexual men and women
49.H65	Hours of labor
49.H68	Housing
49.I52	Incentive awards

TABLES

Government. Public administration
Executive branch
Departments. Ministries
Civil service
Special topics, A-Z -- Continued
49.I6 In-service training. Interns
49.J66 Job satisfaction
49.L53 Life insurance
49.M35 Mental disabilities, People with
49.M54 Minorities
49.O4 Older employees. Age and employment
49.P35 Part-time employment
Pensioners see J8 49.Z2
People with disabilities see J8 49.H35
People with mental disabilities see J8 49.M35
49.P44 Personnel management
49.P64 Political activity
Problem employees see J8 49.E48
49.P7 Promotions
Propaganda see J8 49.P85
Public relations see J8 49.P85
49.P85 Publicity and propaganda. Public relations. Government publicity
49.R3 Rating of employees
49.R47 Relocation of employees
Removals see J8 49.A6
Selection and appointment see J8 49.A6
49.S45 Sexual activity. Sexual harassment
49.S56 Shift systems
49.T57 Titles of officials
49.T67 Total quality management
49.T7 Travel
49.T85 Turnover of employees
49.V35 Vacations. Annual leave. Sick leave
49.V64 Volunteer workers
49.W6 Women in the civil service
49.W68 Work sharing
49.Z2 Salaries. Pensions. Retirement
Individual departments or ministries
50 Department of the Interior
Other departments or ministries see the subject
Legislative branch
51 Directories. Registers
54 General works

	Government. Public administration
	Legislative branch -- Continued
(56)	Constitution. Prerogatives. Powers see class K
(59)	Procedure see class K
59.5	Legislative reference bureaus
	Upper house
61.A4	Directories. Registers
61.A5	General works
	Lower house
63.A4	Directories. Registers
65	General works
67	Election districts
69.A-Z	Special topics, A-Z
69.B74	Broadcasting of proceedings
69.E45	Employees
69.E85	Ethics
69.F34	Filibusters
(69.L39)	Legislative power see class K
(69.L4)	Legislative process see class K
	Lobbying see J8 69.P7
69.O6	Opposition
69.P53	Political planning. Public policy
69.P7	Pressure groups. Lobbying
69.P8	Publication of proceedings
	Reporters and reporting see J8 69.P8
69.S65	Speaker. Presiding officer
(70-76)	Judiciary see class K
79	Government property. Public buildings
	Political rights. Political participation. Practical politics
81	General works
83	Citizenship
(86)	Naturalization see class K
	Elections. Voting. Suffrage. Right to vote
92	General works
93.A-Z	Local results of national elections. By place, A-Z
94	Election statistics. Election returns
(95)	Election law see class K
97	Election fraud. Corrupt practices
	Political parties

Government. Public administration
Political parties -- Continued
98.A1 General works
98.A2-Z Special parties, A-Z
State, provincial, prefecture government (General and comparative)
98.8 General works
99.A-Z By state, province, prefecture, A-Z
For local government, see JS

	History see J9 10.A4+
1.A1	Periodicals. Societies. Serials
1.A11-.A19	Directories. Registers
1.A25	Dictionaries
(1.A3-3)	Constitutional history. Constitutional law. Constitutions see class K
	Treatises see J9 10.A4+
5	Separation of powers
6.A-Z	Special topics, A-Z
6.C58	Civil-military relations
	Federal and state relations see J9 6.S8
	Language question see P119.32
6.M5	Minorities
6.R43	Regionalism
6.S8	State rights. Federal-state relations. Central-local government relations
	Government. Public administration
	Directories. Registers see J9 1.A11+
	History see J9 10.A4+
9.5.A-Z	Special topics, A-Z
9.5.A8	Automatic data processing. Electronic data processing Including use of the Internet for the delivery of government services
	Benchmarking see J9 9.5.T67
	Business and politics. Pressure groups see J9 14.P7
9.5.C54	Communication systems
	Confidential information see J9 9.5.S4
9.5.C55	Consultants
9.5.C57	Correspondence
9.5.C6	Corruption. Political corruption
9.5.C75	Crisis management
9.5.D42	Decentralization
9.5.D45	Decision making
	Electronic data processing see J9 9.5.A8
9.5.E8	Ethics. Political ethics
9.5.I6	Intelligence service. Espionage
9.5.I63	Investigations
9.5.M37	Marketing
9.5.O35	Office practice
9.5.O4	Ombudsman
9.5.O73	Organizational change
9.5.P37	Paperwork
9.5.P64	Political planning. Public policy
9.5.P75	Productivity
9.5.R4	Records. Public records

	Government. Public administration
	Special topics, A-Z -- Continued
9.5.S4	Secret and confidential information. Government information
9.5.T4	Telecommunication systems
9.5.T67	Total quality management. Benchmarking
9.5.T7	Transportation
9.5.W55	Whistle blowing
(10.A3)	Administrative law
	see class K
10.A4-Z	General works
	Executive branch
11	General works
	Civil service
12.A-.Z1	General works
12.Z13A-.Z13Z	Special topics, A-Z
12.Z13A25	Accidents
12.Z13A4	Alcoholism
12.Z13A6	Appointments and removals
12.Z13C53	Charitable contributions
12.Z13C55	Classification
12.Z13D4	Details. Transfers
12.Z13D5	Discipline
12.Z13D77	Drug abuse. Drug testing
12.Z13E48	Employee assistance programs. Problem employees
12.Z13E87	Examinations
12.Z13E9	Executives. Government executives
12.Z13F55	Financial disclosure
12.Z13H35	Handicapped. People with disabilities
12.Z13H39	Health and hygiene. Medical care
12.Z13H4	Health insurance
12.Z13H6	Homosexual men and women
12.Z13H65	Hours of labor
12.Z13H68	Housing
12.Z13I52	Incentive awards
12.Z13I6	In-service training. Interns
12.Z13J66	Job satisfaction
12.Z13L53	Life insurance
12.Z13M35	Mental disabilities, People with
12.Z13M54	Minorities
12.Z13O4	Older employees. Age and employment
12.Z13P35	Part-time employment
	Pensioners see J9 12.Z2
	People with disabilities see J9 12.Z13H35
	People with mental disabilities see J9 12.Z13M35
12.Z13P44	Personnel management
12.Z13P64	Political activity

Government. Public administration
Executive branch
Civil service
Special topics, A-Z -- Continued
Problem employees see J9 12.Z13E48
12.Z13P7 Promotions
Propaganda see J9 12.Z13P85
Public relations see J9 12.Z13P85
12.Z13P85 Publicity and propaganda. Public relations. Government publicity
12.Z13R3 Rating of employees
12.Z13R47 Relocation of employees
Removals see J9 12.Z13A6
Selection and appointment see J9 12.Z13A6
12.Z13S45 Sexual activity. Sexual harassment
12.Z13S56 Shift systems
12.Z13T57 Titles of officials
12.Z13T7 Travel
12.Z13T85 Turnover of employees
12.Z13V35 Vacations. Annual leave. Sick leave
12.Z13V64 Volunteer workers
12.Z13W6 Women in the civil service
12.Z13W68 Work sharing
12.Z2 Salaries. Pensions. Retirement. Fringe benefits
Including legislators' salaries and pensions
Individual departments or ministries
12.Z3 Department of the Interior
Other departments or ministries
see the subject
Legislative branch
13 General works
13.5 Legislative reference bureaus
13.7 Upper house
13.8 Lower house
14.A-Z Special topics, A-Z
14.B74 Broadcasting of proceedings
14.C65 Committees
14.E45 Employees
14.E85 Ethics
14.F34 Filibusters
(14.L39) Legislative power
see class K
(14.L4) Legislative process
see class K
Lobbying see J9 14.P7
14.O6 Opposition

TABLES

	Government. Public administration
	Legislative branch
	Special topics, A-Z -- Continued
14.P53	Political planning. Public policy
14.P7	Pressure groups. Lobbying
14.P8	Publication of proceedings
	Reporters and reporting see J9 14.P8
14.S65	Speaker. Presiding officer
14.W65	Women legislators
(15.A-.Z2)	Judiciary
	see class K
15.Z3-.Z7	Government property. Public buildings
	Political rights. Political participation. Practical politics
16	General works
17.A2	Citizenship
(17.A3)	Naturalization
	see class K
	Elections. Voting. Suffrage. Right to vote
18	General works
18.5.A-Z	Local results of national elections. By place, A-Z
19.A15	Election statistics. Election returns
(19.A2)	Election law
	see class K
19.A4	Election fraud. Corrupt practices
	Political parties
19.A45	General works
19.A5-.A59	Special parties
	Assign one Cutter to each party
	State, provincial, prefecture government (General and comparative)
19.A598	General works
19.A6-.Z8	By state, province, prefecture, A-Z
	For local government, see JS

	History see J10 5.A7+
1.A1	Periodicals. Societies. Serials
1.A11-.A19	Directories. Registers
1.A25	Dictionaries
(1.A3-3)	Constitutional history. Constitutional law. Constitutions see class K
3.2	Separation of powers
3.5.A-Z	Special topics, A-Z
3.5.C58	Civil-military relations
	Federal and state relations see J10 3.5.S8
	Language question see P119.32
3.5.M5	Minorities
3.5.P65	Political development
3.5.R43	Regionalism
3.5.S8	State rights. Federal-state relations. Central-local government relations
	Government. Public administration
	Directories. Registers see J10 1.A11+
	History see J10 5.A7+
5.A55A-.A55Z	Special topics, A-Z
5.A55A8	Automatic data processing. Electronic data processing Including use of the Internet for the delivery of government services
	Benchmarking see J10 5.A55T67
	Business and politics. Pressure groups see J10 7.9.P7
5.A55C37	Capital. Seat of government. Site of the capital
5.A55C54	Communication systems
	Confidential information see J10 5.A55S4
5.A55C55	Consultants
5.A55C57	Correspondence
5.A55C6	Corruption. Political corruption
5.A55C75	Crisis management
5.A55D42	Decentralization
5.A55D45	Decision making
	Electronic data processing see J10 5.A55A8
5.A55E8	Ethics. Political ethics
5.A55I6	Intelligence service. Espionage
5.A55I63	Investigations
5.A55M37	Marketing
5.A55O35	Office practice
5.A55O4	Ombudsman
5.A55O73	Organizational change
5.A55P37	Paperwork
5.A55P64	Political planning. Public policy
5.A55P75	Productivity

	Government. Public administration
	Special topics, A-Z -- Continued
5.A55R4	Records. Public records
5.A55S4	Secret and confidential information. Government information
5.A55T4	Telecommunication systems
5.A55T67	Total quality management. Benchmarking
5.A55T7	Transportation
5.A55W55	Whistle blowing
(5.A6)	Administrative law see class K
5.A7-Z	General works
	Executive branch
6	General works
	Departments. Ministries
	Civil service
6.Z1	General works
6.Z13A-.Z13Z	Special topics, A-Z
6.Z13A25	Accidents
6.Z13A4	Alcoholism
6.Z13A6	Appointments and removals
6.Z13C53	Charitable contributions
6.Z13C55	Classification
6.Z13D4	Details. Transfers
6.Z13D5	Discipline
6.Z13D77	Drug abuse. Drug testing
6.Z13E48	Employee assistance programs. Problem employees
6.Z13E87	Examinations
6.Z13E9	Executives. Government executives
6.Z13F55	Financial disclosure
6.Z13H35	Handicapped. People with disabilities
6.Z13H39	Health and hygiene. Medical care
6.Z13H4	Health insurance
6.Z13H6	Homosexual men and women
6.Z13H65	Hours of labor
6.Z13H68	Housing
6.Z13I52	Incentive awards
6.Z13I6	In-service training. Interns
6.Z13J66	Job satisfaction
6.Z13L53	Life insurance
6.Z13M35	Mental disabilities, People with
6.Z13M54	Minorities
6.Z13O4	Older employees. Age and employment
6.Z13P35	Part-time employment
	Pensioners see J10 6.Z2
	People with disabilities see J10 6.Z13H35
	People with mental disabilities see J10 6.Z13M35

Government. Public administration
Executive branch
Departments. Ministries
Civil service
Special topics, A-Z -- Continued

6.Z13P44 Personnel management
6.Z13P64 Political activity
Problem employees see J10 6.Z13E48
6.Z13P7 Promotions
Propaganda see J10 6.Z13P85
Public relations see J10 6.Z13P85
6.Z13P85 Publicity and propaganda. Public relations. Government publicity
6.Z13R3 Rating of employees
6.Z13R47 Relocation of employees
Removals see J10 6.Z13A6
Selection and appointment see J10 6.Z13A6
6.Z13S45 Sexual activity. Sexual harassment
6.Z13S56 Shift systems
6.Z13T57 Titles of officials
6.Z13T67 Total quality management
6.Z13T7 Travel
6.Z13T85 Turnover of employees
6.Z13V35 Vacations. Annual leave. Sick leave
6.Z13V64 Volunteer workers
6.Z13W6 Women in the civil service
6.Z13W68 Work sharing
6.Z2 Salaries. Pensions. Retirement
Individual departments or ministries
6.Z3 Department of the Interior
Other departments or ministries
see the subject
Legislative branch
7 General works
7.5 Legislative reference bureaus
7.7 Upper house
7.8 Lower house
7.9.A-Z Special topics, A-Z
7.9.B74 Broadcasting of proceedings
7.9.E45 Employees
7.9.E85 Ethics
7.9.F34 Filibusters
(7.9.L39) Legislative power
see class K
(7.9.L4) Legislative process
see class K

TABLES

	Government. Public administration
	Legislative branch
	Special topics, A-Z -- Continued
	Lobbying see J10 7.9.P7
7.9.O6	Opposition
7.9.P53	Political planning. Public policy
7.9.P7	Pressure groups. Lobbying
7.9.P8	Publication of proceedings
	Reporters and reporting see J10 7.9.P8
7.9.S65	Speaker. Presiding officer
7.9.W66	Women legislators
(8)	Judiciary
	see class K
9.A13	Government property. Public buildings
	Political rights
	Including political culture, political participation, practical politics
9.A15	General works
9.A2	Citizenship
(9.A3)	Naturalization
	see class K
	Elections. Voting. Suffrage. Right to vote
9.A5	General works
9.A53A-.A53Z	Local results of national elections. By place, A-Z
9.A55	Election statistics. Election returns
(9.A6)	Election law
	see class K
9.A79	Election fraud. Corrupt practices
	Political parties
9.A795	General works
9.A8A-.A8Z	Special parties, A-Z
	State, provincial, prefecture government (General and comparative)
9.A88	General works
9.A9-.Z8	By state, province, prefecture, A-Z
	For local government, see JS

.A1 Periodicals. Societies. Serials
.A12 Directories. Registers
.A127 Dictionaries
(.A13-.A32) Constitutional history. Constitutional law. Constitutions
see class K
Treatises see J11 .A58
.A36 Separation of powers
.A38A-.A38Z Special topics, A-Z
.A38C58 Civil-military relations
Federal and state relations see J11 .A38S8
Language question
see P119.32
.A38M5 Minorities
.A38R43 Regionalism
.A38S8 State rights. Federal-state relations. Central-local government relations
Government. Public administration
Directories. Registers see J11 .A12
History see J11 .A58
.A56A-.A56Z Special topics, A-Z
.A56A35 Accountability
.A56A8 Automatic data processing. Electronic data processing
Including use of the Internet for the delivery of government services
Benchmarking see J11 .A56T67
Business and politics. Pressure groups see J11 .A792P7
.A56C54 Communication systems
Confidential information see J11 .A56S4
.A56C55 Consultants
.A56C57 Correspondence
.A56C6 Corruption. Political corruption
.A56C75 Crisis management
.A56D42 Decentralization
.A56D45 Decision making
Electronic data processing see J11 .A56A8
.A56E8 Ethics. Political ethics
Government purchasing see J11 .A56P87
.A56I6 Intelligence service. Espionage
.A56I63 Investigations
.A56M37 Marketing
.A56O35 Office practice
.A56O4 Ombudsman
.A56O73 Organizational change
.A56P37 Paperwork
.A56P64 Political planning. Public policy
.A56P75 Productivity

	Government. Public administration
	Special topics, A-Z -- Continued
.A56P87	Purchasing. Government purchasing
.A56R4	Records. Public records
.A56S4	Secret and confidential information. Government information
.A56T4	Telecommunication systems
.A56T67	Total quality management. Benchmarking
.A56T7	Transportation
.A56W55	Whistle blowing
(.A57)	Administrative law see class K
.A58	General works
	Executive branch
.A61	General works
	Departments. Ministries
.A63	General works
	Civil service
.A67	General works
.A69A-.A69Z	Special topics, A-Z
.A69A25	Accidents
.A69A4	Alcoholism
.A69A6	Appointments and removals
.A69C53	Charitable contributions
.A69C55	Classification
.A69D4	Details. Transfers
.A69D5	Discipline
.A69D77	Drug abuse. Drug testing
.A69E48	Employee assistance programs. Problem employees
.A69E87	Examinations
.A69E9	Executives. Government executives
.A69F55	Financial disclosure
.A69H35	Handicapped. People with disabilities
.A69H39	Health and hygiene. Medical care
.A69H4	Health insurance
.A69H6	Homosexual men and women
.A69H65	Hours of labor
.A69H68	Housing
.A69I52	Incentive awards
.A69I6	In-service training. Interns
.A69J66	Job satisfaction
.A69L53	Life insurance
.A69M35	Mental disabilities, People with
.A69M54	Minorities
.A69O4	Older employees. Age and employment
.A69P35	Part-time employment
	Pensioners see J11 .A691

	Government. Public administration
	Executive branch
	Departments. Ministries
	Civil service
	Special topics, A-Z -- Continued
	People with disabilities see J11 .A69H35
	People with mental disabilities see J11 .A69M35
.A69P44	Personnel management
.A69P64	Political activity
	Problem employees see J11 .A69E48
.A69P7	Promotions
	Propaganda see J11 .A69P85
	Public relations see J11 .A69P85
.A69P85	Publicity and propaganda. Public relations. Government publicity
.A69R3	Rating of employees
.A69R47	Relocation of employees
	Removals see J11 .A69A6
	Selection and appointment see J11 .A69A6
.A69S45	Sexual activity. Sexual harassment
.A69S56	Shift systems
.A69T57	Titles of officials
.A69T67	Total quality management
.A69T7	Travel
.A69T85	Turnover of employees
.A69V35	Vacations. Annual leave. Sick leave
.A69V64	Volunteer workers
.A69W6	Women in the civil service
.A69W68	Work sharing
.A691	Salaries. Pensions. Retirement
	Individual departments or ministries
.A693	Department of the Interior
	Other departments or ministries see the subject
	Legislative branch
.A7	Directories. Registers
.A71	General works
(.A72)	Constitution. Prerogatives. Powers see class K
(.A75)	Procedure see class K
.A76	Legislative reference bureaus
.A77	Upper house
.A78	Lower house
.A792A-.A792Z	Special topics, A-Z
.A792B74	Broadcasting of proceedings

	Government. Public administration
	Legislative branch
	Special topics, A-Z -- Continued
.A792E45	Employees
.A792E85	Ethics
.A792F34	Filibusters
(.A792L39)	Legislative power see class K
(.A792L4)	Legislative process see class K
	Lobbying see J11 .A792P7
.A792O6	Opposition
.A792P53	Political planning. Public policy
.A792P7	Pressure groups. Lobbying
.A792P8	Publication of proceedings
	Reporters and reporting see J11 .A792P8
.A792S65	Speaker. Presiding officer
(.A8-.A87)	Judiciary see class K
.A9	Government property. Public buildings. Government purchasing
	Political rights. Political participation. Practical politics
.A91	General works
.A92	Citizenship
(.A93)	Naturalization see class K
	Elections. Voting. Suffrage. Right to vote
.A95	General works
.A953A-.A953Z	Local results of national elections. By place, A-Z
.A956	Election statistics. Election returns
(.A96)	Election law see class K
.A975	Election fraud. Corrupt practices
	Political parties
.A979	General works
.A98A-.A98Z	Special parties, A-Z
	State, provincial, prefecture government (General and comparative)
.A988	General works
.A99-.Z8	By state, province, prefecture, A-Z For local government, see JS

	Apply this table to regions that are larger than a single country
.A1	Periodicals. Societies. Serials
.A12	Directories. Registers
.A127	Dictionaries
(.A13-.A32)	Constitutional history. Constitutional law. Constitutions see class K
	Treatises see J11a .A58
.A36	Separation of powers
.A38A-.A38Z	Special topics, A-Z
.A38C58	Civil-military relations
	Federal and state relations see J11a .A38S8
	Language question see P119.32
.A38M5	Minorities
.A38R43	Regionalism
.A38S8	State rights. Federal-state relations. Central-local government relations
	Government. Public administration
	Directories. Registers see J11a .A12
	History see J11a .A58
.A56A-.A56Z	Special topics, A-Z
.A56A33	Accountability
.A56A8	Automatic data processing. Electronic data processing Including use of the Internet for the delivery of government services
	Benchmarking see J11a .A56T67
	Business and politics. Pressure groups see J11a .A792P7
.A56C54	Communication systems
	Confidential information see J11a .A56S4
.A56C55	Consultants
.A56C57	Correspondence
.A56C6	Corruption. Political corruption
.A56C75	Crisis management
.A56D42	Decentralization
.A56D45	Decision making
	Electronic data processing see J11a .A56A8
.A56E8	Ethics. Political ethics
.A56I6	Intelligence service. Espionage
.A56I63	Investigations
.A56M37	Marketing
.A56O35	Office practice
.A56O4	Ombudsman
.A56O73	Organizational change
.A56P37	Paperwork
.A56P64	Political planning. Public policy
.A56P75	Productivity

TABLES

Government. Public administration
Special topics, A-Z -- Continued
.A56R4 Records. Public records
.A56S4 Secret and confidential information. Government information
.A56T4 Telecommunication systems
.A56T67 Total quality management. Benchmarking
.A56T7 Transportation
.A56W55 Whistle blowing
(.A57) Administrative law
see class K
.A58 General works
Executive branch
.A61 General works
Departments. Ministries
.A63 General works
Civil service
.A67 General works
.A69A-.A69Z Special topics, A-Z
.A69A25 Accidents
.A69A4 Alcoholism
.A69A6 Appointments and removals
.A69C53 Charitable contributions
.A69C55 Classification
.A69D4 Details. Transfers
.A69D5 Discipline
.A69D77 Drug abuse. Drug testing
.A69E48 Employee assistance programs. Problem employees
.A69E87 Examinations
.A69E9 Executives. Government executives
.A69F55 Financial disclosure
.A69H35 Handicapped. People with disabilities
.A69H39 Health and hygiene. Medical care
.A69H4 Health insurance
.A69H6 Homosexual men and women
.A69H65 Hours of labor
.A69H68 Housing
.A69I52 Incentive awards
.A69I6 In-service training. Interns
.A69J66 Job satisfaction
.A69L53 Life insurance
.A69M35 Mental disabilities, People with
.A69M54 Minorities
.A69O4 Older employees. Age and employment
.A69P35 Part-time employment
Pensioners see J11a .A691
People with disabilities see J11a .A69H35

Government. Public administration
Executive branch
Departments. Ministries
Civil service
Special topics, A-Z -- Continued
People with mental disabilities see J11a .A69M35
.A69P44 Personnel management
.A69P64 Political activity
Problem employees see J11a .A69E48
.A69P7 Promotions
Propaganda see J11a .A69P85
Public relations see J11a .A69P85
.A69P85 Publicity and propaganda. Public relations. Government publicity
.A69R3 Rating of employees
.A69R47 Relocation of employees
Removals see J11a .A69A6
Selection and appointment see J11a .A69A6
.A69S45 Sexual activity. Sexual harassment
.A69S56 Shift systems
.A69T57 Titles of officials
.A69T67 Total quality management
.A69T7 Travel
.A69T85 Turnover of employees
.A69V35 Vacations. Annual leave. Sick leave
.A69V64 Volunteer workers
.A69W6 Women in the civil service
.A69W68 Work sharing
.A691 Salaries. Pensions. Retirement
Individual departments or ministries
.A693 Department of the Interior
Other departments or ministries
see the subject
Legislative branch
.A7 Directories. Registers
.A71 General works
(.A72) Constitution. Prerogatives. Powers
see class K
(.A75) Procedure
see class K
.A76 Legislative reference bureaus
.A77 Upper house
.A78 Lower house
.A792A-.A792Z Special topics, A-Z
.A792B74 Broadcasting of proceedings
.A792E45 Employees

	Government. Public administration
	Legislative branch
	Special topics, A-Z -- Continued
.A792E85	Ethics
.A792F34	Filibusters
(.A792L39)	Legislative power see class K
(.A792L4)	Legislative process see class K
	Lobbying see J11a .A792P7
.A792O6	Opposition
.A792P53	Political planning. Public policy
.A792P7	Pressure groups. Lobbying
.A792P8	Publication of proceedings
	Reporters and reporting see J11a .A792P8
.A792S65	Speaker. Presiding officer
(.A8-.A87)	Judiciary see class K
.A9	Government property. Public buildings
	Political rights. Political participation. Practical politics
.A91	General works
.A92	Citizenship
(.A93)	Naturalization see class K
	Elections. Voting. Suffrage. Right to vote
.A95	General works
.A956	Election statistics. Election returns
(.A96)	Election law see class K
.A975	Election fraud. Corrupt practices
	Political parties
.A979	General works
.A98A-.A98Z	Special parties, A-Z
.A988	State, provincial, prefecture government (General and comparative)

.xA1-.xA3	Periodicals. Societies. Serials
.xA4-.xA49	History
	General works see J12 .x2
	Public administration
.x2	General works
.x25A-.x25Z	Special topics, A-Z
.x25A8	Automatic data processing. Electronic data processing Including use of the Internet for the delivery of government services
	Benchmarking see J12 .x25T67
.x25C54	Communication
	Confidential information see J12 .x25S43
.x25C58	Consultants
.x25C59	Correspondence
.x25C6	Corruption. Political corruption
.x25D42	Decentralization
	Electronic data processing see J12 .x25A8
.x25I6	Intelligence service. Espionage
.x25M37	Marketing
.x25O4	Ombudsman
.x25P37	Paperwork
.x25P64	Political planning. Public policy
.x25P75	Productivity
	Public relations see J12 .x25P95
.x25P95	Publicity and propaganda. Public relations
.x25R43	Records. Public records
.x25S43	Secret and confidential information. Government information
.x25T67	Total quality management. Benchmarking
.x25T7	Transportation
.x25W55	Whistle blowing
	Executive branch
.x3	General works
.x4	Civil service
.x5	Legislative branch
.x58	Government property. Public buildings
	Political rights. Political participation. Practical politics
.x59	General works
.x6	Civics. Citizenship
.x65	Elections. Voting. Suffrage. Right to vote
	Political parties
.x7	General works
.x73A-.x73Z	Special parties, A-Z
.x8A-.x8Z	Other topics, A-Z
.x8C58	Civil-military relations
.x8D4	Decentralization
	Federal and State relations see J12 .x8S8

TABLES

Other topics, A-Z -- Continued

Military power see J12 .x8C58

.x8S8 State rights. Federal and State relations. Central-local government relations. Regionalism

.x9A-.x9Z By state, province, prefecture, A-Z

For local government, see subclass JS

1	Periodicals. Societies. Serials
12	Directories. Registers
(18)	Laws, ordinances, codes
	see class K
	History
20	General works
	By period
23	To 1800
25	19th century
27	20th century
28	21st century
33	General works
35	Local government and the state. Home rule. Central-local government relations
	Local finance
	see HJ9011+
37.A-Z	Other special, A-Z
37.A56	Annexation
37.C7	Commission government. Municipal government by commission
	Correspondence see J13 37.R42
37.E4	Electronic data processing
	Federal and city relations see J13 35
(37.I3)	Incorporation. Charters
	see class K
(37.L2)	Land use. Public land
	see HD166+
37.L7	Limits, Territorial. Administrative and political divisions
37.P7	Publicity and propaganda. Public relations. Government publicity
37.P8	Punched card systems
37.R42	Records and correspondence. Public records
38	Local government other than municipal. County government. Township government. Village government
	Executive branch. Mayor. Administration
40	General works
41.A-Z	Individual departments and agencies, A-Z
	For other departments or agencies limited to a particular subject, see the subject
	Civil service
47	General works
(48)	Rules
	see class K
49	Salaries. Pensions. Retirement
50	Legislative branch. Aldermen. City councils
(60)	Judiciary. Municipal courts
	see class K

69 Government property. Government purchasing
70 Political participation
Elections. Local elections. Municipal elections
(83-85) Election law
see class K
86 General works
87 Statistics. Election returns
90 Political corruption

1	Periodicals. Societies. Serials
2	Directories. Registers
(4)	Laws, ordinances, codes see class K
	History
5.A5-Z	General works
	By period
6	To 1800
7	19th century
8	20th century
9	21st century
10	General works
11	Local government and the state. Home rule. Central-local government relations
	Local finance see HJ9011+
12.A-Z	Other special, A-Z
12.A56	Annexation
12.C7	Commission government. Municipal government by commission
	Correspondence see J14 12.R42
12.E4	Electronic data processing
	Federal and city relations see J14 11
(12.I3)	Incorporation. Charters see class K
(12.L2)	Land use. Public land see HD166+
12.L7	Limits, Territorial. Administrative and political divisions
12.O4	Ombudsman
12.P7	Publicity and propaganda. Public relations. Government publicity
12.P8	Punched card systems
12.R42	Records and correspondence. Public records
13	Local government other than municipal. County government. Township government. Village government
	Executive branch. Mayor. Administration
14.A1	General works
14.A13A-.A13Z	Individual departments and agencies, A-Z For other departments or agencies limited to a particular subject, see the subject
	Civil service
14.A2	General works
(14.A3)	Rules see class K
14.A4	Salaries. Pensions. Retirement
15	Legislative branch. Aldermen. City councils

(16)	Judiciary. Municipal courts see class K
16.A9	Government property. Government purchasing
17.A2	Political participation
	Elections. Local elections. Municipal elections
(18.A2-.A5)	Election law see class K
18.3	General works
18.5	Statistics. Election returns
19	Political corruption
20.A-Z	Local. By city, borough, parish, district, ward, etc., A-Z

1	Periodicals. Societies. Serials
2	Directories. Registers
(4)	Laws, ordinances, codes see class K
	History
5.A5-Z	General works
	By period
6	To 1800
7	19th century
8	20th century
9	21st century
10	General works
11	Local government and the state. Home rule. Central-local government relations
	Local finance see HJ9011+
12.A-Z	Other special, A-Z
12.A56	Annexation
12.C7	Commission government. Municipal government by commission
	Correspondence see J14a 12.R42
12.E4	Electronic data processing
	Federal and city relations see J14a 11
(12.I3)	Incorporation. Charters see class K
(12.L2)	Land use. Public land see HD166+
12.L7	Limits, Territorial. Administrative and political divisions
12.O4	Ombudsman
12.P7	Publicity and propaganda. Public relations. Government publicity
12.P8	Punched card systems
12.R42	Records and correspondence. Public records
13	Local government other than municipal. County government. Township government. Village government
	Executive branch. Mayor. Administration
14.A1	General works
14.A13A-.A13Z	Individual departments and agencies, A-Z For other departments or agencies limited to a particular subject, see the subject
	Civil service
14.A2	General works
(14.A3)	Rules see class K
14.A4	Salaries. Pensions. Retirement
15	Legislative branch. Aldermen. City councils

(16) Judiciary. Municipal courts
see class K
16.A9 Government property. Government purchasing
17.A2 Political participation
Elections. Local elections. Municipal elections
(18.A2-.A5) Election law
see class K
18.3 General works
18.5 Statistics. Election returns
19 Political corruption

1.A1	Periodicals. Societies. Serials
1.A3	Directories. Registers
(1.A9)	Laws, ordinances, codes see class K
	History
2.A2	General works
	By period
2.A3	To 1800
2.A5	19th century
2.A8-Z	20th century
2.2	21st century
3.A2	General works
3.A3	Local government and the state. Home rule. Central-local government relations
	Local finance see HJ9011+
3.A6A-.A6Z	Other special, A-Z
3.A6A56	Annexation
3.A6C7	Commission government. Municipal government by commission
	Correspondence see J15 3.A6R42
3.A6E4	Electronic data processing
	Federal and city relations see J15 3.A3
(3.A6I3)	Incorporation. Charters see class K
(3.A6L2)	Land use. Public land see HD166+
3.A6L7	Limits, Territorial. Administrative and political divisions
3.A6P7	Publicity and propaganda. Public relations. Government publicity
3.A6P8	Punched card systems
3.A6R42	Records and correspondence. Public records
3.A8	Local government other than municipal. County government. Township government. Village government
	Executive branch. Mayor. Administration
4.A1	General works
4.A13A-.A13Z	Individual departments and agencies, A-Z For other departments or agencies limited to a particular subject, see the subject
	Civil service
4.A2	General works
(4.A3)	Rules see class K
4.A4	Salaries. Pensions. Retirement
5	Legislative branch. Aldermen. City councils
(6)	Judiciary. Municipal courts see class K

TABLES

6.A9	Government property. Government purchasing
7.A15	Political participation
	Elections. Local elections. Municipal elections
(7.A7-.A8)	Election law
	see class K
7.3	General works
7.5	Statistics. Election returns
8	Political corruption
9.A-Z	Local. By city, borough, parish, district, ward, etc., A-Z

1.A1	Periodicals. Societies. Serials
1.A3	Directories. Registers
(1.A9)	Laws, ordinances, codes see class K
	History
2.A2	General works
	By period
2.A3	To 1800
2.A5	19th century
2.A8-Z	20th century
2.2	21st century
3.A2	General works
3.A3	Local government and the state. Home rule. Central-local government relations
	Local finance see HJ9011+
3.A6A-.A6Z	Other special, A-Z
3.A6A56	Annexation
3.A6C7	Commission government. Municipal government by commission
	Correspondence see J15a 3.A6R42
3.A6E4	Electronic data processing
	Federal and city relations see J15a 3.A3
(3.A6I3)	Incorporation. Charters see class K
(3.A6L2)	Land use. Public land see HD166+
3.A6L7	Limits, Territorial. Administrative and political divisions
3.A6P7	Publicity and propaganda. Public relations. Government publicity
3.A6P8	Punched card systems
3.A6R42	Records and correspondence. Public records
3.A8	Local government other than municipal. County government. Township government. Village government
	Executive branch. Mayor. Administration
4.A1	General works
4.A13A-.A13Z	Individual departments and agencies, A-Z For other departments or agencies limited to a particular subject, see the subject
	Civil service
4.A2	General works
(4.A3)	Rules see class K
4.A4	Salaries. Pensions. Retirement
5	Legislative branch. Aldermen. City councils
(6)	Judiciary. Municipal courts see class K

6.A9 Government property. Government purchasing
7.A15 Political participation
Elections. Local elections. Municipal elections
(7.A7-.A8) Election law
see class K
7.3 General works
7.5 Statistics. Election returns
8 Political corruption

.A1 Periodicals. Societies. Serials
.A12 Directories. Registers
(.A3) Laws, ordinances, codes
see class K
History
.2.A2 General works
By period
.2.A3 To 1800
.2.A5 19th century
.2.A8-Z 20th century
.25 21st century
.3.A2 General works
.3.A3 Local government and the state. Home rule. Central-local government relations
Local finance
see HJ9011+
.3.A6A-.A6Z Other special, A-Z
.3.A6A56 Annexation
.3.A6C7 Commission government. Municipal government by commission
Correspondence see J16 .3.A6R42
.3.A6E4 Electronic data processing
Federal and city relations see J16 .3.A3
(.3.A6I3) Incorporation. Charters
see class K
.3.A6I55 Information resources management
(.3.A6L2) Land use. Public land
see HD166+
.3.A6L7 Limits, Territorial. Administrative and political divisions
.3.A6P7 Publicity and propaganda. Public relations. Government publicity
.3.A6P8 Punched card systems
.3.A6R42 Records and correspondence. Public records
.3.A8 Local government other than municipal. County government. Township government. Village government
Executive branch. Mayor. Administration
.4.A1 General works
.4.A13A-.A13Z Individual departments and agencies, A-Z
For other departments or agencies limited to a particular subject, see the subject
Civil service
.4.A2 General works
(.4.A3) Rules
see class K
.4.A4 Salaries. Pensions. Retirement
.5 Legislative branch. Aldermen. City councils

TABLES

(.6)	Judiciary. Municipal courts see class K
.6.A9	Government property. Government purchasing
.7.A15	Political participation
	Elections. Local elections. Municipal elections
(.7.A7-.A8)	Election law see class K
.73	General works
.75	Statistics. Election returns
.8	Political corruption
.9.A-Z	Local. By city, borough, parish, district, ward, etc., A-Z

This table is used for countries that have been assigned a decimal number. Append the appropriate number from the table to the base number assigned to the country. For example, Lebanon has been assigned the base number JS7501.5. For general works, append 3.A2 to JS7501.5, resulting in the number JS7501.53.A2.

	History
2.A2	General works
	By period
2.A3	To 1800
2.A5	19th century
2.A8-.Z8	20th century
2.Z9	21st century
3.A2	General works
3.A3	Local government and the state. Home rule. Central-local government relations
	Local finance see HJ9011+
3.A6A-.A6Z	Other special, A-Z
3.A6A56	Annexation
3.A6C7	Commission government. Municipal government by commission
	Correspondence see J16a 3.A6R42
3.A6E4	Electronic data processing
	Federal and city relations see J16a 3.A3
(3.A6I3)	Incorporation. Charters see class K
(3.A6L2)	Land use. Public land see HD166+
3.A6L7	Limits, Territorial. Administrative and political divisions
3.A6P7	Publicity and propaganda. Public relations. Government publicity
3.A6P8	Punched card systems
3.A6R42	Records and correspondence. Public records
3.A8	Local government other than municipal. County government. Township government. Village government
	Executive branch. Mayor. Administration
4.A1	General works
4.A13A-.A13Z	Individual departments and agencies, A-Z For other departments or agencies limited to a particular subject, see the subject
	Civil service
4.A2	General works
(4.A3)	Rules see class K
4.A4	Salaries. Pensions. Retirement

5	Legislative branch. Aldermen. City councils
(6)	Judiciary. Municipal courts
	see class K
6.A9	Government property. Government purchasing
7.A15	Political participation
	Elections. Local elections. Municipal elections
7.A73	General works
7.A75	Statistics. Election returns
8	Political corruption
9.A-Z	Local. By city, borough, parish, district, ward, etc., A-Z

.xA1-.xA19	Periodicals. Societies. Serials
.xA2	Directories. Registers
.xA6-.xZ	General works
.x3A3-.x3A39	Executive branch. Mayor
.x3A4-.x3A49	Civil service
.x3A5-.x3A59	Legislative branch. City councils
.x3A7-.x3A79	Political participation
.x3A8-.x3A89	Elections. Local elections. Municipal elections
.x3A9-.x3A99	Political corruption. Corruption
.x4A-.x4Z	Local, A-Z

1	Periodicals. Serials
2	Societies
3	Congresses
3.5	Museums. Exhibitions
7	Dictionaries. Encyclopedias
(8)	Atlases
	see G1000+
	Study and teaching
	see JV57
	Biography
9.A2	Collective
9.A3-Z	Individual
	History
11	General works
	By period
14	Early to 1600
15	17th century
16	18th century
17	19th century
18	20th century
27	General works
(29)	Colonial companies
	see HF481+
35	Relations with indigenous peoples
	Relation to central government
41	General works
43	Colonial Office
45	Relation to legislature
(53-59)	Law
	see class K
	Administration. Colonial administration
60	General works
(63)	Economic policy
	see HC94+
	Executive
	Including viceroy, governor
71	General works
75	Civil service
85	Legislative bodies
(91-95)	Judiciary
	see class K
96	Political rights. Political participation. Citizenship
97	Elections

1.A2	Societies
1.A3-.Z7	General works
3.A-Z	Local, A-Z

.A2	Societies
.A3-.Z7	General works

2 Periodicals. Societies. Serials
For immigrant relief societies, see HV4013
Serial documents see J20 2
(5) Laws
see class K
Emigration
10 General works
History. By period
12 To 1800
14 19th century
15 20th century
(18) Emigration to individual countries, regions, etc.
see classes D, E, F
19 Aid to emigrants. Information bureaus. Manuals
Immigration
20 General works
History. By period
22 To 1800
24 19th century
25 20th century
25.2 21st century
25.5 Statistics
33 Immigration policy. Government policy
(41-45) Regulation and control. Legislation
see class K
(51-55) Restriction and exclusion
see class K
(71-75) Services for immigrants. Social work with immigrants
see HV4013
Special groups of immigrants
81 Children
82 Refugees
84 Women
(85) By ethnic group
see classes D, E, F
Local
90.A-Z By state or province, A-Z
95.A-Z Other local, A-Z

0.A1	Periodicals. Societies. Serials
	For immigrant relief societies, see HV4013
	Serial documents see J21 0.A1
(0.A7-.A8)	Laws
	see class K
	Emigration
1	General works
(1.Z79)	Emigration to individual countries
	see classes D, E, F
1.Z8	Aid to emigrants. Information bureaus. Manuals
	Immigration
2.A-.Z2	General works
2.Z5	Statistics
3	Immigration policy. Government policy
(4)	Regulation and control. Legislation
	see class K
(5)	Restriction and exclusion
	see class K
(7)	Services for immigrants. Social work with immigrants
	see HV4013
8	Special groups of immigrants (children, refugees, women, etc.)
	By ethnic group
	see classes D, E, F
	Local
9.A2-.Z5	By state or province, A-Z
9.Z6A-.Z6Z	Other local, A-Z

(.A1-.A19) General collections
Foreign relations and diplomatic correspondence
Secretary of State, Minister of Foreign Affairs
(.A2-.A29) Reports
Including bureau reports and documents
(.A3) Diplomatic correspondence
Class here general collections, routine correspondence
For correspondence covering special affairs, negotiations, wars, etc., see classes D, E, F, etc.
(.A4-.A48) Legislative documents
Including Senate (Upper house), House (Lower house), and Other
(.A5) Other documents
Treaties and Conventions
(.A58) Official serials
(.A6) Collections, by imprint date of first volume
(.A7) Separate treatises. By date
(.A75) Indexes
Cases, claims, etc.
(a) Place claims under defendant nation, unless the United States or an American citizen is a party, in which case prefer JX238+ (b) Prefer JX238 and (.A8) using JX239 and (.A85) only for claims which can not be otherwise disposed of; (c) Group claims under name of plaintiff nation, e. g. .C5 Chilean claims, .C7 Colombian claims, .M5 Mexican claims, etc.; (d) Under each claim subarrange using successive Cutter numbers (for material not dealing with a particular claim, arrange in a single chronological series)
(.A8A-.A8Z) By name, A-Z
(.A85) By date
(.A9-.Z) States which at some time maintained independent foreign relations, treaty rights, etc.
e. g. Under German Empire: Bavaria, Hanover, Saxony, Wurttemberg, etc.
e. g. Under Italy: Venice, Kingdom of the Two Sicilies, etc.

(1) General collections
Foreign relations and diplomatic correspondence
Secretary of State, Minister of Foreign Affairs
(2) Reports
Including bureau reports and documents
Diplomatic correspondence
Class here general collections, routine correspondence
For correspondence covering special affairs, negotiations, wars, etc., see classes D, E, F, etc.
(3.A1-.A4) Serial
(3.A5) Special (not limited to special countries). By date
(3.A6-Z) Relations with particular countries
(4) Legislative documents
Including Senate (Upper house), House (Lower house), and Other
Other documents
(5.A1-.A5) Administrative
(5.A6) Digests of decisions, opinions, etc.
Treatises and Conventions
(5.8) Official serials
(6) Collections, by imprint date of first volume
(7) Separate treaties. By date
(7.5) Indexes
Cases, claims, etc.
(a) Place claims under defendant nation, unless the United States or an American citizen is a party, in which case prefer JX238+ (b) Prefer JX238 and (8) using JX239 and (9) only for claims which can not be otherwise disposed of; (c) Group claims under name of plaintiff nation, e. g. .C5 Chilean claims, .C7 Colombian claims, .M5 Mexican claims, etc.; (d) Under each claim subarrange using successive Cutter numbers (for material not dealing with a particular claim, arrange in a single chronological series)
(8.A-Z) By name, A-Z
(8.A2) General collections
(9) By date
(10) States which at some time maintained independent foreign relations, treaty rights, etc.
e. g. Under German Empire: Bavaria, Hanover, Saxony, Wurttemberg, etc.
e. g. Under Italy: Venice, Kingdom of the Two Sicilies, etc.

(1) General collections
Foreign relations and diplomatic correspondence
Secretary of State, Minister of Foreign Affairs
(2) Reports
Including bureau reports and documents
Diplomatic correspondence
Class here general collections, routine correspondence
For correspondence covering special affairs, negotiations, wars, etc., see classes D, E, F, etc.
(3.A1-.A4) Serial
(3.A5) Special (not limited to special countries). By date
(3.A6-Z) Relations with particular countries
(4) Legislative documents
Including Senate (Upper house), House (Lower house), and Other
Other documents
(5.A1-.A5) Administrative
(5.A6) Digests of decisions, opinions, etc.
Treatises and Conventions
(5.8) Official serials
(6) Collections, by imprint date of first volume
(7) Separate treaties. By date
(7.5) Indexes
Cases, claims, etc.
(a) Place claims under defendant nation, unless the United States or an American citizen is a party, in which case prefer JX238+ (b) Prefer JX238 and (8) using JX239 and (9) only for claims which can not be otherwise disposed of; (c) Group claims under name of plaintiff nation, e. g. .C5 Chilean claims, .C7 Colombian claims, .M5 Mexican claims, etc.; (d) Under each claim subarrange using successive Cutter numbers (for material not dealing with a particular claim, arrange in a single chronological series)
(8.A-Z) By name, A-Z
(8.A2) General collections
(9) By date

(.A2)	Collections
(.A28)	History of the science
	History and other general works
(.A3)	To 1800
(.A4-.Z4)	1800-
(.Z5)	Contemporary works. By date
(.Z6A-.Z6Z)	Special topics, A-Z
(.Z7A-.Z7Z)	Relations with particular powers, A-Z

(.A2-.A4)	Collections
(.A5)	Organization. Administration
(.A6-.Z)	General works. By author

(1)	Collections
(2)	Organization. Administration
(3)	General works. By author

	Manuals, yearbooks, diplomatic lists
(1.A15-.A19)	Serials
(1.A2)	Nonserials. By date
	Periodicals
	see JX1+
	General works
(1.A3)	Early, to 1860. By date
(1.A5A-Z)	1860- . By author, A-Z
	Organization and administration
	Documents
(2.A2)	Serial
	Including budget, estimates and appropriations, and other general special
	For the annual reports of the State Department with or without diplomatic correspondence, and other general serial documents, see JX200+ subdivisions 1, 2, 3, etc. under each country
(2.A3)	Special. By date
(2.A33)	Upper House (Senate). By date
(2.A34)	Lower House (Representatives, etc.). By date
(2.A37)	Other. By date
(2.A4)	Department of foreign affairs, Minister of state, etc. By date
	Legations, etc.
(2.A5)	General
	Legations, etc. in particular regions
(2.A52)	North America
(2.A53)	South America
(2.A54)	Europe
(2.A55)	Asia
(2.A56)	Other
(2.A58A-.A58Z)	By place, A-Z
(2.A585)	Foreign legations
(2.A59)	Ambassadors, ministers, envoys, etc.
	Consular service
	Documents
(2.A6)	Serial
	Cases
(2.A65)	Collections
(2.A65Z5)	Particular cases. By date
(2.A7)	Organization, duties, regulations, forms, etc.
(2.A75)	Special. By date (inspection, etc.)
(2.A8-.Z3)	General works. By author, A-Z
(2.Z4)	Consular courts
	see class K
(2.Z5)	Civil service
	For lists, see JX6 1.A15+

TABLES

	Organization and administration -- Continued
(2.Z55)	Messengers, interpreters, etc.
(2.Z6)	Examinations for diplomatic and consular service
(2.Z7A-.Z7Z)	Other works. By author, A-Z
(2.Z8)	States
(2.Z9)	Miscellaneous uncataloged material

(1) Collections and selections

(3-8) Separate works

Separate works are to have separate numbers, 3-8, arranged by alphabetical order of original titles

Texts in original language: .A1 and date

Translations to be arranged alphabetically by language: .E5, English; .F5, French; .G5, German; .I5, Italian; .S5, Spanish

(9) Criticism

(1.A1) Collections and selections

(1.A3-Z) Separate works

Arrange using successive Cutter numbers for translations, e. g. JX2542.P3 1915 Lawrence, Principles of international law, 1915; JX2542.P35 1920 a French translation, 1920

(2) Criticism

Table JX9 has been discontinued

TABLES

(0)	Preliminaries. By date
	Proceedings
(0.2)	Indexes and digests
(0.3)	General. By editor
(0.4)	Statements by participants. By author Including indictments, speeches by prosecution and defense, proceedings in chambers
(0.5)	Evidence. By date
(0.6)	Judgments and minority opinions. By author
(0.7)	Post-trial. By author
(0.8)	General works on the trial. By author

(.xA15)	Preliminaries. By date
	Proceedings
(.xA2-.xA29)	Indexes and digests
(.xA3-.xA39)	General. By editor
(.xA4-.xA49)	Statements by participants. By author Including indictments, speeches by prosecution and defense, proceedings in chambers
(.xA5)	Evidence. By date
(.xA6-.xA69)	Judgments and minority opinions. By author
(.xA7-.xA79)	Post-trial. By author
(.xA8-.Z)	General works on the trial. By author

The numbers <5>-<10> are provided in this table as an alternative arrangement for libraries using this classification. At the Library of Congress, the material indicated by these numbers is classed in KZ

1 General collections

Foreign relations and diplomatic correspondence

Secretary of State, Minister of Foreign Affairs

2 Reports. Memoranda. Correspondence

Including bureau reports and documents, press releases, etc.

Diplomatic correspondence and papers (General)

Class here general collections, routine correspondence, etc.

Cf. Classes D, E, F, etc. for correspondence covering special affairs, negotiations, wars, etc.

3 Serials

3.5 Monographs. By date

3.6.A-Z Relations with particular countries. By country, A-Z

3.7 Indexes. Lists of documents, etc.

4 General legislative papers. By date

Including Senate (Upper house), House (Lower house), and other

General administrative and executive papers

see subclass J

Digests of decisions, opinions, etc. By date

see "Digests of decisions, opinions, etc. By date," below

Treaties and conventions

see subclass KZ

<5> Indexes. Registers

Collections

<5.3> Serials

Including official and non-official

<6> Monographs. By date

<6.3.A-Z> By country, A-Z

<7> Individual treaties

Indexes. Registers see JZ1 5

<7.7> Digests of decisions, opinions, etc. By date

<8> Cases, claims, etc.,

see subclass KZ

<8.A2> General collections

<8.A4-Z> By name of plaintiff nation, A-Z

<9> By date

Including private claims

<10.A-Z> States which at some time maintained independent foreign relations, treaty rights, etc.

e. g. under German Empire: Bavaria, Hanover, Saxony, Wurttemburg, etc.; under Italy: Venice, Kingdom of the Two Sicilies, etc.

see subclass KZ

1 General collections
Foreign relations and diplomatic correspondence
Secretary of State, Minister of Foreign Affairs
2 Reports. Memoranda. Correspondence
Including bureau reports and documents, press releases, etc.
Diplomatic correspondence and papers (General)
Class here general collections, routine correspondence, etc.
Cf. Classes D, E, F, etc. for correspondence covering special affairs, negotiations, wars, etc.
3 Serials
3.5 Monographs. By date
3.6.A-Z Relations with particular countries. By country, A-Z
3.7 Indexes. Lists of documents, etc.
4 General legislative papers. By date
Including Senate (Upper house), House (Lower house), and other
General administrative and executive papers
see subclass J

TABLES

The numbers <.A5>-<.A9-.Z> are provided in this table as an alternative arrangement for libraries using this classification. At the Library of Congress, the material indicated by these numbers is classed in KZ

.A1-.A19 General collections

Foreign relations and diplomatic correspondence

Secretary of State, Minister of Foreign Affairs

.A2-.A29 Reports. Memoranda

Including bureau reports and documents, press releases, etc.

.A3 Diplomatic correspondence and papers

Class here general collections, routine correspondence, etc.

Cf. Classes D, E, F, etc. for correspondence covering special affairs, negotiations, wars, etc.

.A4-.A48 General legislative papers

Including Senate (Upper house), House (Lower house), and other

General administrative and executive papers

see subclass J

Treaties and conventions

see subclass KZ

<.A5> Indexes. Registers

Collections

<.A58> Serials

Including official and non-official

<.A6> Monographs. By date

<.A7> Individual treaties

Indexes. Registers see JZ2 .A5

Cases, claims, etc.

see subclass KZ

<.A82> General collections

<.A84A-.A84Z> By name of plaintiff nation, A-Z

<.A85> By date

Including private claims

<.A9-.Z> States which at some time maintained independent foreign relations, treaty rights, etc.

e. g. under German Empire: Bavaria, Hanover, Saxony, Wurttemburg, etc.; under Italy: Venice, Kingdom of the Two Sicilies, etc.

see subclass KZ

Periodicals
see JZ5.5+
Manuals, yearbooks, diplomatic lists
.A15 Serials
.A19 Monographs. By date
General works. History see JZ3 .A9+
Organization and administration
General collections
.A2 Serials
Including budget, estimates and appropriations, etc.
For the annual reports of the State Department with or without diplomatic correspondence, and other general serial documents, see JZ200+
.A3 Monographs. By date
.A33 Upper House (Senate). By date
.A34 Lower House (Representatives, etc.). By date
.A4 Department of foreign affairs, Minister of state, etc. By date
Foreign relations and legations
.A5 General works
Particular regions and countries
.A52 North America
.A53 South America
Including Latin America in general
.A54 Europe
.A545 Mediterranean Region
.A55 Asia and Pacific area
Including Middle East
.A56 Africa
.A57A-.A57Z By country, A-Z, and date
Do not subarrange by main entry
.A58 Foreign legations
.A59 Ambassadors, ministers, envoys, etc.
Consular service
Documents
.A6 Serials
Cases
.A65 Collections. By date
.A65A-.A65Z Particular cases. By first named defendant or best known name
.A7 Organization, duties, regulations, forms, etc.
.A8 Messengers, interpreters, etc.
.A82 Examinations for diplomatic and consular service
.A9-.Z General works. History
Including early (contemporary) works

Periodicals
see JZ5.5+
Manuals, yearbooks, diplomatic lists, etc. see JZ4 .xA6+
.xA2 Collections. By date
History (including all periods) of foreign relations and diplomacy
see JZ4 .xA6+
Contemporary works see JZ4 .xA6+
.xA5 Organization. Administration
Including foreign service and consular service
.xA6-.xZ6 General works
Relations with particular powers see JZ4 .xA6+

NUMERALS

A

INDEX

H

INDEX

INDEX

N

O

P

INDEX

V

Y

Z

GPO U.S. GOVERNMENT PRINTING OFFICE: 2012–378–911/40022